RESEARCH STUDIES IN HIGHER EDUCATION

Educating Multicultural College Students

Edited by
Terence Hicks
and
Abul Pitre

D0970786

Issues in Black Education Series

University Press of America,® Inc.
Lanham · Boulder · New York · Toronto · Plymouth, UK

Copyright © 2012 by
University Press of America,® Inc.
4501 Forbes Boulevard
Suite 200
Lanham, Maryland 20706
UPA Acquisitions Department (301) 459-3366

Estover Road
Plymouth PL6 7PY
United Kingdom

Library of Congress Control Number: 2011945408
ISBN: 978-0-7618-5813-3 (clothbound : alk. paper)
ISBN: 978-0-7618-5778-5 (paperback : alk. paper)
eISBN: 978-0-7618-5779-2

Issues in Black Education Series

Dedication

As every achievement and plateau, I have attained in my life-time, the success of this effort is dedicated to my wife Rox-anne and to our beautiful children, Cordarius, Tyrice and Alexus.

Terence Hicks

I am deeply indebted to my parents, wife, and children for their encouragement. This book is a result of your inspiration!

Abul Pitre

Contents

Figures

Tables

Series Foreword

Historically, the state of Black education has been at the center of American life. When the first Blacks arrived to the Americas to be made slaves, a process of *mis-education* was systematized into the very fabric of American life. Newly arrived Blacks were dehumanized and forced through a process that has been described by a conspicuous slave owner named Willie Lynch as a "breaking process": "Hence the horse and the nigger must be broken; that is, break them from one form of mental life to another—keep the body and take the mind" (Hassan-EL, 2007, p. 14). This horrendous process of breaking the African from one form of mental life into another included an elaborate educational system that was designed to kill the creative Black mind. Elijah Muhammad called this a process that made Black people blind, deaf, and dumb—meaning the minds of Black people were taken from them. He proclaimed, "Back when our fathers were brought here and put into slavery 400 years ago, 300 [of] which they served as servitude slaves, they taught our people everything against themselves" (Pitre, 2008, p.6). Woodson (2008) similarly decried, "Even schools for Negroes, then, are places where they must be convinced of their inferiority. The thought of inferiority of the Negro is drilled into him in almost every class he enters and almost in every book he studies" (p. 2).

Today, Black education seems to be at a crossroads. With the passing of the *No Child Left Behind Act of 2001,* schools that serve a large majority of Black children have been under the scrutiny of politicians who vigilantly proclaim the need to improve schools while not realizing that these schools were never intended to educate or educe the divine powers within Black people. Watkins (2001) posits that after the Civil War, schools for Black people—particularly those in the South—were designed by wealthy philanthropists. These philanthropists designed "seventy five years of education for blacks" (pp. 41-42). Seventy-five years from 1865 brings us to 1940, and today we are seventy years removed from 1940. The sum of these numbers does not equal seventy-five years of scripted education; to truly understand the plight of Black education, one has to consider the historical impact of seventy-five years of scripted education and its influence on the present state of Black education.

Presently, schools are still controlled by ruling class Whites who hold major power. Woodson (2008) saw this as a problem in his day and argued, "The education of the Negroes, then, the most important thing in the uplift of Negroes, is almost entirely in the hands of those who have enslaved them and now segregate them" (p.22). Here, Woodson cogently argues for historical understanding: To point out merely the defects as they appear today will be of little benefit to the present and future generations. These things must be viewed in their historic setting. The conditions of today have been determined by what has taken place in the past. . . (p. 9) Watkins (2001) summarizes that the "white architects of black education. . . carefully selected and sponsored knowledge, which contributed to obedience, subservience, and political docility" (p. 40). Historical knowledge is essential to understanding the plight of Black education.

A major historical point in Black education was the famous *Brown v. the Board of Education Topeka Kansas,* in which the Supreme Court ruled that segregation deprived Blacks of educational equality. Thus, schools were ordered to integrate with all deliberate speed. This historic ruling has continued to impact the education of Black children in myriad and complex ways.

To date, the landmark case of *Brown v. the Board of Education Topeka Kansas* has not lived up to the paper that it was printed on. Schools are more segregated today than they were at the time of the *Brown* decision. Even more disheartening is that schools that are supposedly desegregated may have tracking programs such as "gifted and talented" that attract White students and give schools the appearance of being integrated while actually creating segregation within the school. Spring (2006) calls this "second-generation segregation" and asserts: Unlike segregation that existed by state laws in the South before the 1954 *Brown* decision, second generation forms of segregation can occur in schools with balanced racial populations; for instance, all White students may be placed in one academic track and all African American or Hispanic students in another track (p. 82). In this type of setting, White supremacy may become rooted in the subconscious minds of both Black and White students. Nieto and Bode (2008) highlight the internalized damage that tracking may have on students when they say students "may begin to believe that their placement in these groups is natural and a true reflection of whether they are 'smart,' 'average,' or 'dumb'" (p. 119). According to Oakes and Lipton (2007), "African American and Latino students are assigned to low-track classes more often than White (and Asian) students, leading to two separate schools in one building— one [W]hite and one minority" (p. 308). Nieto and Bode (2008) argue the teaching strategy in segregated settings "leaves its mark on pedagogy as well. Students in the lowest levels are most likely to be subjected to rote memorization and static teaching methods" (p. 119). These findings are consistent with Lipman's (1998): "scholars have argued that desegregation policy has been framed by what is in the interest of [W]hites, has abstracted from excellence in education, and has been constructed as racial integration, thus avoiding the central problem of institutional racism" (p. 11). Hammond (2005) is not alone, then, in observing that "the school experiences of African American and other minority students in the United States continue to be substantially separate and unequal" (p. 202).

Clearly, the education of Black students must be addressed with a sense of urgency like never before. Lipman (1998) alludes to the crisis of Black education, noting that "The overwhelming failure of schools to develop the talents and potentials of students of color is a national crisis" (p.2). In just about every negative category in education, Black children are over-represented. Again Lipman (1998) alludes, "The character and depth of the crisis are only dimly depicted by low achievement scores and high rates of school failure and dropping out" (p. 2). Under the guise of raising student achievement, the *No Child Left Behind Act* has instead contributed to the demise of educational equality for Black students. Hammond (2004) cites the negative impact of the law: "The Harvard Civil Rights Project, along with other advocacy groups, has warned that the law threatens to increase the growing dropout rate and pushout rates for students of color, ultimately reducing access to education for these students rather than enhancing it" (p. 4). Asante (2005) summarizes the situation thus: "I cannot honestly say that I have ever found a school in the United States run by whites that adequately prepares black children to enter the world as sane human beings . . . an exploitative, capitalist system that enshrines plantation owners as saints and national heroes cannot possibly create sane black children" (p. 65). The education of Black students and its surrounding issues indeed makes for a national crisis that must be put at the forefront of the African American agenda for liberation.

In this series, *Issues in Black Education,* I call upon a wide range of scholars, educators, and activists to speak to the issues of educating Black students. The series is designed to not only highlight issues that may negatively impact the education of Black students but also to provide possibilities for improving the quality of education for Black students. Another major goal of the series is to help pre-service teachers, practicing teachers, administrators, school board members, and those concerned with the plight of Black education by providing a wide range of scholarly research that is thought-provoking and stimulating. The series will cover every imaginable aspect of Black education from K-12 schools to higher education. It is hoped that this series will generate deep reflection and catalyze action-praxis to uproot the social injustices that exist in schools serving large numbers of Black students.

In the past, significant scholarly research has been conducted on the education of Black students; however, there does not seem to be a coherent theoretical approach to addressing Black education that is outside of European dominance. Thus, the series will serve as a foundation for such an approach—an examination of Black leaders, scholars, activists, and their exegeses and challenge of power relations in Black education. The idea is based on the educational philosophies of Elijah Muhammad, Carter G. Woodson, and others whose leadership and ideas could transform schools for Black students. One can only imagine how schools would look if Elijah Muhammad, Carter G. Woodson, Marcus Garvey, or other significant Black leaders were in charge. Additionally, the election of Barack Hussein Obama as the first Black president of the United States of America offers us a compelling examination of transformative leadership that could be inculcated into America's schools. The newly elected president's history of working for social justice, his campaign theme of "Change We Can Believe In," and his inaugural address that challenged America to embrace a new era are similar to the ideas embodied in *Critical Black Pedagogy in Education.*

This series is a call to develop an entirely new educational system. This new system must envision how Black leaders would transform schools within the context of our society's diversity. With this in mind, we are looking not only at historical Black leaders but also at contemporary extensions of these great leaders. Karen Johnson et al. (in press) describes the necessity for this perspective: "There is a need for researchers, educators, policy makers, etc. to comprehend the emancipatory teaching practices that African American teachers employed that in turn contributed to academic success of Black students as well as offered a vision for a more just society." Freire (2000) also lays a foundation for critical Black pedagogy in education by declaring, "it would be a contradiction in terms if the oppressors not only defended but actually implemented a liberating education" (p. 54). Thus, critical Black pedagogy in education is a historical and contemporary examination of Black leaders (scholars, ministers, educators, politicians, etc.) who challenged the European dominance of Black education and suggested ideas for the education of Black people.

This ground breaking book by Terence Hicks, a quantitative research professor and Abul Pitre, a qualitative research professor builds upon the usefulness of each research method and integrates them by providing valuable findings on a diverse group of college students. This book provides the reader with a mixture of quantitative and qualitative research studies surrounding nine chapters. Drawing from major quantitative and qualitative theoretical research frameworks found in multicultural education, this book, "*Research Studies in Higher Education: Educating Multicultural College Students*" is a must read. The editors feel that their book contributes much to the research literature regarding the role that educational leaders have in educating multicultural college students.

The book is a welcome addition to the literature on Black education. Similar to Joyce King's (2005) *Black Education: A Transformative Research and Action Agenda for the New Century,* this book addresses research issues raised in *The Commission on Research in Black Education* (CORIBE). Like CORIBE's agenda, *it* focuses on "using culture as an asset in the design of learning environments that are applicable to students' lives and that lead students toward more analytical and critical learning" (p. 353). The book is indeed provocative, compelling, and rich with information that will propel those concerned with equity, justice, and equality of education into a renewed activism.

Abul Pitre
Series Editor

References

Asante, K. (2005). *Race, rhetoric, and identity: The architecton of soul.* Amherst, NY: Humanity Books.

Freire, P. (2000). *Pedagogy of the oppressed.* New York: Continuum.

Hammond-Darling, L. (2004). From "separate but equal" to "no child left behind": The collision of new standards and old inequalities. In Meier, D. & Wood, G.

(Eds.), *Many children left behind: How the no child left behind act is damaging our children and our schools (pp. 3-32).* Boston: Beacon Press.

Hammond-Darling, L. (2005). New standards and old inequalities: School reform and the education of African American students. In King, J. (Ed.), *Black education: A transformative research and action agenda for the new century (pp. 197-224).* Mahwah, NJ: Lawrence Erlbaum Associates.

Hassan-EL, K. (2007). *The Willie Lynch letter and the making of slaves.* Besenville, IL: Lushena Books.

Johnson, K., Pitre, A. and Johnson, K. (Eds.). (in press). African American women educators*: A critical examination of their pedagogies, educational ideas, and activism from the nineteenth to the mid-twentieth centuries.* Lanham, MD: University Press of America.

King, J.E. (Ed). (2005). *Black education: A transformative research and action agenda for the new century.* Mahwah, NJ: Lawrence Erlbaum Associates.

Lipman, P. (1998). *Race and the restructuring of school.* Albany, NY: SUNY Press.

Nieto, S. and Bode, P. (2008). *Affirming diversity: The sociopolitical context of multicultural education* (Fifth edition). Boston: Allyn and Bacon.

Oakes, J. and Lipton, M. (2007). *Teaching to change the world.* (Third edition). Boston: McGraw-Hill.

Pitre, A. (2008). *The education philosophy of Elijah Muhammad: Education for a new world.* (Second edition). Lanham, MD: University Press of America.

Spring, J. (2006). *American education.* New York: McGraw-Hill.

Watkins, W. (2001). *The White architects of Black education: Ideology and power in America 1865-1954.* New York: Teachers College Press.

Woodson, C.G. (2008). *The mis-education of the Negro.* Drewryville, VA: Kha Books.

Foreword

Our nation is not operating at its full potential. Every day we are missing out on the latent contributions of bright, talented, academically promising students. These students are primarily students of color, first-generation students and students from low-income backgrounds who never graduate from college. Many of them never get the opportunity to attend college—we are failing them throughout the PreK-16 educational pipeline. Many of the under-served students who enter college are not achieving at high levels or to their full potential. We now see a trend that is especially troubling—African American and Latino males are not achieving at the same levels as their female counterparts.

There are numerous reasons we find ourselves in this predicament. Nationwide standardized tests scores of our public school students have increased for all subgroups, but there remains an achievement gap—in fact the gap between white students and African American students in reading assessments has remained virtually unchanged since 1992. This gap follows our students on to college—they often begin their post-secondary careers with an academic deficit. All too often college faculty members do not know what is necessary to ensure the success of under-served students; they are neither certain what strategies are successful when working with under-served and under-represented students nor are they informed of the types of support that these students need.

As the Vice President for Diversity and Community Engagement at The University of Texas at Austin, I have the pleasure of overseeing a number of projects and programs that support under-served and under-represented students. We have some phenomenal students in our programs—students who make a difference at the university and who are sure to become outstanding leaders during their careers and in their communities. We would not have the successful programs without implementation of the research-based best practices and strategies that form the foundation of our programs. I would like to see all students of color, first-generation students, and students from low-income backgrounds not only have a shot at attending the college or university of their choice, but the chance to be academically successful.

Through current research, there is hope that faculty and staff can achieve a better understanding of what our under-served and under-represented students at the post-secondary level need. A good place to begin or continue our search for understanding is in *Research Studies in Higher Education: Educating Multicultural College Students*. Editors Dr. Terence Hicks and Dr. Abul Pitre present a series of qualitative and quantitative studies, all focusing on educational attainment, access and equity for college students who are under-served or under-represented given their race, ethnicity, low-income, first-generation, or nontraditional student status. The selection of studies represents a cross-section of institutions and provides an examination of what is and what is not working with regard to policies and structures that are meant to assist our under-served and under-represented students at colleges across the country. The research focuses on programs and policies from community colleges, and public and private universities. The researchers themselves come from a variety of academic backgrounds and institutional settings that help inform their findings.

Research Studies in Higher Education: Educating Multicultural College Students. is one in a series titled *Issues in Black Education.* Eight books are planned for the series and they will address topics ranging from black males in special education to issues around the STEM subjects. With help from researchers whose findings are included in *Research Studies in Higher Education* and the entire *Issues* series edited by Dr. Abul Pitre, faculty and staff should be able to tap into practices that make a difference.

Dr. Gregory J. Vincent
Vice President for Diversity and Community Engagement
W.K. Kellogg Professor in Community College Leadership
Professor of Law
The University of Texas at Austin
Austin, Texas

Acknowledgments

Many people made this book possible. First, we would like to thank the production and marketing staff at the University Press of America division of Rowman & Littlefield Publishers Inc. for endorsing and assisting with this important project. We are grateful for the assistance of Sylvia Macey with this project. We thank all of the contributors for their enthusiasm and insights, as well as willingness to engage in dialogue about their ideas. It has been a privilege to collaborate with this exceptional group of colleagues.

Finally, while it is not possible to acknowledge everyone, we would like to thank our colleagues and others who have maintained an interest and enthusiasm for this project concerning research studies on multicultural college students.

Introduction

Terence Hicks
Fayetteville State University
Abul Pitre
North Carolina A&T State University

Expanding equity and access to higher education for minorities and low-income students continues to be a major focus in the twenty-first century. So, what are the advantages of a book on quantitative and qualitative research studies on a diverse population of college students in higher education? For one, integrating quantitative and qualitative approaches to transit research provides an innovative tool in both determining and understanding college students and their needs to transition into an institution. Researchers have consistently engaged in critical policy and equity research through quantitative and qualitative research methods, addressing issues of race, sex, diversity, and ethnicity in their research and publications. This ground breaking book edited by Terence Hicks, a quantitative research professor and Abul Pitre, a qualitative research professor builds upon the usefulness of each research method and integrates them by providing valuable findings on a diverse group of college students.

The editors provide a unique mixture of quantitative and qualitative research studies conducted on African American, first-generation, undecided and non-traditional college students. There is an apparent gap in the knowledge of college administrators and faculty concerning the educational expectations that are held by incoming African American, first-generation, undecided and non-traditional college students and how these expectations may relate to their persistence, or lack thereof, at a post-secondary institution. Until more accurate methods are developed to identify which college students are at risk of failing and leaving college, little can be done to intervene and avoid the undesired consequences of poor educational performances and attrition that affect college students and the institutions. Thus, it would be helpful to know what educational challenges exist for these students upon entering a college setting. Such information is needed to assess more fully the at-risk potential of these students for non-completion of college.

Given that a relatively large percentage of African Americans, first-generation, undecided and non-traditional college students are entering college and considering the low completion rate among these groups, it is of importance to explore means to improve their college completion rates. Furthermore, it is imperative that these college students receive appropriate support in and out of the classroom in order to navigate successfully the educational pathway. In this important book on quantitative and qualitative research studies surrounding the African American, first-generation, undecided and non-traditional college students, the chapter authors provide important recommendations for university administrators, faculty and staff in supporting the adjustment to college life of these students. Most importantly, the recommendations focused primarily on these college students, and ways in which university administrators and faculty could provide support to address the low college retention rate among this group due to their educational challenges.

This book offers three dynamic sections. In the first section, the contributing chapter authors provide qualitative research findings on the African American and Latino college student population. In Chapter One, Desiree' Vega and James Moore III chapter focuses on the lived experiences of African American and Latino first-generation college students encounters throughout their elementary and secondary educational process and its impact on their pursuit and completion of a higher education. Chapter Two, by Pamela Larde uses the phenomenological research approach to capture the lived experiences and essence of why and how African American first-generation college students decided to pursue higher education. In Chapter Three, J. Luke Wood and Adriel A. Hilton discusses the factors affecting the academic success of African American male students in the community college. This study employed a qualitative research design using semi-structured interviews conducted with twenty-eight Black male community college students. Chapter Four by Ron Brown discusses the perceived influence of racialized discrimination (societal dissonance) on the academic success of seven academically successful African American male undergraduate students at a predominantly White institution of higher education. Through the lived experiences of these students, the chapter provides insight into issues of societal perception, persistence, support, and access through the perspective of African American males.

In the second section of the book, the chapter authors provide a mixture of quantitative and qualitative research studies on the first-generation college student. Chapter Five by Bryan Andriano uses quantitative data collected by the Center for Post-secondary Study (CPS) at Indiana University-Bloomington through the National Survey of Student Engagement (NSSE) College Survey Report to examine engagement practices and study abroad participation among first-generation American college students. Bryan Andriano uses a logistic regression model to predict study abroad participation among the first-generation American college students. In Chapter Six, Ashley Rondini uses a grounded theory analytical approach and uses in-depth interviews with low-income first-generation college students and parents of these students to study the lived experiences of educational mobility for low income first-generation students on an elite campus. Chapter Seven by Mona Davenport uses analysis of variance (ANOVA) and regression analyses to examine nine critical factors that affect persistence of ethnic minority first-generation and non-first-generation college students.

In the third section of the book, the chapter authors provide quantitative research findings on undecided and non-traditional college students. Chapter Eight by Kimberly Brown uses the t-test and chi-square analysis to determine if there were statistically significant differences between Specific Majors (SMs) and Non-Specific Majors (NSMs) college students in terms of background characteristics, self-perception of abilities, degree aspirations and academic achievement (first year GPA). In Chapter Nine, J. Michael Harpe and Theodore Kaniuka uses quantitative data to analyze retention and persistence rates among North Carolina Community College traditional and non-traditional students.

Qualitative Research Studies on the African American and Latino College Student

Chapter One
African American and Latino First-Generation Students: Implications for Teachers, School Counselors, University Officials, Parents, and Students

Desireé Vega, Ph.D. and
James L. Moore III, Ph.D.
The Ohio State University

Introduction

In many high schools across the United States, students from various backgrounds and school settings aspire to attend college. Unfortunately, many never achieve this goal. Students of color (e.g., African American and Latino) and those students who come from low-income backgrounds often find themselves in this predicament (Bell, Rowan-Kenyon, and Perna, 2009; Choy, Horn, Nuñez, and Chen, 2000; Ishitani, 2003; Martinez and Klopott, 2005; Noeth and Wimberly, 2002), and, if they are successful in matriculating to college, these students are frequently the first in their families to ever achieve this accomplishment (Cho, Hudley, Lee, Barry, and Kelly, 2008; Farmer-Hinton, 2008; Noeth and Wimberly). Generally speaking, first-generation college students tend to have less access to family, friends, and mentors who are knowledgeable about college and the college-going process. They also frequently attend public schools, where three-quarters of the student population is comprised of ethnic minorities (Horn and Neville, 2006), with very few of these students who are academically prepared to go to college (Kimura-Walsh, Yama-mura, Griffin, and Allen, 2009; Perna et al., 2008; Reid and Moore, 2008).

According to the National Center for Education Statistics (NCES), the percentage of tenth graders across racial and ethnic groups who indicated that they aspired to attain a bachelor's degree or higher doubled from 40 percent in 1980 to 80 percent in 2002 (Roderick, Nagaoka, and Coca, 2009). Nonetheless, despite high college aspirations and a rise in college enrollment rates, African American and Latino students still lag behind their white counterparts. In 2005, Solórzano, Villalpando, and Oseguera examined the educational pipeline among Latino students and found that, although their college enrollment has increased, attendance at two-year community colleges accounted for the growth. Further, the authors reviewed data from the U.S. Bureau of the Census (2000) and found that, despite Latinos representing the largest ethnic/racial group in the United States, they had the poorest educational transition rates in comparison to African American, Native American, White, and Asian American students. Education researchers have identified the challenges that contribute to the disparities in college enrollment and attendance among first-generation African American and Latino students, such as poor academic preparation, lack of access to college counseling, and inadequate social capital (Engle, 2007; Kimura-Walsh, Yamamura, Griffin, and Allen, 2009; Perna et al., 2008; Reid and Moore, 2008; Thompson and Joshua-Shearer, 2002; Venezia and Kirst, 2005).

With this in mind, the post-secondary educational process for first-generation students starts long before they enter college. It is essential that efforts are attempted to make information available for students and families early in their academic careers. Therefore, early exposure to college preparatory resources is helpful in increasing the number of first-generation students that enroll and graduate from college (Engle, 2007; Holcomb-McCoy, 2010; Horn and Nuñez, 2000; Wimberly and Noeth, 2004). Because African American and Latino students are more often first-generation students, educators should work to better understand the challenges they face in accessing post-secondary education and develop more effective measures, at both the elementary and secondary levels, to prepare them for college (Reid and Moore, 2008). This chapter focuses on the experiences first-generation African American and Latino students encounter throughout their elementary and secondary educational process that subsequently impact their pursuit and completion of a higher education. Recommendations for educators (e.g., teachers, school counselors, etc.) are also discussed.

Pre-College Factors

Academic Preparation

At the preK-12 education level, it is critical that educators are keenly aware of the need for rigorous academic preparation for African Americans and Latino students. Academic rigor increases the likelihood that these students, as well as any other student demographic group, will obtain a bachelor's degree but reduces the likelihood of students having to complete remedial coursework in college (Harrell and Forney, 2003). In a past study by Horn and Nuñez (2000), they found that first-generation students who completed advanced mathematics courses in high school doubled their chances of enrolling in a four-year college. Nonetheless, they also reported that first-generation students were less likely to complete eighth grade algebra even when they were academically qualified to take the course. Therefore, it is important that first-generation students are aware of the importance of taking rigorous courses, and they are informed of the implications of taking such courses as early as middle school to avoid being underprepared for college (Smith, 2009).

In 2008, Reid and Moore found that seven of the thirteen first-generation participants felt less prepared for college than their freshman college peers. For example, one student stated, "I feel like I was less prepared than those who attended [suburban] schools because they have different resources. . . . They have ACT/SAT preparation. . . . They knew what to expect once they got to college" (p. 252). Additionally, many of the students in the study thought that they lacked certain academic skills, study skills, and time management skills. The students also suggested that they missed out on opportunities that could have better prepared them for college. Regardless of students' high-achieving status, many of the student interviewees asserted that their urban public high schools did not provide adequate preparation for their postsecondary pursuits. However, several mentioned those teachers who were doing an outstanding job preparing their students for college.

In a past study about college undergraduates' high school educational experiences, Thompson and Joshua-Shearer (2002) found that African American and Latino students wished they had greater access to college preparation courses. Such students significantly increased their chances of attaining a college degree, when they took rigorous courses in high school (Warburton, Bugarin, and Nunez, 2001). To this end, advanced placement (AP) courses afford high school students, including those who are first-generation, the opportunity to prepare for college-level work (Moore and Slate, 2008).

In 2004, Solórzano and Ornelas conducted a study examining the access and availability of AP courses for African American and Latino students. The two researchers discovered three themes, such as (a) African American and Latino students were disproportionately underrepresented in AP enrollment in the schools with the lowest ratio of students to AP courses in California in general and the Los Angeles Unified School District (LAUSD) in particular; (b) schools that served urban, low-income African American and Latino communities had low student enrollment in AP courses; and (c) even when African American and Latino students attended high schools with high numbers of students enrolled in AP courses, they were not proportionately represented in AP enrollment. Based on these findings, it is reasonable to believe that AP courses play a major role in preparing students for college courses and strengthening their qualifications for college admissions applications. AP courses are strong indicators of a high-quality high school curriculum (Solórzano and Ornelas, 2004). Therefore, it is necessary for schools to offer a variety of AP courses to ensure African American and Latino students, especially first-generation students, are ready for the rigor of college-level work.

In 2006, Griffin and Allen examined the college preparatory experiences of high-achieving African American students in a well-resourced, suburban school and an under-resourced, urban high school. Despite the differential access to college preparation, students in both school settings encountered inhibitory barriers. For instance, Twin Oaks High School, the suburban school, offered 39 AP and 11 honors courses. While the African American students felt that the school had high-quality teachers and strong curricula, they still believed that their race served as a barrier in their academic courses. As an example of this, one African American student expressed how he had to fight for access into more rigorous courses because he was seen as an athlete, not a scholar. Another African American student shared the difficulty of being the only black person in his AP courses. The following quote captured this point:

> Sometimes it's hard when you're in honors or AP classes and there are not very many minorities in it. Cause it, psychologically, it's like you can't afford to be wrong. Cause then everybody's like, he don't know what he's talking about. (p. 485).

The high-achieving students at Bennett High School indicated very few AP classes were offered; however, they felt it was sufficient to prepare them for college. The students also felt they had high-quality teachers who supported their college goals. One student shared, "I feel like the teachers we have teach us about college. They teach us the things about what we need to know about college and then they prepare you for life in general." (p. 485).

Griffin, Allen, Kimura-Walsh, and Yamamura (2007) found comparable results in their study of high-achieving African American and Latino students attending magnet and non-magnet public high schools. The students at both schools reported having supportive and encouraging teachers; however, the students at the magnet school had access to more AP courses and a more rigorous college preparatory environment. School resources are extremely important for first-generation students, without any other access to college information. The school climate may also play a significant role in how students utilize those available resources. Although Twin Oaks offered a large number of AP courses and employed seven school counselors, the students thought that their school counselors had little confidence in them and provided little support. On the contrary, Bennett High School students believed that they received a great deal of support from school personnel. Further, they believed that the support offered by their school counselors and teachers compensated for any resources not available in school. The Latina students, in the study of Kimura-Walsh et al. (2009), also thought their teachers were doing their best, although the school was overcrowded and lacked resources (e.g., textbooks). Nonetheless, these inadequacies in school prevent students from receiving the personalized attention they desperately needed.

Roderick et al. (2009) recommends that teachers provide classroom environments that "deeply engage students in acquiring the skills and knowledge they will need to gain access to and succeed in college" (pp. 202-203). As a way of doing this, school personnel should invest some of their efforts in ensuring that students are offered a strong school curriculum indicative of college. Wiggan (2008) found that teacher practices, such as high-quality instruction, encouragement of critical thinking, and interactive teaching and learning, had the most significant impact on school success for African American high school students. Unfortunately, many first-generation students—who tend to be from communities of color and working poor or low-income communities (Cho et al., 2008)—report having teachers with low academic expectations and negative perceptions. In their meta-analyses, Tenenbaum and Ruck (2007) found that teachers held the highest expectations for Asian American students in comparison to other student demographic groups and held more positive expectations for European American than Latino and African American students.

Based on popular and social science literature, the relationships that students develop with their teachers and school counselors are critical as they transition from high school to college, particularly when students rely solely on these persons to provide them with college information and guidance (Holland, 2010). Holland and Farmer-Hinton (2009) emphasize the importance of a college culture within urban school contexts. The researchers define the college culture as an environment saturated with information and resources and on-going formal and informal conversations that help students comprehend the aspects associated with preparing for, enrolling in, and graduating from post-secondary institutions. An important ingredient to a school, which promotes a college culture, is social support. Social support promotes positive and meaningful connections between students and school personnel. With this in mind, it is critical that all public schools—urban, rural, and suburban—provide students with strong college counseling and guidance (Moore, 2006; Moore, Henfield, and Owens, 2008; Moore and Owens, 2008), as well as print and electronic resources that will help develop student academic and social skills to excel in preK-12 school environments and beyond (Holland and Farmer-Hinton, 2009; Moore, 2006).

Generally speaking, public high schools should align their curricula to prepare students for the demands of college. This includes providing equal access to AP classes, as well as the AP examinations that offer students the opportunity to gain college credit, while in high school (Moore and Slate, 2008). Roderick and his colleagues (2009) advocate for a preK-16 education alignment, as a way of improving college readiness and increasing graduation standards. The researchers acknowledged the limitations of increasing graduation standards when many students do not graduate now, but felt they must be supplemented with a data system to track student progress across educational level. A data system will enable educators to monitor students' academic progress and address their needs early in their educational experiences.

College Counseling

The American School Counselor Association (ASCA) recommends a school counselor-to-student ratio of 1:250 (ASCA, 2008); however, the national average for the 2008-2009 school year was 1:457, nearly double the recommended figure ("Student-to-Counselor Ratios," n.d.). School counselors in many American public schools across the country, particularly urban and rural, are often relegated to clerical duties and consumed with non-counseling responsibilities, which prevents them from providing students with much needed college support, guidance, and information needed for preparing for post-secondary (Martin, 2002; Moore et al., 2008; Perna et al., 2008). In 2008, Farmer-Hinton argued that, unless the dissemination of college information is structured in a way that provides access to all students, African American and Latino students lacking other networks to access this knowledge will continue to fall short of attending college.

Due to their often first-generation status, African American and Latino students frequently lack the needed social capital in their homes to access specific information about college (Reid and Moore, 2008), even when it is consistently offered. According to the research literature, a social capital framework is often used to understand first-generation students' pathways to college (Holland, 2010; Pérez and McDonough, 2008; Strayhorn, 2010). It refers to relationships that "have the potential to advance an individual's goals" (Holland 2010, pp. 112-113). In public schools around the country, these relationships are often absent for African American and Latino students or reserved for the brightest students among them (Kimura-Walsh et al., 2009), which often puts first-generation students at a further disadvantage. First-generation students require access and will benefit greatly from social networks that prepare them for college in the absence of familial college knowledge.

Kimura-Walsh et al. (2009) examined the college preparation experiences of Latina high and non-high achieving students attending an urban, public school. They found that Latina students relied almost exclusively on school-based resources to access college information. Due to their family's often lack of experiences with higher education, they did not obtain specific advice in preparation for college. Therefore, these students depended heavily on information received from school personnel to make decisions about the college selection process. Kimura-Walsh et al. found that 33 percent of the Latina students indicated that they used teachers and 27 percent used school counselors as their primary resource in attaining college information. Generally speaking, the students described their school counselors as helpful. For instance, one student shared, "my counselor, every time I needed something, I needed a recommendation letter or anything. . . I go to her and I ask her about it and she always gives me a straight answer." (p. 308). However, other students, such as this Latina student, shared the mistakes their school counselors made with the follow quote: "My counselor has been great to me, he guided me throughout high school. . . . But there's been times when they give you the wrong information [and] you get the consequences, not them" (p. 308). Many of the Latino participants believed that their school counselors served as useful resources in navigating their high school experiences and the college preparation process; however, some believed that their school counselors gave inaccurate information to their own personal detriment.

The latter finding is consistent with previous studies highlighting the lack of academic and college preparation available to first-generation students at the secondary level (Chen, 2005; Perna et al., 2008; Reid and Moore, 2008; Vega, 2011; Warburton, Bugarin, and Nuñez, 2001). For example, Chen (2005) found that 55 percent of first-generation students enrolled in remedial courses compared to only 27 percent of students whose parents held college degrees. The researcher also found that first-generation students performed poorly compared to their peers as early as their first year in college and were more likely to withdraw or repeat courses. In 2011, Vega found that many first-generation students in her qualitative study did not feel that their teachers were adequately preparing them for college and that their school counselors did not have enough time to offer necessary individual-ized support. For example, Lisa, a participant in the study, explained, "They [school counselors] don't do anything. . . . That's another thing that I hate because we miss out on a lot of opportunities, a lot of programs, a lot of things to do because of the counselors."

Chen (2005) found that such students struggled academically in college, due to the lack of vital information offered in high school. Kimura-Walsh et al. (2009) discovered that the school counselor-student ratio at Radcliffe High School was 1:725. Further, the high school had a college corner or a college counseling center on its campus, which only served the top 10 percent of students. These students benefitted from individualized and specialized college guidance, such as academic workshops, scholarship information, and college representative visits. Yet, the remaining 90 percent of the students were denied access to this resource. It is reasonable to believe that those students—who were not able to partake in these comprehensive services—were mostly African American and Latino. They more than likely would have been the first in their families to matriculate in college. Further, it is quite likely that the students not afforded the opportunities to access the college corner would be greatly penalized.

Stated differently, first-generation college students need information about the college application process that neither their parents nor their school could provide (Kimura-Walsh et al., 2009). Programs like the college corner at Radcliffe High School are excellent ways to expose first-generation college students to the college process. Pre-college outreach programs, such as Upward Bound, are also an effective approach. Strayhorn (2010) found that participation in outreach programs was associated with higher grades in college for African American and Latino males. In a past study of Kimura-Walsh et al. (2009), they found that high-achieving students tend to participate in these outreach programs. Their findings suggest that students who were not high-achievers did not readily access this additional source of college preparation information.

Further, in their examination of high-achieving, African American students attending urban and suburban schools, Griffin and Allen (2006) found stark differences in the availability of college preparatory resources. Twin Oaks, the suburban and well-resourced school, employed eight school counselors to assist students with the college decision-making process. Students reported that the school emphasized college attendance early in their high school careers, as early as freshman year. One student stated:

> So, going to this school, I know the first day, freshman year, [you] set up an appointment with your counselor and from then on, I've had a plan to go to college. I've known classes I need to take. I know what I have to do for my path. And that's one thing I think about this school is really good (p. 486).

However, this was not the consensus among the students. Some reported that their school counselors had low expectations and encouraged them to apply to community colleges, even when they were academically capable students. Students at Bennett High School, the low-resourced school with only three school counselors, reported being less satisfied with access to college information than students at Twin Oaks. Nevertheless, the students shared that they appreciated the school counselors' efforts to help them navigate the college preparation process. Consistent with this sentiment, one student shared "it may not be all those that other schools have, but they're here" (p. 488). Griffin et al. (2007) also found that students attending a magnet high school had more access to school counselors' knowledge about the college application process, college/university representatives, and opportunities to explore career options in the form of summer internships. On the contrary, students at the non-magnet high school felt their school counselors lacked the college preparation information they needed. Regardless of the reason for these perceptions, it is clear that these disparities in resources can influence the college preparation and success of African American and Latino, first-generation students.

According to the research literature, African American and Latino students may not fully understand the significance of their school counselors (Moore et al., 2008; Moore and Owens, 2008). For example, Moore, Sanders, Bryan, Gallant, and Owens (2009) found that less than half of the African American male participants in their study reported visiting the school counselor at least once for college preparation, career and personal, social, and emotional services. Most of the participants visited the school counselor to receive academic services; however, over half admitted being unaware of the availability of non-academic services (i.e., career, personal, social, and emotional services). Without a systematic process in place to provide college and career guidance, many students lose out on much needed information. Unfortunately, African Americans and Latinos—who will potentially be the first in their families to go to college—often are the students who lose out on these resources and opportunities. Aligned with this notion, Perna et al. (2008) found that students who do not take the initiative to contact their school counselors and/or attend a school without a college culture are less likely to receive sufficient college counseling. Thus, those students with the greatest need for support face the most barriers to receiving such counseling.

Familial, Peer, and Personal Factors

Research documents the importance of parental involvement in the academic success of youth. However, it is widely understood that first-generation students from African American and Latino communities require more support because their families frequently do not possess the needed social capital and personal experiences to help their children navigate the college-going process (Ceja, 2006; Holland, 2010; Kimura-Walsh et al., 2009). On another note, parents—who have attended college or graduated from college—are often better equipped to offer support in completion of admissions applications, financial aid forms, scholarship applications, as well as registering for classes (Harrell and Forney, 2003). First-generation students require access to specific information about college, so that they are not left behind and caught off guard. It is also important that students feel that they are being supported and encouraged throughout their schooling.

Research has documented the importance of support and encouragement from parents, regardless of their educational attainment and socioeconomic status (Griffin and Allen, 2006; Holland, 2010; Moore, 2006; Vega, 2011). Kimura-Walsh et al. (2009) found that Latina students endorsed their families as strong sources of emotional support for their educational goals. For instance, one Latina stated, "When my dad was in Mexico, he said it was hard because . . . they were poor . . . . So he said it was hard and I have the chance here . . . that I have . . . everything and to take advantage of it." In a past study, Ceja (2006) explored the role of parents in the college choice process of first-generation Chicana students and found similar results. The Chicana students explained that their parents lacked an understanding of the college selection process; however, they did indicate that their parents provided emotional and financial support. This support demonstrated to the students that their parents strongly valued a college education. Another student in the study indicated that her father attended college workshops to obtain information about college, but his limited understanding of English restricted his full comprehension. In other words, language barriers can prevent parents from becoming more involved in the college choice process.

In a past study focused on African American students, Holland (2010) examined the manner in which the college-bound accessed post-secondary information while in high school. Based on the findings, some students reported that their family and friends greatly influenced their decision to attend college, while others reported their families expected them to go to college. The majority of the African American participants identified their families as their primary source of inspiration and encouragement as they pursued their post-secondary educational plans. Such support helped them stay focused and motivated to succeed. In addition to emotional support, some students indicated their family provided assistance with academic assignments and financial support. The students, in the study, also indicated that their peers were inspirational and helpful in staying on track with their post-secondary plans. Griffin and Allen discovered that students' close peers held similar educational goals, which helped them to persist in the face of challenges. For example, one student shared:

> All my friends are going to college. . . . We all, we help each other out with, with the college process on those applications and scholarships. We do what we have to do so that all of us will have a better life and future (p. 489).

For Latino students in general, Pérez and McDonough (2008) found that they received strong support from their parents, relatives, and friends. A unique finding was the large degree to which these students relied on members of their extended family for college information. As an example of this, one student reported utilizing his cousin, a college graduate, as a resource for college planning. For African American males in science, technology, engineering, and mathematics, Moore (2006) found similar results.

Over the years, most research demonstrates the positive forms of support parents and relatives supply to first-generation students. On the contrary, Pérez and McDonough (2008) found that family members sometimes provided negative advice about the college selection process. For instance, a Latina interviewee shared that her older brother told her to stay in California because going out-of-state would be more expensive and that she would be away from her family. Another interviewee reported feeling conflicted by her brother's suggestion to go away to college, and her mother's advice to stay close to home. Although this advice may have been well-intended, it can cause students to make choices they do not want to make. This information underscores the need for schools and families to increase their communication about the college process and the opportunities and benefits of attending colleges that match students' need, regardless of their distance from home.

In Fordham and Ogbu's (1986) seminal study on "acting White," the two researchers documented how African American students are negatively affected by peer relationships. To this end, they asserted, "that *one major reason* black students do poorly in school is that they experience inordinate ambivalence and affective dissonance in regard to academic effort and success" (p. 177). Low-income, students of color, as well as those who are the first in their families to attend college, were often rejected or ostracized by their high school peers because of their high academic aspirations. Thus, they coped with the burden of "acting White" by forgoing their racial identity to achieve success. Fordham and Ogbu described the strategies utilized by students at Capital High. In essence, the strategies were used to resolve the tension between the desire to do well and conform to their peer group's collective identity. African American students participated in athletics and group activities, camouflaged their academic effort by clowning around, associated with bullies, and chose not to brag about their success or bring attention to themselves. In a later study, Fordham (1988) posited that high-achieving African American students developed a "raceless" persona to be academically successful. Her study demonstrated that high-achieving African American students possessed an inability to maintain a strong racial identity and achieve success simultaneously; a pyrrhic victory occurred in that their success came at the expense of a collective identity. The raceless persona developed, due to the tensions experienced by Black students as they tried to define their dual relationship to their racial group and the individualistic culture of school and society. The incompatibility of the two identities—racial and academic—led to a raceless persona. Nonetheless, researchers, over the years, have found that the responses to accusations of acting white vary among African American and Latino students. Horvat and Lewis (2003) found that supportive peer groups were associated with the pursuit of academic goals among African American students. Accordingly, all students, even African American and Latino first-generation students, are able to better adjust to college, if they perceive their high school peers to support high academic achievement and aspirations (Hudley, Moschetti, Gonzalez, Cho, Barry, and Kelly, 2009).

Steele's (1997) stereotype threat theory posits that out of fear of confirming negative racial stereotypes related to intellectual ability, African American students do not perform well academically. As a result, they identify and engage less with academics. This disengagement from school alleviates the anxiety by removing the student from the anxiety-provoking situation. Therefore, academically identified students of color are at a significant risk of dropping out or disidentifying from school due to stereotype threat (Osborne and Walker, 2006). Additionally, Majors and Billson (1992) argue that African American males adopt a "cool pose" or the attitudes and behaviors that position African American males as calm, emotionless, and tough. This permits them to cope in an environment of social oppression and racism, such as what many students of color experience in today's public schools. Although academic withdrawal—due to stereotype threat and adopting a cool pose—may protect the self-concept of students of color by preventing the development of negative feelings and barring the negative effects of racial discrimination, these coping mechanisms are often counterproductive to academic outcomes. In closing, these strategies often weaken students' motivational attitudes and behaviors that lead to academic success.

College Persistence

Pascarella, Pierson, Wolniak, and Terenzini (2004) found that parental level of education influenced the type of post-secondary institution students attended, the experiences students had in college, and their outcomes. In spite of high academic credentials and motivation identical to that of students whose parents attained a college degree, first-generation students were at a greater risk of being left behind academically, socially, and economically. Further, first-generation students were more likely to attend less selective post-secondary institutions, complete fewer credit hours in three years, and work more hours per week than their non-first-generation peers. They also were less likely to live on campus, enroll part-time, and be less academically and socially integrated in the campus community (Pascarella et al., 2004).

First-generation students benefit more from academic and social interactions with faculty and their peers. Yet, due to the limited time they often spend on campus, these students do not always access these resources enough. Additionally, first-generation students drop out of college at rates twice that of their non-first-generation counterparts over the course of their first three years (Hudley et al., 2009). The lack of academic and social integration puts these students at a greater risk for early departure from college (Tinto, 1993). The findings from Cho et al.'s (2008) study suggested that psychosocial factors, such as perceived safety, positive social climate, and having friends present on campus as important components when choosing a college for first-generation students. Further, for African American and Latino first-generation students, the ethnic composition of the campus and community were also important variables for their college choice process. It quite possible that social connections with other students of color in college may ease the transition and isolation felt by providing a sense of belonging for African American and Latino first-generation students. Student participation is related to positive academic and social benefits. Thus, the following section explores how African American and Latino first-generation students persist in college, in spite of barriers.

Familial Support, Peer Encouragement, and Student Resiliency

Throughout the secondary education literature on first-generation students, the benefits of emotional support from parents, relatives, and peers have been documented as discussed earlier in this chapter. The encouragement that these persons offer, after first-generation students enroll in college, often remains strong and has lasting benefits. A study by Dennis, Phinney, and Chuateco (2005) also demonstrated that personal characteristics, such as self-efficacy, can lead to positive outcomes in college.

In their examination of motivational characteristics and social supports, Dennis et al. (2005) found that the need for peer and family support was correlated with college adjustment. However, peer support was found to be a stronger predictor of college grades and adjustment than family support. This finding suggests that, while families can provide emotional support to first-generation students, they feel their peers were more equipped to provide the support needed to perform well in college. In terms of self-efficacy, the researchers also found that motivation to attend college on the basis of personal interest, intellectual curiosity, and the desire to attain a fulfilling career predicted college adjustment among African American and Latino first-generation college students. Both personal and career motivation variables predicted their commitment to attend college. Similarly, Gardenhire-Crooks, Collado, Martin, and Castro (2010) found that African American, Latino, and Native American men were motivated to attend college because it provided them with a means to social mobility. Further, a post-secondary education would afford them the opportunity to obtain high-paying jobs. In the study, the male participants identified earning respect, being a role model, earning academic credentials, and overcoming negative life experiences as motivators for attending college. The researchers also reported that the males did not allow negative stereotypes to discourage them from pursuing their educational and career goals.

Moore, Madison-Colmore, and Smith (2003) investigated the persistence of African American males in an engineering school at a predominantly white institution (PWI). These students encountered discrimination as the males in Gardenhire-Crooks et al. (2010) study did. Their personality characteristics aided them in persevering in college. The prove-them-wrong syndrome was used as an emerging framework to explain how these students persisted in engineering. In essence, the African American males in the study coped with adversity by working hard to prove others wrong and show that they were capable of academic success. As an example of this, one participant explained, "You have to deal with stereo-types . . . you push harder. There is always the feeling that you have to perform better than anybody else" (p. 69). Another student shared:

> Basically, you're working twice as hard not only to overcome what they [White engineering professors, students, and administrators] think of you but to eventually to rise to what you know you can do . . . work twice as hard proving someone wrong as opposed to proving someone right (p. 67).

The African American males in the study developed personality traits that represented the prove-them-wrong syndrome. Despite facing discrimination and stereotypes, the students remained determined and committed to achieving academic success and attaining their goals.

Mentoring and Outreach Programs

Positive relationships between first-generation students and teachers play an important part in building the social capital these students oftentimes lack because their parents did not attend college. Morales (2009) explored the effects of mentoring relationships on the academic progress of male, Latino, first-generation college students. In this study, the students reported that their mentors provided them with inside information concerning academic and professional matters, such as developing critical thinking skills, taking effective notes in class, applying to graduate school, finding internships, and securing scholarship funding. The students also felt their mentors supported their future educational and career goals.

In regard to student-faculty relationships, Guiffrida (2005) found that that black faculty provided high-achieving African American students with comprehensive academic, career, and personal support. Although they expressed that the African American faculty advocated for them and believed in their ability to achieve, many of the students also expressed positive relationships with white faculty; however, the nature of the relationships differed from the African American faculty. The African American students in the study felt white faculty members were less willing to go above and beyond to guide them towards success. Based on the findings, it seemed that these students desired strong academic guidance and personal advice. The African American students, in the study, perceived their black faculty members as more willing to take on this mentorship role in comparison to their white faculty. On another note, Guiffrida and Douthit (2010) suggested that participation in African American student organizations offer many advantages in the form of locating Black mentors and students who have dealt with similar feelings of transitioning to a new environment and networking with African American professionals on campus and in the community. Similarly, Strayhorn (2010) found that African American males gained academic and social benefits through their involvement in college activities such as student government and volunteer opportunities.

Grant-Vallone, Reid, Umali, and Pohlert (2003-2004) surveyed first-generation college students participating in college support programs, such as Educational Opportunity Program (EOP), Academic Support Program for Intellectual Rewards and Enhancement (A.S.P.I.R.E.), and Faculty Mentoring Program (FMP) to understand how these programs influenced their academic and social integration, self-esteem, and commitment to college. The results indicated that students who utilized these programs the most were more likely to report higher levels of social adjustment. Stated differently, students' involvement with these campus programs facilitates positive adjustment to college life. More programs, such as those mentioned, should be created on college campuses to help first-generation college students reap the benefits of the college experience.

Recommendations

While many African American and Latino first-generation students aspire to attend college, a small number are successful in attending and graduating from college. These students' first-generation status often challenges their ability to access the information necessary to compete with their non-first-generation peers. The common goal should be to provide these first-generation students the opportunities they deserve to prepare for college and persist in college, while being competitive with their non-first-generation college peers. Thus, the following recommendations provide teachers, school counselors, university personnel, parents, and first-generation students with tips to create positive learning experiences throughout their schooling.

Recommendations for Teachers

1. Teachers should provide first-generation African American and Latino students with the experiences, resources, and knowledge that allow them to compete with non-first-generation African American, Latino, and White students. Therefore, it is important that these students have ongoing access to rigorous curricula throughout their preK-12 education (Harrell and Forney, 2003; Smith, 2009).
2. Teachers should work to develop positive, encouraging relationships with African American and Latino first-generation students that are supportive, encouraging, and validating (Hudley et al., 2009. This type of trusting relationship enables these students, as well as any other demographic group, to feel comfortable talking to their teachers about their college-going goals and asking for academic assistance (Harrell and Forney, 2003).
3. It is important for teachers to hold high expectations for their students and deliver high-quality instruction (Moore, 2006; Moore and Owens, 2008). The development of a college culture demonstrates to African American and Latino first-generation students that their schools are committed to their academic success and helping them go to college (Perna and Thomas, 2009).
4. Teachers should create and sustain personal connections with parents (Fann, Jarsky, and McDonough, 2009) and assume parents want their children to persist academically. They should also work closely with students' parents to ensure that African American and Latino first-generation students stay on track for college (Smith, 2009).

Recommendations for School Counselors

1. School counselors should find ways to equitably disseminate college preparation information (Farmer-Hinton 2008), including courses students should enroll in (e.g., AP and honors courses), college application resources, financial aid resources, and college placement exams. Such information truly makes a difference in the college preparation process for first-generation African American and Latino students.
2. School counselors should inform all students of their post-secondary educational and career options rather than discouraging them from applying to college. Therefore, school counselors should work aggressively to establish rapport with their students.
3. School counselors should offer special seminars and workshops for parents to increase their familiarity with the college-planning process. Such practices can help families enhance their knowledge base on the college process and be able to provide their children with concrete and specific assistance.
4. School counselors should translate, when necessary, their materials and handouts in multiple languages. With the increase of Spanish-speaking Latino

and other immigrant families in America's prek-12 schools, there is a strong need for these kinds of materials.

5. When planning college-related activities and workshops, school counselors should be sensitive to the schedules of parents of first-generation students. Oftentimes, these parents of students work multiple jobs or are employed in positions that are not always flexible with their hours.

6. School counselors should consider establishing parent volunteer programs, where parents can serve as ambassadors for the school counseling office. In these kinds of programs, parent volunteers can help with reaching "hard to reach" parents, as well as assist with coordinating and delivering workshops that focus on the college-going process (Downs et al., 2008; Holcomb-McCoy, 2010).

Recommendations for University Administrators, Faculty, and Staff

1. Mentors and role models in the form of faculty and staff support are significant for first-generation students to facilitate their academic and social integration into the campus community, as well as completion of their degree (Harrell and Forney, 2003; Morales, 2005). These relationships can help first-generation students locate resources on campus, such as math labs, writing centers, and the counseling center (Reid and Moore, 2008).

2. First-generation African American and Latino college students in their junior and senior years may have experienced difficulty fitting in at the start of their college careers due to their generational status and race/ethnicity. Therefore, they are equipped to help first-generation African American and Latino freshmen acclimate to college, both socially and academically. For that reason, connecting first-generation African American and Latino freshmen with upper-class first-generation to African American and Latino students as mentors can be beneficial in helping these students navigate the resources in their new environment (Reid and Moore, 2008).

3. Bridge programs that facilitate the transition from high school to college should be extended to African American and Latino first-generation students (Saunders and Serna, 2004). Such programs can assist students with getting familiar with the campus and meeting important university administrators, faculty, and staff who can help them navigate the campus.

3. Professional development should be offered to faculty and administrators to gain a deep understanding of the isolation first-generation students of color often experience in college. To this end, professional development can provide college personnel with the opportunity to develop strategies for helping students adjust to college (Guiffrida and Douthit, 2010).

Recommendations for Parents

1. At an early age, parents should instill in their children the notion that they have the ability to attend and succeed in college. Continued support and encouragement throughout their children's educational careers is vital to their development. Throughout the research literature, first-generation students, including African American and Latino, have acknowledged the significant role that parents play in their education.
2. Parents should get to know their children's teachers and school counselors to become informed about required courses, activities to prepare their children for college, and college applications and admissions policies. Such relationships have been found to be beneficial for students.
3. Research demonstrates the strong value first-generation African American and Latino students place on emotional support received from their parents (Ceja, 2006; Griffin and Allen, 2006; Holland, 2010; Kimura-Walsh et al., 2009; Moore, 2006; Vega, 2011). Therefore, parents can continue to influence their children's motivation through discussions concerning their future educational and career goals.
4. Holland (2010) discussed the importance of a college culture in preparing underrepresented students for college enrollment and persistence. This type of school environment communicates to students the schools' investment and dedication in helping them acquire the knowledge and skills needed for the demands of college. Therefore, parents should seek out schools that are dedicated to academic excellence and have a strong college culture.

Recommendations for African American and Latino First-Generation Students

1. In middle and high school, first-generation students need to be aware of the courses that best prepare them for the rigor of college. Therefore, it is important that these students are self-regulated and able to comfortably ask questions, when they do not know the answers.
2. They should also learn how to maximize the benefits of their formal and informal networks, including with their teachers, school counselors, and peers, to become college ready (Holland, 2010). Such relationships have been found to play a major role in students' academic journeys throughout the educational pipeline (i.e., elementary, secondary, and post-secondary).
3. First-generation college students should seek out academic and social networking resources on their college campuses to increase their chances of persistence. Many first-generation students are not integrated on their college campuses because they enroll part-time, work full-time, and only come to campus for classes. This disconnection between the student and the college culture oftentimes leads these students to depart college early (Tinto, 1993). If

students are involved with organizations and support groups on their campuses, their chances of leaving college early are likely to decrease.

Conclusion

First-generation students of color face many barriers throughout their educational careers that affect their ability to attend and succeed in college, including poor academic instruction, lack of access to college counseling, and a lack of knowledge about navigating their education. These students require access to the social capital that will allow them to achieve post-secondary and career success. Schools play a large role in providing students with necessary information to reach their educational goals of enrolling in and graduating from college. However, poor educational experiences make it difficult for first-generation students to do so. First-generation college students feel they lack critical thinking skills, study skills, time management, and adequate academic preparation compared to their peers (Reid and Moore, 2008).

Pre-college outreach programs are successful in preparing students for college; however, these programs are not accessible to all students (Kimura-Walsh et al., 2009). Familial and peer support provide first-generation youth with encouragement and motivation; nonetheless, they also need concrete and specific college preparation guidance. Thus, school personnel—teachers and school counselors— must address the knowledge gap by creating school environments that embrace a college culture, high-expectations, positive relationships, high-quality instruction, access to a rigorous curriculum, college counseling, and outreach to parents. Once these first-generation students enter college, their academic and social integration is vital to their post-secondary success. Support from family, peers, faculty, in addition to participation in outreach programs and student organizations, influences these students' chances of developing a college identity and commitment to persisting at their academic institutions.

Limitations in the current research concerning first-generation college students include an examination of their experiences by racial and ethnic identity as well as gender. Less is known about the differences between first-generation college students from various backgrounds. Although every group is heterogeneous, this information is a helpful starting point in expanding the discussion about African American and Latino first-generation students. To this end, there is a strong need for more research examining first-generation college students' perspectives of how their high school experiences prepared them for college. Such studies should examine how African American and Latino first-generation students succeed, despite facing challenges in their educational experiences.

Extant literature falls short of closely examining the experiences of undocumented Latino students. This type of investigation is needed and is likely aid parents and educational professionals, at both the preK-12 and post-secondary levels, in helping these students be successful.

References

Auerbach, S. (2007). From moral supporters to struggling advocates: Reconceptualizing Parent roles in education through the experience of working-class families of color. *Urban Education, 42*, 250-283.

Bell, A.D., Rowan-Kenyon, H.T., and Perna, L.W. (2009). College knowledge of 9th and 11th grade students: Variation by school and state context. *The Journal of Higher Education, 80*, 663-685.

Ceja, M. (2006). Understanding the role of parents and siblings as information sources in the college choice process of Chicana students. *Journal of College Student Development, 47*, 87-104.

Chen, X. (2005). *First-generation students in post-secondary education: A look at their college transcripts* (NCES 2005–171). U.S. Department of Education, National Center for Education Statistics. Washington, DC: U.S. Government Printing Office.

Cho, S., Hudley, C., Lee, S., Barry, L., and Kelly, M. (2008). Roles of gender, race, and SES in the college choice process among first-generation and non first-generation students. *Journal of Diversity in Higher Education, 1*, 95-107.

Choy, S.P., Horn, L.J., Nuñez, A., and Chen, X. (2000). Transition to college: What helps at-risk students and students whose parents did not attend college. *New Directions for Institutional Research, 107*, 45-63.

Dennis, J.M., Phinney, J.S., and Chuateco, L.I. (2005). The role of motivation, parental support, and peer support in the academic success of ethnic minority first-generation college students. *Journal of College Student Development, 46*, 223-236.

Downs, A., Martin, J., Fossum, M., Martinez, S., Solorio, M., and Martinez, H. (2008). Parents teaching parents: A career and college knowledge program for Latino families. *Journal of Latinos and Education, 7*, 227-240.

Engle, J. (2007). Post-secondary access and success for first-generation college students. *American Academic, 3*, 25-48.

Fann, A., Jarsky, K. M., and McDonough, P. M. (2009). Parent involvement in the college planning process: A case study of P-20 collaboration. *Journal of Hispanic Higher Education, 8*, 374-393.

Farmer-Hinton, R. L. (2008). Social capital and college planning students of color using school networks for support and guidance. *Education and Urban Society, 41*, 127-157.

Fordham, S. (1988). Racelessness as a factor in black students' school success: Pragmatic strategy or pyrrhic victory? *Harvard Educational Review, 58*(1), 54-84.

Fordham, S., and Ogbu, J. (1986). Black students' school success: Coping with the"burden of 'acting White.'" *The Urban Review, 18*(3), 176-206.

Gardenhire-Crooks, A., Collado, H., Martin, K., and Castro, A. (2010). *Terms of engagement: Men of color discuss their experiences in community college.* New York: MDRC.

Grant-Vallone, E., Reid, K., Umali, C., and Pohlert, E. (2003-2004). An analysis of the effects of self-esteem, social support, and participation in student support services on students' adjustment and commitment to college. *Journal of College Student Retention, 5,* 255-274.

Griffin, K., and Allen, W. (2006). Mo' money, mo' problems? High-achieving black high school students' experiences with resources, racial climate, and resilience. *The Journal of Negro Education, 75,* 478-494.

Griffin, K., Allen, W., Kimura-Walsh, E., and Yamamura, E.K. (2007). Those who left, those who stayed: Exploring the educational opportunities of high-achieving black and Latina/o students at magnet and nonmagnet Los Angeles high schools (2001-2002). *Educational Studies, 42,* 229-247.

Guiffrida, D.A. (2005). Othermothering as a framework for understanding African American students' definitions of student-centered faculty. *The Journal of Higher Education, 76,* 701-723.

Guiffrida, D. A., and Douthit, K. Z. (2010). The Black student experience at predominantly White colleges: Implications for school and college counselors. *Journal of Counseling and Development, 88,* 311-318.

Harrell, P. E., and Forney, W. S. (2003). Ready or not, here we come: Retaining Hispanic And first-generation students in post-secondary education. *Community College Journal of Research and Practice, 27,* 147-156.

Holcomb-McCoy, C. (2010). Involving low-income parents and parents of color in college readiness activities: An exploratory study. *Professional School Counseling, 14,* 115-124.

Holland, N. E., and Farmer-Hinton, R. L. (2009). Leave no schools behind: The importance of a college culture in urban public schools. *The High School Journal, 92,* 24-43.

Holland, N. E. (2010). Post-secondary education preparation of traditionally underrepresented college students: A social capital perspective. *Journal of Diversity in Higher Education, 3,* 111-125.

Horn, L., and Nevill, S. (2006). *Profile of undergraduates in U.S. post-secondary education institutions: 2003-04: With a special analysis of community college students* (Rep. No. NCES 2006-184). Washington, DC: U.S. Department of Education, National Center for Education Statistics.

Horvat, E.M., and Lewis, K.S. (2003). Reassessing the "burden of 'acting White'": The importance of peer groups in managing academic success. *Sociology of Education, 76*(4), 265-280.

Hudley, C., Moschetti, R., Gonzalez, A., Cho, S., Barry L., and Kelly, M. (2009). College freshmen's perceptions of their high school experiences. *Journal of Advanced Academics, 20,* 438-471.

Ishitani, T. T. (2003). A longitudinal approach to assessing attrition behavior among first-generation students: time-varying effects of pre-college characteristics. *Research in Higher Education, 44*, 433-449.

Kimura-Walsh, E., Yamamura, E. K., Griffin, K.A., and Allen, W. R. (2009). Achieving the college dream? Examining disparities in access to college information among high-achieving and non-high achieving Latina students. *Journal of Hispanic Higher Education, 8*, 298-315.

Majors, R., and Billson, J.M. (1992). *Cool pose: The dilemmas of Black manhood in America.* New York: Lexington Books.

Martin, P. J. (2002). Transforming school counseling: A national perspective. *Theory into Practice, 41*, 148-153.

Martinez, M., and Klopott, S. (2005). *The link between high school reform and college access and success for low-income and minority youth.* Washington, DC: American Youth Policy Forum and Pathways to College Network. Retrieved January 9, 2011, from http://www.aypf.org/publications/HSReform CollegeAccessandSuccess.

Moore, G. W., and Slate, J. (2008). Who's taking the advanced placement courses and how are they doing: A statewide two-year study. *The High School Journal, 92*, 56-67.

Moore, J. L., III. (2006). A qualitative investigation of African American males' career trajectory in engineering: Implications for teachers, counselors, and parents. *Teachers College Record, 108*, 246-266.

Moore, J. L., III, Henfield, M. S., and Owen, D. (2008). African American males in special education: Their attitudes and perceptions toward high school counselors and school counseling services. *American Behavioral Scientist, 51*, 907-927.

Moore, .L., III, Madison-Colmore, O., and Smith, D.M. (2003). The prove-them-wrong syndrome: Voices from unheard African-American males in Engineering disciplines. *The Journal of Men's Studies, 12*(1), 61-73.

Moore, J. L., III, and Owens, D. (2008). Educating and counseling African American students: Recommendations for teachers and school counselors. In L. Tillman (Ed.), *Handbook for African American education* (pp. 351-366). Thousand Oaks, CA: Sage.

Moore, J. L., III, Sanders, K., Bryan, D., Gallant, D. J., and Owens, D. (2009). African American male students' perceptions of the availability and use of high school counseling services. *The National Journal of Urban Education and Practice, 3*, 13-23.

Morales, E.E. (2009). Legitimizing hope: An exploration of effective mentoring for Dominican American male college students. *Journal of College Student Retention, 11*, 385-406.

Noeth, R. J., and Wimberly, G. L. (2002). *Creating seamless educational transitions for urban African American and Hispanic students* (Rep.). Iowa City, IA: ACT.

Osborne, J.W., and Walker, C. (2006). Stereotype threat, identification with academics, and withdrawal from school: Why the most successful students of colour might be most likely to withdraw. *Educational Psychology, 26*(4), 563-577.

Pascarella, E. T., Pierson, C. T., Wolniak, G. C., and Terenzini, P. T. (2004). First-generation college students: Additional evidence on college experiences and outcomes. *The Journal of Higher Education, 75*, 249-284.

Pérez, P.A., and McDonough, P. M. (2008). Understanding Latina and Latino college choice: A social capital and chain migration analysis. *Journal of Hispanic Higher Education, 7*, 249-265.

Perna, L. W., Rowan-Kenyon, H. T., Thomas, S. L., Bell, A., Anderson, R., and Chunyan, L. (2008). The role of college counseling in shaping college opportunity: Variations across high schools. *The Review of Higher Education, 31*, 131-159.

Perna, L. S., and Thomas, S. L. (2009). Barriers to college opportunity: The unintended consequences of state-mandated testing. *Educational Policy, 23*, 451-479.

Reid, M. J. and Moore, J. L., III (2008). College readiness and academic preparation for post-secondary education: Oral histories of first-generation urban college students. *Urban Education, 43*, 240-261.

Roderick, M., Nagaoka, J., and Coca, V. (2009). College readiness for all: The challenge for urban high schools. *The Future of Children, 19*, 185-210.

Saunders, M., and Serna, I. (2004). Making college happen: The college experiences of first-generation Latino students. *Journal of Hispanic Higher Education, 3*, 146-163.

Smith, M. J. (2009). Right directions, wrong maps: Understanding the involvement of low-SES African American parents to enlist them as partners in college choice. *Education and Urban Society, 41*, 171-196.

Solórzano, D. G., and Ornelas, A. (2004). A critical race analysis of Latina/o and African American advanced placement enrollment in public high schools. *The High School Journal, 87*, 15-26.

Solórzano, D. G., Villalpando, O., and Oseguera, L. (2005). Educational inequities and Latina/o undergraduate students In the United States: A critical race analysis of their educational progress. *Journal of Hispanic Higher Education, 4*, 272-294.

Steele, C.M. (1997). A threat in the air: How stereotypes shape intellectual identity and performance. *American Psychologist, 52*(6), 613-629.

Strayhorn, T. L. (2010). When race and gender collide: Social and cultural capital's influence on the academic achievement of African American and Latino males. *The Review of Higher Education, 33*, 307-332.

Tenenbaum, H. R., and Ruck, M.D. (2007). Are teachers' expectations different for racial minority than for European American students? A meta-analysis. *Journal of Educational Psychology, 99*, 253-273.

Thompson, G. L., and Joshua-Shearer, M. (2002). In retrospect: What college undergraduates say about their high school education. *The High School Journal, 85*, 1-15.

Tinto, V. (1993). *Leaving college: Rethinking the causes and cures of student attrition* (Second edition). Chicago, IL: University of Chicago Press.

Vega, D. (2011). *"With a little faith and support, you could really do anything":* *A study of urban youth.* Unpublished doctoral dissertation, The Ohio State University.

Venezia, A., and Kirst, M. W. (2005). Inequitable opportunities: How current education systems and policies undermine the chances for student persistence and success in college. *Educational Policy, 19*, 283-307.

Warburton, E. C., Bugarin, R., and Nunez, A. M. (2001). *Bridging the gap: Academic Preparation and post-secondary success of first-generation students* (Rep. No. NCES 2001-153). Washington, DC: U.S. Department of Education, National Center for Education Statistics.

Wiggan, G. (2008). From opposition to engagement: Lessons from high achieving African American students. *The Urban Review, 40*, 317-349.

Wimberly, G. L., and Noeth, R. J. (2004). *Schools involving parents in early Post-secondary planning: ACT policy report* (Rep.). Iowa City, IA: ACT.

Chapter Two
Inspired to Be the First:
How African American First-Generation
Students are Predisposed to Pursue
Higher Education

Pamela A. Larde, Ph.D.,
Mercer University

Introduction

Two African American boys of the same bloodline are raised in the same household of an urban Detroit neighborhood—a neighborhood rich with drugs and slim with educational opportunities. One shows signs early on that he's going to go somewhere in life and is even given the nickname "Professor" at an early age. The other, somehow lost in his brother's shadow, succumbs to the fast money of the streets. Professor wins the spotlight in the neighborhood, is adored by his church community, and captures the hearts of his teachers, yet his brother finds a way to simply get by and survive.

As a teen and young adult, Professor finds himself in a tough predicament after fathering a child out of wedlock, but he is resilient and decides to pursue a college education to better support his son and does not stop until he has earned his PhD. His brother, long lost in the shadows, finds himself in the wrong place at the wrong time and is convicted of murder and sent to prison for life.

Professor goes on to become who we know today as Dr. Michael Eric Dyson, renowned minister, distinguished Howard University professor, and best-selling author—his heart aching every step of the way over the fate of his beloved brother whom he believes did not receive the nurturing and support needed to seize the right opportunities in life (Dyson, 2008).

How is it that two boys raised together can take such different paths in life, with one going to college and the other to prison for a life sentence? Dyson addresses this question by saying:

> The temptation is to believe that individual choice alone accounts for such differences in destiny. Successful black family members did their work and played

by the rules; suffering family members ran afoul of the law and were justly locked away. Of course, that is true in many cases, but in far too many cases, it's not the entire truth (Dyson, 2008).

Sadly, the story of the Dyson brothers is not uncommon. This study seeks to uncover some of this truth by focusing in on a group of African American youth who beat the odds through the most challenging of circumstances to become the first in their families to pursue higher education.

Purpose

It is well documented that students whose parents did not attend college are less likely to pursue a college education than their peers. Yet, many find ways to get to college despite the odds that stand against them: poor academic preparation, minimal moral support from family, limited financial resources, a lack of college knowledge, and cultural norms that do not support the pursuit of higher education. Derived from a larger study on African American and Mexican American first-generation students, this chapter focuses specifically on the pre-college experiences of the African American students to develop a greater understanding of the journey to higher education.

Though the presence of first-generation students at institutions of higher education across the nation continues to increase (Terenzini et al., 1996), the problem of college access for this population has yet to be resolved. Even with the services that pre-college programs provide to first-generation students, a great number of college-qualified youth still miss out on the opportunity to go to college (Horn and Nunez, 2000). In order to grasp a full understanding of the barriers that limit students' opportunities to pursue a college education and how these students have overcome these barriers, further study is needed.

In 2001, Choy and MPR Associates reported that only 34 percent of the entering student population at four-year institutions were first-generation students. In most cases, first-generation students attend community colleges, as access to four-year institutions remains a challenge (London, 1992). However, the greatest problem rests in the fact that a significant portion of first-generation students still choose not to attend college at all. "Students whose parents have not attended college and/or have not earned a college degree are much less likely to go to college than their peers, particularly in the four-year sector" (Engle et al., 2006, p. 13).

A number of racial trends have also been identified among the first-generation population. First-generation students are more likely to be Black or Latino (Chen and Carroll, 2005), are typically older Latina females, and are often working mothers (Engle et al., 2006; Inman and Mayes, 1999; McConnell, 2000). Additionally, McCarron and Inkelas (2006) found a difference in college graduation rates among first-generation students of different racial backgrounds. In their study, 42 percent of Asian American students earned a bachelor's degree, compared to 31 percent of White students, 21 percent of African American students, and 19 percent of Latino students. Of greatest concern is the African American population because the number of African American first-generation college students has experienced a dramatic decline, dropping from 62.9 percent in 1971 to 22.6 percent in 2005 (Saenz et al., 2007). Unfortunately, this decline is not attributed to a growing number of students with college-educated parents. It instead, reflects a decline in enrollment from members of this population. To compound these figures, social economic status is another factor that affects the college-going disparity between the privileged and the underprivileged still exists. High school students who come from higher socioeconomic backgrounds attend college at a rate 30 percent higher than their peers who come from lower socioeconomic backgrounds (Walpole, 2007).

To take one step further, it is important to not only understand the barriers but also to understand the ways in which students have overcome them. Such information can provide the basis for a model that outlines what first-generation students may need in order to successfully enroll in and graduate from college. Pascarella and Terenzini (1980) asserted that future studies on successful students of color should take race and the interrelationship between social and academic integration into account. The current study took these factors into account by focusing on the experiences of African American students. It examines strategies for negotiating cultural background while in an academic environment and places significant emphasis on social and academic integration within the college predisposition framework created for this study.

Significance

This study is significant for two reasons: it brings forth the strengths that African American first-generation students possess and it explores how they became predisposed to go to college. Clifton and Anderson (2002) proposed that educators, particularly those in higher education, move away from deficit models, which focus primarily on problems, concerns and defects and that an increased focus is placed on success and achievement. As stated by the authors, "To produce excellence, you must study excellence" (Clifton and Anderson, pg. ix). The intent of this chapter is to zero in on excellence. Acquiring an understanding of the successes of African American first-generation students, the strategies they employ to overcome challenges and the resources they used to access a college education can lead to more effective college preparation initiatives and services within secondary and post-secondary institutions of education, as well as in government-funded and privately owned pre-college programs.

Literature Review

The First-Generation College Student

A number of definitions have been used to describe *first-generation* status. In general, it refers to the level of education obtained by a student's parents; however, when defining the specific level of education parents have received, researchers have had differing views. Pike and Kuh (2005), for example, stated that a student could be considered first-generation if his or her parent or guardian never earned a bachelor's degree, meaning that the parent may have had a great deal of college experience, just short of earning a bachelor's degree, or that they completed an associate's degree or certificate program. Other researchers (Choy, Horn, Nunez, and Chen, 2000; Pascarella et al., 2004; Terenzini et al., 1996) have defined *first-generation* status as having parents who did not earn more than a high school diploma, leaving open the possibility of having some college experience, short of earning specialized certification or an associate's degree. A host of other researchers have defined *first-generation students* as explicitly those whose parents never attended college at all (Chen and Carroll, 2005; Engle et al., 2006; Horn and Nunez, 2000; Volle and Federico, 1997). Brooks (1998) articulated a definition that combines the three into what can be considered a summarization of the most common understanding of first-generation status among academic researchers. First-generation students may fall under one of the following two scenarios: (a) Neither parent has completed a college degree, or (b) the student is the first member of the family to attend college (Walpole, 2007). The current study used option B as its operational definition.

Overall, first-generation students are less likely to have aspirations to pursue a college education (Saenz et al., 2007; Terenzini et al., 2001). In 1996, only 26 percent of first-generation students applied to a four-year institution, whereas 71 percent of their peers whose parents are college educated applied to a four-year institution. Even when first-generation students are qualified for admission, they are more likely to delay their enrollment, taking some time in between high school and college to work. In comparison, Saenz and associates (2007) found that 73 percent of non-first-generation students enrolled in college immediately after high school, whereas only 29 percent of first-generation students enrolled immediately after high school (Saenz et al., 2007).

Common Challenges of First-Generation Students

London (1992) described the first-generation student's pursuit of higher education as an act of upward social mobility—a step toward exceeding the educational and financial status of their parents. Some first-generation students pursue upward social mobility with great enthusiasm, while others embark upon the journey with much fear and skepticism. For some, it is neither. The idea of earning a college degree is simply a means to an end: a necessary task to accomplish in order to secure a job. Undoubtedly, the pursuit of upward social mobility is life-changing and requires, as London stated, "the shedding of one social identity and the acquisition of another" (p. 8). In order to cross into the world of higher education, first-generation students must navigate through a new set of norms, values, and expectations while balancing (and sometimes rejecting) the norms, values, and expectations of their families and communities.

The research has identified a number of challenges that inhibit a first-generation student's odds of enrolling in college. These include: having a low level of *academic preparation*, lacking strong *family support*, having limited *financial resources*, not having *college knowledge*, and struggling with the *cultural transitioning* that takes place between high school and college. These challenges have an adverse effect on the decision to enroll in college (Engle et al., 2006).

Academic Preparation

One of the most common challenges that first-generation students face is a poor level of preparation for succeeding academically in the college environment (Inman and Mayes, 1999). Many African American students struggle to access higher education opportunities of higher education in this country due to economic, social, and racial disparities (Nelson Laird, Bridges, Morelon-Quainoo, Williams, and Salinas Holmes, 2007). These disparities are largely attributed to segregated neighborhoods that offer inferior educational resources. African American youth are more likely to attend public schools with high concentrations of students of color from low socioeconomic backgrounds and do not receive the academic preparation needed to advance to college.

Coursework that lacks rigor, teachers with low expectations, and subpar resources (i.e., not enough textbooks or certified teachers) are major contributors to a lack of academic preparation in first-generation students, particularly those who attend schools in low socioeconomic communities. Students who are products of these academic experiences tend to lack the expected level of content knowledge and study skills needed to successfully pursue a college degree (Engle et al., 2006). Additionally, first-generation students often do not participate in academic programs that set them on the path to enrolling in college. For example, most are removed from the college preparation track as early as the eighth grade, a time when they are less likely than their non-first-generation peers to have taken important courses, such as Algebra 1 (Adelman, 2006). These students do not usually have access to the rigorous coursework that will prepare them for college such as AP and Honors courses (Cabrera and LaNasa, 2001). As a result, their academic skills tend to be weaker than those of their peers (Horn and Nunez, 2000). This is evident in their traditionally lower standardized test scores and GPAs (Terenzini et al., 1996).

These schools are also more likely to have fewer college counseling resources that will prepare them for college (Cabrera and LaNasa, 2001; Terenzini et al., 2001). The consequence of not receiving adequate academic preparation for college is a lack of confidence in academic abilities, leading students to believe that they are not "college material." Consequently, many dismiss the prospect of going to college altogether (Engle et al., 2006).

Family Support

Another significant factor affecting students' decision to aspire to and enroll in college is the encouragement and support they receive from family (Hossler, Schmit, and Vesper, 1999). According to Choy and MPR Associates (2001), "The likelihood of enrolling in post-secondary education is strongly related to parents' education even when other factors are taken into account" (p. 7). Parent educational level is also positively related to how far students persist in college. Unlike their second and third-generation peers, many first-generation college students lack the support needed from their parents to foster a successful college experience, from the admissions process through graduation (York-Anderson and Bowman, 1991). Parents who are college educated, on the other hand, are more likely to be involved in their children's education. When parents are more involved, students are more likely to take a rigorous high school curriculum and enroll in college (Horn and Nunez, 2000). Findings in a study of students from low socioeconomic backgrounds indicated that combining parental involvement with a school curriculum that prepares students for college were critical components leading to graduation and college enrollment (Cabrera and LaNasa, 2000).

However, while most studies posit that the families of first-generation students provide the least amount of support, Saenz et al. (2007) identified a new trend in a recent study. In this study, first-generation students actually placed equal importance on their parental support to attend college when compared to their non-first-generation peers. In 2005, almost 50 percent of first-generation students reported the fact that their parents wanted them to go to college was a key reason they pursued higher education. According to Saenz et al., "This trend has reversed for the two groups—first-generation students are now *more* likely to report parental encouragement as a very important reason for going to college" (p. 2). For some students, the very fact that their parents lack a college education served as a motivator to pursue one for themselves. In such cases, students recognized the hardships their parents endured as an opportunity to attend college and make a better life for themselves. The choice to go to college was a gesture of appreciation for their parents' hard work (Engle et al., 2006). According to Engle et al., "First-generation students do not view going to college primarily as a personal pursuit, but rather as the culmination of generations of effort and progress in their families and communities" (p. 22).

Financial Resources

First-generation students, who often come from low socioeconomic backgrounds, are adversely affected by financial constraints. First-generation students and even non-first-generation students from low socioeconomic backgrounds have been found to have lower educational aspirations, persistence rates, and rates of educational attainment than their peers from higher socioeconomic levels (Pascarella and Terenzini, 2005). In a longitudinal study of graduates of the class of 1992, just over half of the first-generation students were from families of low socioeconomic background. Comparatively, less than one-third of the students whose parents were college educated could be classified as low-income (Horn and Nunez, 2000). These factors present a real challenge to student success and college access, as lower incomes are associated with lower high school graduation rates and lower rates of college success (Volle and Federico, 1997).

> More first-generation students than their peers considered financial factors very important to their choice of specific colleges, and at college entry, they are twice more likely than their peers to report having a major concern about financing college. (Saenz et al., 2007, p. 2)

This line of reasoning resonates with human capital theory, which states that students' decisions about pursuing a college education are based on the economic feasibility and benefits of doing so. Specifically, students consider tuition, fees, books, housing, lost wages, and even emotional costs to determine whether or not these costs will reap greater benefits in the end (Walpole, 2007). These considerations affect the type of college they choose, the geographical location of the college, and the decisions about employment. In most cases, first-generation students choose to take on a job to pay for college expenses. This decision often leads them to delay enrollment to work and to choose the more affordable two-year institution (Chen and Carroll, 2005).

College Knowledge

A marked difference between first-generation students and their peers whose parents are college educated is the amount of information they have with regards to preparing for, applying to, and paying for college. This arsenal of information is referred to as *college knowledge* (Engle et al., 2006). Students who are armed with college knowledge often receive this information from parents, guidance counselors, teachers, and other influential adults. York-Anderson and Bowman (1991) found that the amount of college knowledge students have is strongly related to how much support they *perceive* they are receiving. Their findings indicated that those students who perceived that they had more family support "had more factual information about college than did those students who perceived less support" (p. 120).

College knowledge affects awareness on three levels: (a) college benefits awareness, (b) college resources awareness, and (c) college planning awareness. On the college benefits level, first-generation students and their parents are often unaware of the social and economic benefits of attending college (Volle and Federico, 1997). Non-first-generation usually have the advantage of receiving direction and having expectations set by parents who know the benefits of attaining a college degree, have experienced the demands of college, and can pass this knowledge on to them (Volle and Federico, 1997). As a result, they are more likely to be aware of and employ a number of effective strategies to increase higher education opportunities, such as hiring a private consultant to assist with the application requirements, enrolling in test preparation courses, and applying to a large number of colleges to increase the odds of acceptance. It is not surprising that this group is typically from higher socioeconomic backgrounds and tends to have higher rates of attendance at elite and selective universities (McDonough, 1994).

Conversely, first-generation students generally have fewer resources, less understanding of the benefits of a college degree, and less knowledge about different types of colleges and the college admissions process. This lack of college knowledge strongly affects the likelihood that they will attend college at all (Bedsworth, Colby, and Doctor, 2006; Cabrera and LaNasa, 2001; Choy et al., 2000; Terenzini et al., 2001). Most do not have people in their families or social circles who can help them with the college admissions process (Engle et al., 2006). Consequently, they are more likely than their peers whose parents are college educated to perceive the prospect of college as overwhelming and the application process intimidating.

Cultural Transitioning

The fifth challenge is related to the process of transitioning from the home culture to the college culture. Real consequences and challenges are associated with the pressures of shifting from one cultural community to another. The very fear of such change can bring displeasure from family and friends as first-generation students prepare to leave the culture in which they grew up to join an unfamiliar culture on a college campus. This experience of dislocating from one culture and relocating into another can be traumatic when the academic world is drastically different from first-generation students' home communities (Rendón, 1992). The process includes renegotiating old relationships with family and friends as they may question new habits, interests, and peers (London, 1992). For first-generation students, these challenges may come as a shock as they are often unprepared to pay the costs of the personal and social dislocations that take place through this pursuit of upward mobility. According to Inman and Mayes (1999), "First-generation students often feel they have to make an all-or-nothing decision about maintaining their parents' way of life or rejecting their family's culture to pursue an academic goal" (p. 4).

A Theoretical Framework for College Predisposition

Predisposition refers to a condition or quality that is based on natural and environmental factors (Dictionary.com, 2008). Based upon this definition, a student who has a predisposition to pursue higher education does so in response to a natural or innate desire. In other words, such individuals are more inclined than others to have college aspirations, due to a combination of natural and environmental factors. Naturally, they may possess a hunger and desire to learn. Environmentally, they may have received the support, validation, and information needed to nurture that hunger and desire.

The current study employed a three-tier college predisposition framework designed to encapsulate the experiences of first-generation students of color and to acquire a greater understanding of the characteristics possessed and strategies used by these students to pursue college enrollment. The framework was developed for this study in response to the limited scope of academic research that explores the *strengths* of first-generation students. Its purpose was to help the researcher identify the characteristics and background experiences that predispose first-generation students to pursue higher education. The framework pulls together the components of self-determination, academic achievement, and resourcefulness to explore the ways in which first-generation students of color overcame the common challenges that can inhibit the pursuit of a college education. It was constructed using elements of Ryan and Deci's (2000) Self-Determination Theory, a body of research on academic success (Astin, 1975; Griffin, 2006; Harper, 2005; Tinto, 1975; Yazedjian, Toews, Sevin, and Purswell, 2008) and common challenges faced by first-generation students (Horn and Nunez, 2000; London, 1992; Rendón, 1992; Hsaio, 1992; Chen and Carroll, 2005; Engle, Bermeo and O'Brien, 2006; Adelman, 2006).

The theoretical framework, as shown in Figure 2.1, consists of three tiers, each intended to explore the path to enrollment for first-generation students of color. Self-Determination Theory was used to develop the first tier to explore the students' internal drive for educational enhancement. The literature on high-achieving students formulated the second tier to explore the academic strategies students possess to ensure that they qualify for college acceptance. The final tier was derived from research identifying the common challenges first-generation students face to explore resourceful strategies employed to overcome these challenges.

Figure 2.1. College Predisposition Framework

Self-Determination (having college aspirations)	Academic Success (being qualified)	Resourcefulness (successfully enrolling)
Competence	Classroom Performance	Getting Academically Prepared
		Securing Financial Resources
Autonomy	Sense of Responsibility	Learning the Admission Process
	Stereotype Threat Resistance	
Relatedness	Social and Academic Integration	Shutting Out Negative Cultural Norms
		Building a network of human support

Self-Determination

The first tier of the framework is self-determination. As was indicated in the research, first-generation students face a number of challenges that make it difficult to pursue higher education, including lacking academic preparation, family support, financial resources, college knowledge, and an environment that embraces the pursuit of a college education to enable smooth cultural transitioning. Thus, if first-generation students who face these challenges manage to develop college aspirations and follow through on those aspirations, it can be said that they *choose* to take these challenges on, rather than conform to the pressure to not go to college. Self-Determination Theory (Ryan and Deci, 2000) was used to explore the extent to which self-determination played a role in this decision-making process.

Self-Determination Theory posits that all human beings have a natural propensity to pursue growth and integration. The authors explained that even as infants, humans are self-motivated to learn and progress and will continue in this motivation as long as the three psychological needs—competence, autonomy, and relatedness—continue to be met. Self-determination is interrupted only when at least one of these needs goes unfulfilled.

The first psychological need, *competence*, refers to believing that one is capable of accomplishing a goal. This term resonates with Nasim, Roberts, Harnell, and Young's (2005) characterization of positive self-concept as possessing qualities such as strength of character, motivation, independence, confidence, and a strong feeling of self.

Ryan and Deci (2000) described *autonomy,* the second psychological need, in terms of having a sense of personal control, freedom, and choice. In their words, it is "the feeling of volition that can accompany any act, whether dependent or independent, collectivist or individualist" (Ryan and Deci, p. 74). A group of high-achieving African American students in one study described the sense of autonomy they felt through the ability to be "agents of their own success" and to rely on their own "will, effort and resourcefulness" (Griffin, 2005, p. 11).

The final psychological need, *relatedness,* refers to having social support or strong connections to other people. Schlossberg's transition theory identifies five types of social support, including intimate relationships, family units, networks of friends, institutions, and communities (Evans, Forney, and Guido-DiBrito, 1998). It has been noted that students who are successful in college have found ways to connect themselves with the community through service and extracurricular activities (Harper, 2005). When students interact with others and feel accepted within the environment, the likelihood of achieving academic success increases (Astin, 1984; Harper, 2005; Tracey and Sedlacek, 1984; White and Sedlacek, 1986).

To consider how the psychological needs of competence, autonomy, and relatedness affect college aspirations of first-generation students, the self-determination tier in this framework explores the connection between these key supportive conditions and the disposition to aspire to a college education. However, while this theory serves to explore the internal drive that a first-generation student may possess, it cannot stand alone in uncovering the academic and resourceful strategies that these students employ to enable them to progress from having college-going aspirations to actually setting foot on a college campus. Hence, it is necessary to also examine how these students might ensure that they are qualified for college and how they might go about securing the resources necessary to make a college education possible.

Academic Success

The second tier of the theoretical framework explores the strategies students employ to gain acceptance into a four-year university. *Academic success* is a collective term that embodies both in-class and out-of-class success (Harper, 2005). The academic success tier in the framework includes four specific components that enable students to navigate the wide range of experiences they have in the academic environment. These components are rooted in the work of Astin, 1975; Griffin, 2006; Harper, 2005; Tinto, 1975; and Yazedjian, Toews, Sevin, and Purswell, 2008. The four components used to explore academic success strategies included: (a) successful classroom performance, (b) a sense of responsibility, (c) an ability to resist stereotype threat, and (d) social and academic integration. These four components are rooted in the vast amount of literature that examines academic success strategies and characteristics in college students. The underlying assumption here is that college-bound high school students may utilize these same characteristics in order to be successful enough to gain acceptance into the institution of their choice. This tier of the framework sought to explore the existence of these components, and any strategies employed to maintain academic success.

Resourcefulness

The final tier of the framework is resourcefulness. This tier enabled the researcher to explore the decisions students made and the strategies employed that enabled them to overcome common educational barriers. Like academic success, resourcefulness must also precede college enrollment. Students who have college aspirations and the grades to qualify for college admission may not make it to college if they are not resourceful enough to overcome barriers (i.e., not having the funding to pay tuition or not knowing the college admissions process). Therefore, overcoming barriers must precede college enrollment.

Resourcefulness is an action-oriented term and relates to college preparation strategies. First-generation students face a number of challenges that prevent many from pursuing a college education. It is important to understand how students who make it to college navigate these challenges. For example, if a resourceful first-generation student was challenged by insufficient academic preparation, the student would need to find ways to get academically prepared. If faced with the challenge of not having the financial resources to attend college, the student would need to address the problem by seeking out ways to pay for college. It is important to note that not all first-generation students face every challenge described, but as the literature indicates, many face at least some of the challenges. This final tier of the framework serves as a tool to explore the strategies the first-generation students used to address the five common challenges in order to successfully enroll into college.

This college predisposition framework is multidimensional in nature because, as described above, the college enrollment puzzle has many pieces. As Griffin (2005) put it, "A multidimensional framework best explains these students' motivation patterns" (p. 391). A student cannot make it to college on self-determination alone if he or she is not academically prepared. Likewise, a student cannot make it on academic achievement alone if he or she does not have the resourcefulness needed to figure out how to get to college. The three categories work together to illustrate what a first-generation student who can successfully make it to college might look like. This framework serves as a starting point from which researchers, educators, pre-college program staff, and policymakers can gain a greater understanding of the strategies used and strengths possessed by first-generation students who go to college.

Methodology

This chapter addresses the following research question: What set of factors predispose African American first-generation students to pursue a college education? The related research questions were as follows: (1) To what degree were the three innate psychological needs that cultivate self-determination met for these students? (2) What skills and assets do these students possess that enabled them to be academically successful enough to qualify for college? (3) What strategies did these students employ to successfully enroll into college?

Given the purpose of exploring the nature of a first-generation college student's decision to attend college, the research approach was phenomenological to capture the essence of the students' lived experiences and employed the method of interviewing. The site for this study was "Private University," the pseudonym for a private, religiously affiliated, four-year university in the Midwestern region of the United States. This university reported a total undergraduate population of 8,048 students during the 2007-2008 academic year. Demographically, the university maintains the following average enrollment percentages: 82 percent Caucasian, 4.6 percent African American, 4.5 percent Asian, 4.1 percent Latino, and 0.3 percent American Indian (U.S. College Search, 2008).

The researcher used purposive sampling to identify and select participants (Weiss, 1994). The sample was developed by contacting members of the university's Black student organizations by email to invite them to participate in the study. The email specified the requirement that participants must be the first in the family to attend college. Student affairs administrators were also contacted by email and asked to refer students whom they believed met the qualifications.

To filter out students who do not meet the qualifications of the study, each respondent was asked to complete a short demographic survey that would help determine if the student was in fact, first in the family to pursue a college education. This survey was also used to describe characteristics of the sample. Those students whose questionnaires indicated that their parents had never enrolled in college were invited to participate in one-on-one interviews. When more participants were needed, the researcher used snowball sampling (Weiss, 1994) by asking participants to refer other students who might qualify to participate in the study. The larger study yielded a sample of 17 African American and Mexican American Students. This chapter highlights the experiences of the eight African American students in the sample.

Description of the Participants

The participants described in this chapter are eight African American first-generation college students enrolled at the participating university. Having parents with no college experience was used as the characteristic that defined students as "first-generation" because of the presumed greater lack of knowledge and resources parents would have to help prepare their children for college. Of the study participants, four were female and four were male. The average participant age was 20.2, with ages ranging from nineteen to twenty-four. One participant was a sophomore, two were juniors, and five were seniors. All participants were full time students who were actively involved in student organizations.

High School Background

Of the participants, five attended public high schools before attending Private University, and three attended private high schools. The racial makeup of the students' high schools ranged tremendously. Three reported attending predominantly White high schools, three attended predominantly African American high schools, and the remaining two attended racially diverse high schools. The average cumulative high school grade point average was 3.45. Only two of the students reported involvement with a pre-college program in high school or middle school.

Family Structure and Background

Of the participants, two were raised by both parents, and the remaining six were raised in single-parent homes. Seven of the students had mothers who completed up to a high school diploma, and one had a mother who had less than a high school diploma. Five reported that their fathers had earned a high school diploma, two had fathers who had less than a high school diploma, and one did not know their fathers' educational status. The vast majority of the students came from lower socioeconomic households: six of the students reported a family income of less than $35,000 per year, one reported an income within the $35,000-$49,000 range, and one reported $75,000-$99,000. Table 2.1 shows brief profiles of participants in the study.

Table 2.1. Study Participant Profiles

Partici-pant	Gender	School	Parent	GPA	Pre-College Program?
Nicole	Female	Predominantly White Public School	Mom	3.2	No
Daslyn	Male	Predominantly African American Private School	Both	3.4	No
Jerell	Male	Predominantly White Public School	Grandmother	3.4	No
Nia	Female	Predominantly African American Private School	Mom	3.8	Yes
Shawna	Female	Predominantly African American Public School	Dad	3.1	No
Elijah	Male	Diverse Public School	Mom	3.1	No
Lamar	Male	Predominantly White Private School	Both	3.7	No
Cherise	Female	Diverse Public School	Mom	3.9	Yes

Results

Most of the students were raised in homes headed by single mothers who did not heavily emphasize the pursuit of an education. This was largely due to pressing life challenges that prompted these mothers to focus more on overcoming day-to-day challenges, such as simply putting food on the table. Taking time to plan for the future was not always a feasible option. As children, these students had to be highly resilient to accomplish their educational goals. They had to exercise diligence and persistence to get to college. This was highly reflective of Cherise's experience:

> My mom had me when she was sixteen; my grandmother died probably two years prior to that and she didn't have any guidance at all. I think the only person who graduated directly from high school was my oldest aunt. So, she didn't have any background on this is what you do in life, you go to school and you graduate. And, money, our status is poor. The main thing was having food and lights outside of college. College just wasn't real.

Despite the financial hardships, most of the students were able to find moral support for their academic endeavors within their immediate households. When this type of support was not available (as was the case for both Cherise and Nia), they took measures to receive encouragement from relationships developed outside of the home. Cherise received much encouragement from the Upward Bound staff, and Nia received support from her pre-college coach at school. Thus, all students, regardless of whether they received moral support from within or outside of the home, had each of the three psychological needs fulfilled: competence, autonomy and relatedness.

Findings for Research Question One: Self Determination

Research question one explored the degree to which the three innate psychological needs that cultivate self-determination were met for the students. Based on Ryan and Deci's (2000) Self-Determination Theory, the participants in this study were indeed self-determined, as all three psychological needs were fulfilled in their lives. While there was some evidence of variation in how these needs were met, it was quite clear that based upon the criteria of self-determination set forth by Ryan and Deci (2000), these students were fully provided with the provisions necessary to become self-determined individuals. Most participants were intrinsically motivated to do well, meaning that they were more driven by an internal passion or desire to succeed.

The students simply loved to learn. This love for learning was highly reinforced by important adults in their lives, such as parents and teachers. Parents (and in some cases, other influential adults) played a critical role in meeting the three psychological needs that promote self-determination by providing (a) the encouraging environment needed to feel *competent*; (b) the empowerment needed to feel *autonomous*; and (c) the inclusiveness needed to feel a sense of *relatedness* to others. Figure 2 provides a visual representation of the self-determination themes and how these served to fulfill each of the three psychological needs.

Figure 2.2. Self-Determination Themes

Self-Determination		
Competence	**Autonomy**	**Relatedness**
Strengths that are validated by others	Parents who encourage independence	Assurance of love from significant others
Spiritual assurance	Sense of responsibility	Relationships that are healthy and satisfying
Distinction as "the smart one"	Preference for self-reliance	Sense of acceptance by others within peer group
Desire to pave the way for others	Desire to exceed parents' financial status	

Competence

The participants exhibited a strong sense of competence, which they maintained through a varying combination of the following themes: having (a) strengths that were validated by others, (b) spiritual assurance, (c) distinction as "the smart one" in the family, and (d) a desire to pave the way for others. Elijah described how his ability to do well in school is ultimately tied to his purpose in life, and impels him to continue in his success:

> I always felt like [God] has got big plans for me. And, in my life, if I make some type of difference, I know what it is. But, I am meant to make a difference for somebody. A difference, whether in school or at work, friends, anything . . . . I just had a revelation one day. It was my junior year in high school. He has a purpose for me and ever since then, I've felt that way. I've just always felt that there is a bigger purpose than I can see. But, yeah, he wants me to do something. I don't know what it is, and I can't figure it out, but I've just always felt that way.

It was the combination of his role as mentor to his younger siblings and a belief that God chose him to set the example that reaffirmed his ability and commitment to be successful. The participants knew that they were capable of achieving academic success, and this knowing was validated by important people in their lives who affirmed their strengths and abilities.

Past successes also played a role in validating competence. When they accomplished goals or maintained good grades, this reinforced a sense of competence. The participants' academic abilities, along with the passion and drive to do well, made them stand out among their peers and siblings. As indicated by the literature, competence is characterized by a strong feeling of self, confidence, independence, motivation and strength of character (Nasim et al., 2005). The participants embodied these characteristics through school work, their spiritual connections, as the "smart" one in the family, and through the desire to use their strengths to benefit others.

Autonomy

The participants were highly autonomous, and this was largely reflective of the relationships they had with their parents. In most cases, the parents laid the foundation by instilling values and having high expectations for their children, but did not step in to control their lives. This was largely because parents were unable to. They needed to commit a great deal of time to their jobs to maintain the stability of the home. Instilling the ability to be independent is a parenting strategy driven by cultural norms in which autonomy is necessary for mere survival. The students expressed a sense of autonomy in four ways, which included having (a) parents who encouraged independence, (b) a sense of responsibility, (c) a preference for self-reliance, and (d) a desire to exceed their parents' financial status.

Jerell's story is one that embodies all four of the autonomy themes. Abandoned by both parents at an early age, he was raised by his grandmother, who became terminally ill during his high school years. The challenges he faced in his life required that he exercised a great deal of responsibility at a young age. Here's how he described his experience:

> You know, my grandmother was sick and all . . . her body had shut down and was in the hospital for two months . . . . When she came home, it was just me and her and the roles completely reversed and I was the provider and I was working . . . . I'd get up, go to school, come home, eat and do some homework. Work from 4-11, come home, go to sleep. Grandma would wake me up at 2 am because she didn't feel well and wanted me to sit with her. Literally sit with her until 3 and then go to sleep and get up to get ready to go back to school.

All cases were not as extreme as Jerell's, but all of the participants' parents highly valued autonomy for their children. Unlike the parenting styles of helicopter parents, who hover over their child's every move, the parents of the participants placed more value on allowing their children to solve problems themselves so that they could learn to survive life's harsh realities of discrimination and financial hardship.

More often than not, this was also a result of being unable to spend the time that it would take to manage their children's lives in the way that a helicopter parent would due to the greater amount of effort needed to maintain financial stability for their families. The fact that parents had to work long hours to provide for the family meant that the participants were expected to contribute by taking on roles that may have typically been the parents' responsibility. These responsibilities, as well as the encouragement their parents provided to live independently, were key components that resulted in the participants' sense of autonomy.

Relatedness

All participants felt a strong sense of belonging or connection to a significant individual or group of people. For many, this meant being well-connected to family; for others, it was a church group, an athletic team, an academic group, or a group of friends; for a select few, it meant being connected to extended family members when the immediate household was not stable. There were three dominant themes that reflected the students' experience with relatedness: (a) assurance of love from significant people in their lives, (b) healthy and satisfying relationships, and (c) a sense of acceptance by others within their peer groups.

Nicole spoke with great depth about her family:

> My family's support is extremely important. I feel my drive and determination helps me along the way, but their support helps me go further. They are always there to put things into perspective for me.

It was Nia's grandmother who contributed to her sense of relatedness:

> My grandmother who passed two years ago—I was my grandmother's baby. That's probably the reason I am the person I am versus the way typical people are in my area.

Daslyn's parents modeled what it meant to maintain a healthy and satisfying relationship:

> My parents instilled those important educational values when I was really young. That was a pretty much a big impact on my life. Additionally, the fact that they were still together the whole time I was growing up—I'm pretty much one of the few people I know my age whose parents are still together. Them being married has been a huge part of it and the reason I'm still alive.

Most of the participants had a strong sense of relatedness through their connections to family. There were a few cases in which the students did not feel strongly connected to their parents or other close members of their households. In these cases, the students drew their support from other relationships with teachers, staff, members of the extended family, or friends. Thus, all students were able to maintain relationships that were healthy and satisfying and found a context within which they could feel accepted by others.

Findings for Research Question Two: Academic Success

The central goal of the second research question was to explore the strategies the students employed to be academically successful enough to qualify for college.

Figure 2.3. Academic Success Themes

Academic Success		
Classroom Performance	**Stereotype Threat Resistance**	**Social and Academic Integration**
Earning good grades Having high expectations Nurturing strengths and managing weaknesses	Disproving negative stereotypes Ignoring the threat Avoiding "stereotypical" peers	Getting involved through extracurricular activities Developing relationships with teachers and staff

Academic success is a collective term that embodies both in-class and out-of-class experiences (Harper, 2005). Themes included (a) successful classroom performance, (b) the ability to resist stereotype threat, and (c) social and academic integration. Based upon this understanding of academic success, the participants demonstrated that they were highly successful.

Classroom Performance

Successful classroom performance is an essential component that includes maintaining a strong grade point average and having the ability to score well on tests and writing assignments. Classroom performance is generally strengthened through the students' active involvement in the educational process. The participants demonstrated successful classroom performance in the following three ways: (a) earning good grades, (b) having high expectations, and (c) and nurturing strengths while managing weaknesses.

Making the grade was of utmost importance. The participants were highly committed to getting the most out of their high school careers as a strategy to position themselves as strong college admissions candidates. They were self-aware enough to understand their strengths and weaknesses and tailored their academic and extracurricular decisions accordingly. For example, Cherise, who was not a great test-taker described her strategy to compensate for her weakness:

> Every extra credit assignment, I'd ask for, because my ACT scores weren't great, so I was trying to find all that I could do to get to college. And then coming from [this school district], I never had any AP courses. So I felt like the contending part was my GPA.

The participants took the work that they accomplished in the classroom seriously. They were intentional about establishing a strong academic record and consistently looked for ways to keep their grades up. Many were not willing to settle for average performance and took measures to ensure that they stood out among their peers. The expectations they held for themselves were high, from the work they completed for their classes to the type of colleges that they anticipated attending. Every student was aware of the importance of maintaining good grades and made this a priority, specifically so that they would meet and exceed college admissions requirements.

Stereotype Threat Resistance

Resisting stereotype threat is a task that takes a substantial amount of energy to acknowledge, process, and respond to (Fries-Britt and Griffin, 2007; Griffin, 2005; Solorzano, Allen, and Carroll, 2002; Steele, 1997; Steele and Aronson, 1998). Generally, resisting stereotype threat within an academic setting has a negative impact on academic performance and well-being (Griffin, 2005). Steele asserted that not overcoming the threat can bring down intellectual performance and, if left unchecked over time, can cause a student to seriously question his or her own abilities. This was not the case for the participants in the current study. Not only were they convinced that they did they not suffer academically from the stereotypes they encountered, but many of them were not interested in giving much attention to the idea of being stereotyped or discriminated against. The participants who spoke about encountering stereotype threat resisted the threat in three ways: (a) disproving negative stereotypes, (b) ignoring the threat, and (c) avoiding "stereotypical" peers.

In some cases, the threat seemed to effectively motivate them to maintain a strong academic record. The racial makeup of the participants' schools and the highly diverse set of activities that they became involved with likely reduced the extent to which stereotype threat affected them. Thus, the combination of extracurricular involvement, the ability to develop relationships with teachers and staff, and the ability to maintain a strong academic record seemed to work together as a buffer against stereotype threat, and as a means for academic achievement. Nicole explained that she was always aware of the assumption by others in school that she was the "typical Black girl," which she described as being "bad" or a product of a dangerous urban environment:

> I had this teacher. He was also a basketball coach and he was giving me a ride home. He says to me, "I know you've probably seen people get shot and killed," and I was kind of like, "Okaaaay" [laughter]. I'd get the pity look, you know. The "I feel sorry for you" look.

Situations like these created a drive in her to prove the stereotypes wrong. This is the approach that she often took:

> I always try to make myself known. I am going to talk to you. Shake your hand. Let you know what I am all about. I am always the type where I want you to get to know me. It's typical, I mean, I've been known to do it . . . . I just feel like it's my job to let them know who I am to prove them wrong.

Shawna's response was similar:

> I don't know if it's a personal thing, but I felt that because where I was at in high school, that people viewed us as those that aren't going to do well. . . . I responded in a way that if that's how someone feels about me, that's going to drive me to do better and prove them wrong.

Lamar's approach was to simply ignore or minimize the threat:

> I think our generation is a step above racism, but there were a lot of sheltered people that got to me because they didn't understand our culture. They'd ask stupid questions or act out. Most of the kids came from the [Brook Hills] area and suburbs to Private High and just didn't understand. Not flat out racism as in "I

don't like you because you are Black," but a lot of ignorance. . . . It's not that they try to personally attack me.

Many of the participants reported that they did not experience being stereotyped by peers or teachers, and attributed this to the fact that they attended highly diverse schools or schools that had student populations largely reflective of the participant's racial background. However, even in such cases, while these students easily dismissed the idea that they may have experienced stereotype threat, their stories painted a different picture, indicating that some may have indeed experienced the threat. For those students who did identify situations in which they felt stereotyped, they described two ways in which they actively responded. They would either take measures to prove that the stereotype was not true, or they would avoid peers who seemed to embody the stereotype so that they would not be associated with the behaviors of that group. In every case, however, the students insisted these negative experiences were not powerful enough to negatively impact their grades

Social and Academic Integration

Social and academic integration pertains to becoming fully immersed into the many dynamics of the educational environment. Its concept reaches beyond maintaining a high grade point average and into developing close relationships with faculty and peers, as well as actively engaging in school-related activities. Students who are both socially and academically integrated are more likely to stay in school (Cabrera et al., 1992), experience greater moral and cognitive development, and have clearer vocational aspirations (Astin, 1984). All of the participants were socially and academically integrated and expressed this in two ways: (a) by getting involved through extracurricular activities and (b) by developing relationships with teachers and staff members. Most knew that a strong academic record could be used to participate in programs such as the National Honor Society to further boost the extracurricular resume. Additionally, the students who struggled in a particular subject were intentional about taking the extra time needed with a teacher until they fully understood the concept.

Nicole was involved in basketball, the prom committee, Key Club, and the Young Women Leadership Organization. However, she did not simply join organizations. She was also a mover and shaker on campus. She described an initiative that she and a friend started while in high school:

I started a movement with a friend called INAG. It's an acronym for *It's Not A Game*. We had dress up Thursdays. It started with four people and turned out to be a whole school thing. But, I just couldn't dedicate the time. But I'd like to make it an official thing for the school.

Nia demonstrated academic integration through her deliberate efforts to develop relationships with her teachers by presenting herself as a student who was serious about her studies:

> They would say that I just have this essence about myself that I am all business-y and every time they see me I would be doing something "nerdy." In terms of my teachers, they would see it firsthand. I'm always asking for additional things to do. I am always looking for something more, or start ahead in class.

Becoming an integral part of the campus community was an important strategy for fostering the participants' academic success. Campus involvement allowed the participants to take on leadership roles, test out their strengths and weaknesses, and develop an even stronger sense of self. In the relationships they developed with teachers, the students received affirmation of their strengths and were extended opportunities that other students would not necessarily have. The participants' social and academic integration on campus was pivotal to their academic growth and development.

Findings for Research Question Three: Resourcefulness

The third research question explored how the participants navigated the challenges that prevent many potential first-generation students from pursuing a college education. These challenges include poor academic preparation, limited financial resources, a lack of college knowledge, debilitating cultural norms, and minimal emotional support. Essentially, the students addressed these challenges by ensuring that they (a) were academically prepared for college, (b) had acquired the college knowledge necessary to navigate the admissions and funding processes, and (c) developed the support system necessary to help them achieve their academic goals.

Figure 2.4. Resourcefulness Themes

Resourcefulness		
Academic Preparation	**College Knowledge**	**Support System**
Selecting the right high school Enrolling in competitive courses	Not being intimidated Following the money trail Searching independently Accepting help	Overcoming negative cultural norms Seeking encouragement Seeking resourceful individuals

Academic Preparation

This strategy addresses the challenge of having poor academic preparation for college. The participants identified two ways in which they went about ensuring that they would be prepared for college: (a) selecting the right high school and (b) enrolling in competitive courses.

With the help of an older cousin, Nia enrolled into Conners Academy, a competitive college preparatory school on the opposite end of town. When it was time to choose a high school, she was sure that she did not want to attend the high school in her neighborhood because of its negative reputation:

> I went to an academy near the [local university]. It was a public school in a good neighborhood. It was a well ranked school. You had to be pre-selected into the program because they instilled the No Child Left Behind program my junior year. If you didn't pass or get selected, you had to go to your districts school. They were horrible. I was so excited that I got selected . . . . I was in honors classes . . . it was challenging. My high school kind of helped, as well, because I was in honors courses and the grades are different than regular courses. It was a reality check.

Shawna's high school did not offer advanced courses. As a member of the school's debate team, she learned that the suburban schools she competed against offered much more than what her high school had to offer. She expressed her frustration over the lack of advanced courses offered through her high school and opted to take courses at the local college to boost her transcript and enhance her grade point average:

> It was kind of depressing to see the types of courses that Whites were offered throughout the cities here, versus what I was offered. I already knew when I got to college that I was going to be behind because my school didn't offer particular courses. It was a source of frustration for me. I didn't know if it was just the MPS school district, or if it was because my school was predominantly Black.

Being academically qualified for college was one thing, but being academically competitive was entirely different for the participants. They believed that earning good grades was important, but if they earned good grades in a non-competitive high school or by taking average courses, the grades would not carry as much weight. Therefore, the participants and their families were intentional about the type of schools they attended and the course load they took on. For the parents, it was important that the schools were safe, and for the students, it was important that the schools had the resources necessary to adequately prepare them for college. Many of the schools that the participants chose to attend made it a priority to help students through the college application process and provided them with a wide scope of information to aid them in the decision making process. Shawna's case was the exception because she did not have the option to attend a high school out of her neighborhood. She took measures into her own hands and enrolled in college courses to enhance her course load and contacted the university directly to receive help with the application process. Her actions certainly qualify as resourceful, as she worked within her means to become academically prepared for college.

College Knowledge

Having college knowledge entails possessing the information necessary to successfully enroll into college and to fund the education. This strategy addresses two challenges: the challenge of not having the money to pay for college and the challenge of not having an understanding of the college admissions process. The participants described acquiring college knowledge by employing four different strategies: (a) refusing to be intimidated, (b) following the money trail, (c) searching independently, and (d) accepting help from others.

Most of the participants did not have a plan for financing college, but they were not preoccupied with worry over how college would be paid for. Most stated that a lack of money simply would not be a barrier to their college education, and that they would take out loans as a last resort. All were confident that the money would come somehow. Nicole, for example, did not know how she would pay for school, but she did believe that by applying for as many grants and scholarships as possible, her hard work would pay off:

> When I applied for school, getting scholarships was the whole thing, but I really didn't have a plan. I really did not. It was like, "We'll find some type of way to pay it," and that's kind of how it has been this whole time. "We'll find some type of way." I didn't have any game plan going into this.

Lamar was also unconcerned because of his father's promise to pay for his college education:

> My father and I worked out that I would look and apply for scholarships and he is paying for my tuition. We didn't take out any loans or anything. He is using his pension/savings money; I guess it's his 401k. I get a little financial aid and a scholarship, too. I got a notice about a scholarship competition and I took that opportunity to go for it and I ended up getting an award.

Shawna's father also encouraged her not to worry about college:

> My dad told me not to worry about it and focus on my grades. I always thought I would take out a loan. My dad always said if you get a degree from Private, you'll get a good job and you'll be able to pay your loans back.

Nia, who did not have the moral support of a parent employed her own strategies to make it happen:

I never really knew the steps in terms of paying for college. For me, all I knew was scholarships and grants. I definitely went straight to all the ones that nobody really knew about. Everyone always went to the Tylenol and Coca-Cola scholarships; I went to those ones that didn't have a whole lot of exposure. I had no idea how I was going to pay for Private. I thought that scholarships would be sufficient and the first year comes and you realize it's not enough. But I did get a four-year scholarship funded through [Urban] Public Schools. It is $7,500 a year, and that helped me as well.

Daslyn had parental moral support, but his parents did not have the money to pay for college. He shared some of his creative strategies for financing his education:

The funny thing is my parents told me that I had a college fund, started by my grandpa when I was four or five, and I was relying on that. I was thinking that I had $5,000-$6,000 and then when I get ready to go to college, I only have two $100 bonds. That wasn't enough to cover my books! I was outside of Wal-Mart selling chicken dinners for tuition and I didn't really have a plan. We would be in my kitchen and my aunt would be cooking up a storm. I knew that manager of Wal-Mart and he was cool with me and all and knew what I was trying to do. So, they were supportive as long as I wasn't disruptive or disrespectful. They were all for it because they knew that not a lot of kids in our area could go to college.

Ultimately, Daslyn was able to secure grants and loans to cover his tuition.

The participants made it a point to do as much as possible without seeking out or accepting help, but they were wise enough to utilize the help that was offered to them when it was needed. Lamar was able to get assistance through his school:

Our high school has college prep that has guidance counselors that are on you about deadlines and everything. They were amazing and made sure you were on top of things and deadlines.

Cherise, who was only one of two participants who were a part of a pre-college program, credited her involvement with Upward Bound with providing the most valuable assistance with the college application process:

I was naïve to the whole process and they informed me. My ignorance was evident when I went to do applications. So, it was all upward bound. I knew of scholarships my freshman year and I had a resume by my freshman year. I was working hard to get ready. And there were counselors, but I was always five steps ahead of the counselors in school because of Upward Bound.

Acquiring the information necessary to search for, apply to, and pay for the colleges of their choice did not seem to be a difficult task for the participants, as they had surrounded themselves with a set of teachers, mentors and counselors who were committed to helping them with the college application process. Additionally, they were highly ambitious and primarily pursued this process independently by searching the internet for information about different colleges and how to fund their education. The participants approached the process confidently, and would not allow themselves to become discouraged with the cost of tuition or the competitive nature of the universities they desired to attend. They remained focused, and if faced with a challenge that had the potential of jeopardizing their educational futures, the participants would simply continue to move forward until they found a solution. Many, for example, did not know how college would be paid for, but instead of stagnating in their uncertainty, they moved forward and explored options until the problem was resolved.

Support System

The participants were deliberate about identifying and connecting with a group of people who would morally support them in their college aspirations or serve as resources to help achieve goals. The three strategies that participants used to create a support system included (a) overcoming negative cultural norms, (b) seeking encouragement, and (c) seeking resourceful individuals.

All of the students faced negative feedback from people within their communities regarding their academic aspirations. For Cherise and Nia, it came from their mothers. Nia's response was to use this relationship as a catalyst for doing well in her life:

> It's like me and my mom grew up together and I sometimes feel she feels I am trying to be better than her because I had an opportunity to be exposed to things she has not. She didn't have an opportunity to really have a mother or graduate from high school or go to college. I have to escape that relationship that isn't really there anyway and that negativity. She just doesn't understand—not understanding why I am studying, working so hard. I was kind of the mom in some of the situations—my mom sometimes did drugs and stuff, so I had to step up. That's why I knew I wanted to go to college, regardless of these negative situations in my life. I had to escape that and my escape was school.

For the rest of the participants, the negative feedback came from outside of the household, through relatives or other kids in the neighborhood. Many were accused of "acting white" or being a "sellout." The commitment to their race and culture was consistently being called into question. Here is how Daslyn described his experience:

> For whatever reason, people might have been jealous because they didn't have this opportunity to go. Those are the people who wanted to be in my shoes, or thought I was a sell out because I wanted to get out. I'd get the same flack, being told the same thing that I'm going to the suburbs with all the White people. After a while I got tired of hearing it. One time I did get into a fist fight over it, but after that I realized it wasn't worth it. If they can't see that I'm going to college to help out

the area that I am from, and have more people from where I am from get to where
I am at, I figured it wasn't worth my time and tried to ignore it.

All participants resisted these negative messages, but had various tactics for
doing so and all found ways to barrel through the criticism, so that they could stay
focused on their goals. They were quite instrumental in securing support. The
participants valued the importance of having people in their lives who encouraged
them to pursue their educational dreams, so they placed much more emphasis on
those who supported them than those who did not.

Nia described the people she intentionally surrounded herself with in order to
be successful:

> I had friends and mentors I kind of picked up along the way. One of the post
> secondary coaches that I had in school, I am very close to today. She really pushed
> me with different scholarships and applying for aid and things. It was all of those
> little things like that and networking. We actually had our own office at school to
> go to and fill out the FAFSA and applications and doing personal statements and
> things like that. There were just great things and being in the right place at the
> right time. I can say my teachers and friends motivated me.

Cherise took similar measures to ensure that she was surrounded by the people
who could help her:

> I usually try to seek out and find somebody who will help me and find the most
> simplistic way of getting things. But, what made me different was I was persistent.

It is clear that all participants needed encouragement to aid in their success. If they
already had the encouragement at home, they put less effort into creating a support
system. If the encouragement did not exist at home, they were more deliberate
about surrounding themselves with people who believed in them and would assist
in the achievement of their educational goals. For many of the participants, the
value of education was instilled early on, and they received a great amount of
encouragement from their families. Most families highly valued education and
expected their children to maintain good grades in school. Much of this
encouragement was fueled by the parents' desire to have their children take
advantage of the opportunities that they did not have.

As was previously noted within the findings related to autonomy, the males
were much less likely than the females to ask for help. None of the males indicated
that they would ask for help whereas, all of the females indicated that they would.
For example, when asked about seeking encouragement, Jerell said, "I wouldn't say
that I really turned to anyone, but more or less they gave me the words of
encouragement." The males preferred to work independently over reaching out for
help; however, in cases where they already had resourceful individuals in their
support networks, they were more than willing to accept the resources offered to
them.

Most participants were aware of the importance of networking and used this to their advantage as they employed strategies to achieve their educational and future career goals. With resources ranging from teachers who would write letters of recommendation to mentors who could provide tips about law school, the participants each recognized these opportunities and used them to their advantage.

Discussion

Through an exploration of the factors that contributed to the African American students' decision to pursue a college education, it is apparent that the fulfillment of the students' three innate psychological needs of competence, autonomy and relatedness helped them to maintain the natural human inclination to be self-determined. The high level of self-determination that the students displayed enabled their success by driving them to desire stellar academic performance and to secure the resources necessary to achieve their goals. While the students were active agents of their own success, it was clear that they did not go the journey alone. All were influenced by important people along the way who provided them with the support and resources they needed to accomplish their goals.

The role of the family was critical in providing foundational support. Despite what much of the research says about first-generation students not having parental support, it is clear that this support was central to setting the college aspirations ball into motion. By providing love, support, and high expectations, and by encouraging independence and upward social mobility, the students were armed with the tools necessary to desire a college education.

Because of the foundational support that they received by family and other influential adults, they had the disposition—or the mindset—necessary to aspire toward a college education. Once this disposition was set into place, complete with a strong sense of competence, autonomy and relatedness, the participants had the volition to act upon their aspirations. They engaged in strategies such as selecting the high school that would best prepare them for college, taking the initiative to research college and financial aid information, and developing relationships with people who would help them succeed. These actions were inspired in a variety of ways, including the spiritual assurance that God had provided them with the skills and tools necessary to accomplish their goals, the desire to avoid the financial challenges that their parents struggled to overcome, and the desire to make a difference in the world.

The students credited their schools, the pre-college programs they participated in, and even local colleges and universities with providing them with the information they needed to pursue a college education. Nicole and Shawna chose to directly contact the universities they wished to attend for information. It was clear that the high schools (and in some cases, the middle schools) contributed greatly to providing critical information and support. The students who could not attend college-focused schools were fortunate to have parents who strongly supported them; and similarly, the students who did not have strongly supportive parents were fortunate to attend college-preparatory schools. For Cherise, who had neither the support of her family nor the school she attended, Upward Bound became her safety net. Cherise's story is a prime example of how a pre-college program can provide resources and support for students who may not receive this from home or at school. These programs can serve as a buffer to these deficiencies when the school or family does not provide either moral support or college information. This demonstrates the important role that schools and other institutions can play in providing the foundational support that all students need to be academically successful.

Because the participants in the study were self-determined, they believed that anything was possible. They fully believed in themselves, but also drew upon the support of others to ensure that they had what they needed to succeed. Thus, for these students, having a sense of competence, autonomy and relatedness were important prerequisites to their success.

Self-Determination

Parents played an integral role in cultivating the participants' self-determination. The love and support they provided through such parenting strategies as validating their children's strengths, encouraging independence, and instilling a desire for upward social mobility were pivotal in meeting the three innate psychological needs of competence, autonomy and relatedness. Students who did not have these foundational needs met at home were fortunate enough to find fulfillment from other adults outside of their homes.

Students from nurturing and non-nurturing households alike felt highly competent and credited themselves for their accomplishments. The students who did not grow up in supportive and nurturing homes were grateful for their challenges because they explained that these experiences further emphasized where they did not want to end up in life and prompted them to do all that they could to be successful. They heavily attributed their success to their own academic abilities, and placed great emphasis on their personal drive as the catalyst for their success.

The participants who grew up in highly supportive and nurturing homes were grateful for the sacrifices their parents made to get them into the right schools and provide them with a stable and secure childhood. Like the students who grew up in non-nurturing homes, these students also attributed successes to their own academic abilities and personal drive. They often emphasized that no one forced them to get good grades or to pursue a college education, and did not consider the possibility that their parents' high academic expectations for them may have contributed to the personal drive to succeed academically.

As is indicated in Ryan and Deci's (2000) research, it was indeed necessary for the students to have a sense of competence, autonomy and relatedness to aspire to a college education. Because the participants had a sense of competence, they had the wherewithal to believe that they could succeed in a college environment, and did not fear taking that next step in the educational process. Their competence was planted and reinforced by the important adults in their lives who believed in them and wanted to see them do well. As a result of the participants' sense of autonomy, the students had the freedom to explore their strengths and weaknesses and to take part in important decisions regarding their lives. This level of freedom further developed their aspirations and helped them devise a plan for pursuing a college education. Having a sense of relatedness enabled the participants to share their dreams with others who would support and help them accomplish their goals. It is indisputable that humans are social beings and need one another to accomplish goals. The important connections that the participants were able to maintain kept them in contact with people who would both encourage and assist them as they took the steps necessary to go to college.

Each of the participants had the three innate psychological needs met, and can thus be considered to be self-determined individuals. For first-generation students, self-determination is a necessary characteristic to possess to make it to college, because as the research indicates, this population of students must overcome a number of challenges that their peers often do not face. Overcoming these challenges requires the determination to do so. First-generation students are generally not coerced into pursuing a college education; it takes personal volition—the will do it, which is fueled by self-determination.

Considering these findings about self-determination, a call to implement self-determination initiatives within schools and pre-college programs is in order. Many first-generation students do not have the same level of support from their families that the students in the current student study were privileged to have, and countless others also lack support from their schools. As such support demonstrates the powerful effect it can have on a child's self-perception and educational aspirations, measures must be taken to incorporate similar support structures within the schools in which our children spend much of their childhood. This is not to suggest that parents are off the hook when it comes to ensuring that their children are cared for, but schools also must understand the pivotal role that they play in a child's development.

Academic Achievement

The high level of competence the participants possessed was clear in their academic achievement, particularly in the high expectations that they held for themselves. They were determined to be the best among their peers and were consistently aware of how the activities they engaged in and the grades they achieved would affect their chances of being accepted into a competitive college or university. As they became more academically successful and more involved in their high schools, their competence was more strongly reinforced by teachers, guidance counselors and peers. Experiences that included receiving awards and recognition for academic competitions, being voted class president, and earning high grade point averages fueled them to keep achieving. Lamar said it well when he stated, "My past successes keep me motivated."

For all of the students, being academically successful meant truly valuing their educational experiences. It meant performance. It meant taking classes seriously and employing strategies that would enable them to produce quality results. By understanding their strengths and weaknesses, the students found ways to use their strengths to their benefit and keep the weaknesses from pulling them down. Academic success also meant being resistant to stereotype threat. The participants understood that they would not be successful if they became consumed with or believed that they characterized the stereotypes often held against African Americans. Thus, they took measures to ensure that they would remain academically focused and could become an integrated part of the school without being adversely affected by the constant threat of being stereotyped or discriminated against. While many researchers (this one included) would argue that the strategies they employed were not necessarily healthy ones, it must be acknowledged that as these students advance in their racial identity development through their college experiences, they will find other ways in which to handle stereotype threat. As high school students at this developmental stage, the participants addressed the threat in ways they knew best, and these strategies proved to be successful during this phase in their lives.

Academic success also meant getting involved. It seemed that for this sample, the more students became socially involved and connected with teachers, the more they enjoyed their high school experiences. This did not necessarily result in better grades, but it certainly contributed to a more overall rewarding experience. Cherise, the student who was least involved, had the strongest grade point average, but least favorable high school memories. Toward the end of Cherise's interview, she expressed regret for not being more involved in school as she said, "High school was okay. I wish I could have enjoyed it more."

Being academically successful in high school is, of course, essential for students who wish to attend college. Due to increasingly competitive admissions requirements, the participants took deliberate measures to ensure that they would be qualified for college by their senior year in high school. Taking these measures required that the students upheld high academic expectations, valued responsibility and desired upward social mobility. This disposition was made possible by the foundational support they received by family and other influential adults in their lives who helped to shape them into competent, autonomous and well-connected individuals.

This underscores the importance of personal motivation. When students have a strong foundation of support and are self-determined, they rely less upon others and take matters of achievement into their own hands. Once self-determination is in place, little effort is needed to push these kids to set and accomplish their goals. Parents, schools and pre-college programs can aid in developing academically successful students by teaching them how to address stereotype threat and discrimination, and by ensuring that they are connected with teachers, staff and other students at their schools. Student success is a domino effect that begins with foundational support, is fueled by self-determination, and is propelled from continuous successes that validate a sense of competence.

It is also important to help students discover and utilize their strengths. When they understand what they are good at doing and can match this with extracurricular and co-curricular activities, the chance that they will be academically successful dramatically increases. This not only provides students with direction as they seek out future aspirations, but it also helps to validate them as competent individuals, and will help to set them on track towards the accomplishment of their goals.

Resourcefulness

Taking the measures necessary to overcome potential barriers to college enrollment required that the participants were resourceful enough to come up with solutions to any of the problems they faced as they prepared for college. Many first-generation students face challenges including poor academic preparation, limited financial resources, insufficient college knowledge, a lack of moral support, and negative cultural norms. Most of the participants shared in the struggle to secure financial support to battle debilitating cultural norms, and were strategic in their endeavors to overcome those struggles. However, they did not struggle through poor academic preparation, insufficient college knowledge or a lack of emotional support because they took proactive measures to ensure that they were not deficient in these areas. The decision to carefully select a high school proved to be a wise one, as this instantly placed the participants into college-going environments that maintained college-preparatory curriculums, caring and supportive teachers, and a wealth of information about college. This simplified the participants' efforts to gain college knowledge and to develop a support system, as much of this was already built into their schools. The few who did not have these benefits integrated into their schools were even more deliberate about employing resourceful strategies to ensure that they would matriculate into college.

These students were problem solvers. They did not dwell on challenges, but were driven by them. The people that they were connected to and their own personal volition to "make it happen" (as Shawna would say) enabled the students to take the challenges set before them and find the solutions that would help them move forward. When faced with family or friends who criticized them for their academic achievement and college aspirations, the students made it a point to surround themselves with people who would support them so that the pressure to conform to these negative cultural norms would not be so great.

Self-determination and experiences with past successes helped the students to develop the strength in character that refuses to be unmoved by the challenging circumstances they faced. It is essential that schools and pre-college programs are equipped with the resources that students need to accomplish their goals. Too many schools, especially urban schools, lack even basic resources such as textbooks and computers. It is difficult to understand how any child is expected to succeed in such environments, especially when this is compounded with teachers and staff members who are unsupportive and critical of their students. Self-determined students can only be resourceful to a point—they can only utilize the resources that exist for them. Again, most of the participants in the current study were deliberate about selecting high schools that offered important resources, but this, again, demonstrates what works to aid first-generation students in their preparation for college. If more students had the opportunity to attend schools or participate in pre-college programs that provide college information, offer competitive courses, and enable students to explore educational and career options, a significantly greater number of African American first-generation students would not only enroll, but would graduate from college. So, while it is clear that support is essential to a student's ability to be self-determined, it is also essential that students have access to the resources they need to make a college education possible.

College Predisposition Model

In the spirit of increasing college aspirations in students through solutions grounded in research that explores what works for students (as opposed to following a deficit framework), a College Predisposition Model is proposed. This model suggests that when an individual is exposed to certain environments and elements of support, they develop an inclination to desire and pursue a college education. Essentially, the model identifies the three primary entities that contribute to a first-generation students' successful college enrollment. These entities are: family, which provides foundational support; the individual, who possesses the personal volition to act upon their aspirations; and institutions, which are the bearers of the information and preparation students need to gain college acceptance.

The first entity involves the critical role the family plays in providing foundational support. By providing love, validating strengths, encouraging upward social mobility, racially socializing, and maintaining high academic expectations, families make it possible for children to develop a strong sense of competence, autonomy and relatedness. As the findings of the current study suggest, nurturing the psychological needs that cultivate self-determination are a precursor to desiring a college education. This foundational support of the family is crucial, as it influences the self-determined disposition in students needed to achieve academic success. It should be noted that students who do not receive this foundational support from home can still develop a self-determined disposition if they receive this validation and support from other significant adults.

The second entity involves the students themselves. Complete with a strong sense of competence, autonomy and relatedness, the students are able to develop a self-determined disposition, are driven to be academically successful and have the ability to overcome challenges along the way. This disposition includes the following characteristics: having high expectations, having the ability to resist stereotype threat, not being easily discouraged, not being influenced by negative cultural norms, having a sense of spiritual assurance, being driven to pave the way for others, desiring social mobility, having a sense of responsibility, and having a preference for self-reliance. As self-determined beings, they are equipped with the volition to employ strategies that will help them achieve their goals. Volition makes the difference between the student who simply aspires to go to college and the student who actually makes it to college. Aspirations can exist without self-determination, but volition cannot.

The third entity involves institutions. The institutional role includes P-12 schools, pre-college programs and colleges and universities. These institutions are important for two reasons: they are the keepers of the information needed to successfully qualify for and apply to colleges and universities; and they are the safety net for the encouragement and support that all students need, but do not always receive from home. Secondary schools have the greatest opportunity of the three institutions to provide this information and support because they are the buildings of which the students spend most of their childhood. This is accomplished by maintaining a caring and supportive staff, implementing self-determination based learning, providing college information, offering competitive courses, and engaging in effective outreach to parents.

These roles—that of the family, the individual, and the institution—are all integral to a first-generation student's decision and ability to pursue a college education. The foundational support provided by the family influences the disposition to aspire to a college education. Once that disposition is in place, the student begins to take action—that is, the measures necessary to gain college enrollment. Collectively, they have the potential to provide the moral support, resources and opportunities necessary to make a college education possible.

The College Predisposition Model on is proposed to demonstrate the important role of the family, the individual, and institutions to the first-generation students' desire and ability to go to college. This model reflects the roles that the three entities play to make the transition to college possible.

Summary

By engaging in one-on-one interviews with first-generation college students, this study sought to uncover the factors that may have contributed to the participants' desire and ability to attend college. It was evident that most of the students received parental support and were actively engaged in their educational pursuits. Despite the research that points to a lack of parental support and susceptibility to common challenges of first-generation students, the participants in the current study were well supported and had the volition to move through common challenges. Additionally, institutions played a critical role in providing the students with the information needed to qualify for and apply to college.

Figure 2.5. College Predisposition Model

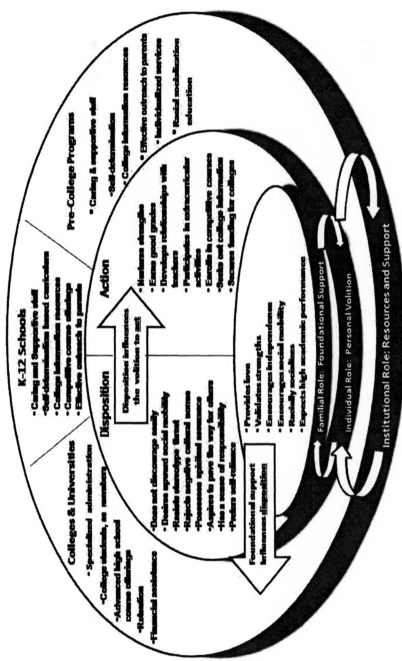

Implications for Practice

This study offers implications that can help P-12 schools, pre-college programs, institutions of higher education, and families assist first-generation students in the pursuit of a college education. It is recommended that P-12 schools strive to transform into college going environments, that pre-college programs evaluate their programs and services to ensure that they continue to meet the needs of first-generation students, and that families recognize and maximize the important role that their support plays in the formation of their children's future aspirations.

Implications for Research

This research invites quantitative inquiry into a larger sample of first-generation students to determine whether or not these factors are also salient to other students. A survey, for example, can determine the level of significance these factors have for other first-generation students and whether or not there are differences for various populations. A quantitative study would be an important follow-up to the current study because such a methodology can test the results found in the current study against a larger population.

Comparative Sibling Study

The fact that many of the participants in the current study had siblings that did not choose to go to college causes one to question why these family members chose two very different directions in life. Having grown up in the same household, it would be valuable to compare each of their experiences to examine whether or not any dominant factors point to an explanation of this phenomenon. This contrast may help to explain personality differences, varying parent-child relationships and academic experiences that may inspire one child to pursue a college education and cause the other to show little interest in such academic pursuits.

Conclusion

The first-generation students represented in this study were resilient, focused and resourceful in their approaches to accomplish their educational goals. Their self-determined nature, made possible by the foundational support they received, was the greatest indicator of the students' success. They understood that they had to take responsibility for their own destiny and did so with great persistence.

This study demonstrated the multidimensional nature of first-generation students and the many pieces of the college enrollment puzzle. Understanding the complex nature of first-generation students and the entities that work together to aid in their success is an important first step toward increasing college enrollment rates for this student population.

The multidimensionality of the students' experiences also underscores the importance of employing a framework that evaluates success to better understand what self-determined students actually do to make a college education possible for themselves. While a deficit model would indeed tell us what they do not receive and what they do not do, understanding what *has* worked for first-generation students places researchers and educators in a much better position to develop solutions to the college access problem. The proposed College Predisposition Model is a starting point. It is the researcher's desire that others will build upon this study to further understand what works for students and how educators can use this knowledge to develop programs that will effectively serve their students. It is important to reemphasize that this study does not attempt to frame the experiences and characteristics of every first-generation student of color, but serves as a foundation from which we can build a greater understanding of the strategies used and strengths possessed by first-generation students who go on to college.

References

Adelman, C. (2006). *The toolbox revisited.* Washington, DC U.S. Department of Education, Office of Educational Research and Improvement.

Astin, A. (1975). *Preventing students from dropping out.* San Francisco: Jossey-Bass.

Astin, A. (1984). Student involvement: A developmental theory for higher education. *Journal of College Student Personnel, 25,* 297-308.

Bedsworth, W., Colby, S., and Doctor, J. (2006). *Reclaiming the American dream.* Retrieved May 29, 2007, from http://www.bridgespangroup.org/kno_ articles americandream.html.

Berkner, L., and Chavez, L. (1997). *Access to post-secondary education for 1992 high school graduates.* Washington, DC: National Center for Educational Statistics.

Cabrera, A., Castañeda, M., Nora, A., and Hengstler, D. (1992). The convergence between two theories of college persistence. *Journal of Higher Education, 63*(2), 143-164.

Cabrera, A., and LaNasa, S. (2001). On the path to college: Three critical tasks facing America's disadvantaged students. *Research in Higher Education, 42,* 119-149.

Chen, X., and Carroll, C. (2005). *First-generation students in post-secondary education: A look at their college transcripts.* Washington, DC: U.S. Department of Education, Institution of Education Sciences.

Choy, S., Horn, L., Nunez, A., and Chen, X. (2000). *Transition to college: What helps at-risk students and students whose parents did not attend college.* San Francisco: Jossey-Bass.

Choy, S. P., and MPR Associates, Inc. (2001). *Students whose parents did not go to college: Post-secondary access, persistence, and attainment.* Washington, DC: U.S. Department of Education, Office of Educational Research and Improvement.

Clifton, D., and Anderson, E. (2002). *Strengths quest: Discover and develop your strengths in academics, career, beyond.* Washington, DC: Gallup.

Dictionary.com. (2008). Retrieved August 5, 2008, from http://www.dictionary. reference.com.

Dyson, M. E. (2008). Commentary: Me and my brother and black America. *CNN.com*. Retrieved August 22, 2008 from: http://www.cnn.com/2008/ US/07/23/bia.michael.dyson/index.html

Engle, J., Bermeo, A., and O'Brien, C. (2006). *Straight from the source: What works for first-generation college students.* Washington, DC: The Pell Institute.

Evans, N., Forney, D., and Guido-DiBrito, F. (1998). *Student development in college: Theory, research, and practice.* San Francisco, California: Jossey-Bass.

Fries-Britt, S., and Griffin, K. (2007). The Black box: How high-achieving Blacks resist stereotypes about Black Americans. *Journal of College Student Development, 48*(5), 509-524.

Griffin, K. (2006). Striving for success: A qualitative exploration of competing theories of high-achieving Black college students' academic motivation. *Journal of College Student Development, 47*(4), 384-400.

Harper, S. (2005, March/April). Leading the way: Inside the experiences of high-achieving African American male students. *About Campus*, 8-16.

Horn, L., and Nunez, A. (2000). *Mapping the road to college: First-generation students' math track, planning strategies, and context of support.* Washington, DC: Office of Educational Research and Improvement.

Hossler, D., Schmit, J. V., and Vesper, N. (1999). *Going to college: How social, economic, and educational factors influence the decisions students make.* Baltimore, MD: Johns Hopkins University Press.

Hsaio, K. (1992). First-generation college students. Retrieved August July 1, 2008 from ERIC Clearinghouse for Junior Colleges: http://www.ericdigests.org/ 1992-1/first.htm.

Inman, W., and Mayes, L. (1999). The importance of being first: Unique charac teristics of first-generation community college students. *Community College Review, 26*(4), 3-22.

London, H. (1992). Transformations: Cultural challenges faced by first-generation students. In L. Zwerling, and H. London (Eds.), *New directions for community colleges.* San Francisco: Jossey-Bass.

McCarron, G., and Inkelas, K. (2006). The gap between the educational aspirations and attainment for first-generation college students and the role of parental involvement. *Journal of College Student Development, 47*(5), 534-549.

McConnell, P. (2000). What community colleges should do to assist first-generation students. *Community College Review, 28*, 75-87.

McDonough, P. (1994). Buying and selling higher education. *Journal of Higher Education, 65*, 427-446.

Nasim, A., Roberts, A., Harnell, J., and Young, H. (2005). Non-cognitive predictors of academic achievement for African American across cultural contexts. *The Journal of Negro Education, 74*(4), 344-358.

Nelson Laird, T., Bridges, B., Morelon-Quainoo, C., Williams, J., and Salinas Holmes, M. (2007). African American and Hispanic student engagement at minority serving and predominantly White institutions. *Journal of College Student Development, 40*(1), 39-56.

Pascarella, E., and Terenzini, P. (1980). Predicting freshmen persistence and voluntary dropout decisions from a theoretical model. *Journal of Higher Education, 51*, 60-75.

Pascarella, E., Pierson, C., Wolniak, G., and Terenzini, P. (2004). First-generation college students: Additional evidence on college experiences and outcomes. *Journal of Higher Education, 75*, 249-251.

Pascarella, E., and Terenzini, P. (2005). *How college affects students: A third decade of research* (Vol. 2). San Francisco: Jossey-Bass.

Pike, G., and Kuh, G. (2005). First- and second-generation college students: A comparison of their engagement and intellectual development. *Journal of Higher Education, 73*(3), 276-300.

Rendón, L. (1992). From the barrio to the academy: Revelations of a Mexican American "scholarship girl." In *First-generation College Students: Confronting the cultural issues* (pp. 55-64). San Francisco: Jossey-Bass.

Ryan, M., and Deci, E. (2000). Self-Determination Theory and the facilitation of intrinsic motivation, social develoment, and well-being. *American Pschologist, 55* (1), 68-78.

Saenz, V., Hurtado, S., Wolf, D., and Yeung, F. (2007). *First in my family: A profile of first-generation college students at four-year institutions since 1971.* Los Angeles: Higher Education Research Institute.

Solorzano, D., Allen, W., and Carroll, G. (2002). Critical race theory, racial microaggressions, and campus racial climate at the University of California Berkeley. *Chicano Latino Law Review, 23*, 15-112.

Steele, C. (1997). A threat in the air: How stereotypes shape intellectual identity and performance. *American Psychologist, 56*(6), 613-629.

Steele, C., and Aronson, J. (1995). Stereotype threat and the intellectual test performance of African Americans. *Journal of Personality and Social Psychology, 69*(5), 787-811.

Terenzini, P., Cabrera, A., and Bernal, E. (2001). *Swimming against the tide: The poor in American higher education.* Princeton, NJ: College Board.

Terenzini, P., Springer, L., Yaeger, P., Pascarella, E., and Nora, P. (1996). First-genertation college students: Characteristics, experiences, and cognitive development. *Research in Higher Education, 37*(1), 1-22.

Tinto, V. (1975). Dropout from higher education: A theoretical synthesis of recent research. *Review of Eductional Research, 45*, 89-125.

Tracey, T., and Sedlacek, W. (1984). Non-cognitive variables in predicting academic success by race. *Measurement and Evaluation, 16*, 171-178.

U.S. College Search. (2008). *Marquette University.* Retrieved August 6, 2008, from U.S. College Search: http://www.uscollegesearch.org/marquette-university. html.

Volle, K., and Federico, A. (1997). *Missed opportunities: A new look at disadvantaged college aspirants.* Washington, DC: Institute for Higher Education Policy.

Weiss, R. (1994). *Learning from strangers: The art and method of qualitative interview studies.* New York: Free.

White, T., and Sedlacek, W. (1986). Non-cognitive predictors of grades and retention for specially admitted students. *Journal of College Admissions, 3*, 20-23.

Walpole, M. (2007). *Economically and educationally challenged students in higher education: Access to outcomes.* San Francisco: Jossey-Bass.

Yazedjian, A. T., Toews, M. L., Sevin, T., and Purswell, K. E. (2008). "It's a whole new world:" A qualitative exploration of college students' definitions and strategies for college success. *Journal of College Student Development, 49*(2), 141-154.

York-Anderson, D., and Bowman, S. (1991). Assessing the college knowledge of first-generation and second-generation college students. *Journal of College Student Development, 32*, 116-122.

Chapter Three
Enhancing Success in the Community College: Recommendations from African American Male Students

J. Luke Wood, Ph.D.,
San Diego State University
Adriel A. Hilton, Ph.D.,
Upper Iowa University

ABSTRACT

This chapter reports on findings from a study which examined factors affecting the academic success of African American male students in the community college. Specifically, this study sought to determine students' perception on recommendations for improving the success of Black males. Data was collected at a mid-sized community college located in the southwestern United States. Through in-depth, semi-structured interviews with twenty-eight participants, this study identified four primary recommendations. Three recommendations were provided for community college personnel (e.g., administrators, faculty, staff), they included: 1) creating awareness of campus resources; 2) bringing role models to campus; and 3) establishing a Black Male academic success program. One recommendation was specific to African American male students themselves. Participants noted the importance of having a 'right frame of mind', which is both committed to and engaged in academic work. Across recommendations, student responses illustrated the importance of improving students' perceptions of collegiate utility.

Introduction

Over the past few decades, there has been a proliferation of research on African American male students in education (the terms Black and African American are used interchangeably) (Baldwin, Fisler and Patton, 2009; Fashola, 2005). While this has resulted in a growing literature base, in general, research on Black males has largely avoided their status and experience in the community college context (Bush and Bush, 2010; Wood and Turner, 2011). For example, Wood (2010) conducted a meta-synthesis of literature on African American males in the community college. This examination identified only twelve manuscripts which were published on this student group between 1971 and 2009. Of these manuscripts, eight were peer-reviewed journal articles and four were book chapters. This is a particularly interesting circumstance given the majority (63.1 percent) of African American males enter post-secondary education through the community college (U.S. Department of Education, 2006). In contrast, the vast majority of literature and knowledge base regarding Black males in post-secondary education is dedicated to the 36.9 percent of these students who attend four-year colleges and universities.

While there may exist some commonalities between Black males in two- and four-year contexts, scholars should be cautious in presupposing homogeny in their experiences as numerous differences exist (e.g., student population, faculty credentials, funding and resourcing, organizational structure, prestige) between institutional types (Wood and Turner, 2011). These differences may serve to impact factors affecting student success, broadly defined, within these institutions. For instance, Flowers (2006) research indicated that Black males in community colleges and universities settings have significant differences in their social integration. He found that African American males in the community college experience lower social integration (e.g., engagement in campus activities, participation in extra-curricular programming) than their counterparts in four year universities. Flowers findings illustrate a need to consider success factors that are unique to Black males in the community college.

Bearing the aforementioned in mind, a larger study was conducted which sought to identify factors that were relevant to the success of Black males in the community college. More specifically, the study examined factors affecting the academic success of Black males in the community college. As with extant research on this topic (e.g., Jordan, 2008; Perrakis, 2008), academic success referred to students' grade point averages and successful completion of courses toward their academic goals. One of the goals of the larger study was to identify recommendations that could improve the status of Black males in the community college. This chapter addresses this goal by reporting Black male students' recommendations for improving the academic success of their population. This study is unique in that it presents recommendations based upon the perspectives of Black male collegians. In this qualitative study, semi-structured interviews were conducted with students which asked them to identify practices that could serve to enhance the academic success of Black male students in the community college. It is the hope of the authors that these recommendations will serve to inform both community college practitioners (e.g., faculty, administration, staff) and Black male students.

Review of Literature

Minimal research has examined African American males in the community college. An even smaller body of literature has focused on academic success factors affecting these students (e.g., Beckles, 2008; Faison, 1993; Hampton, 2002; Perrakis, 2008; Travis, 1994). To date, eight total studies have been conducted on this topic. This limited research indicates a need for scholars and practitioners to better understand: a) factors impeding their academic success; and b) strategies to enhance their status. This study addresses both by overview academic success factors (in this literature review) and strategies for Black male success (in the findings).

Across these studies, several major themes and findings are evident. Academic success was operationalized as it related to students' grades (as is the case in this study). Recurring findings/themes in these investigations indicated several primary factors that may affect student academic success. Both Mosby (2009) and Perrakis (2008) found that Black males were more likely to succeed when they felt a sense of belonging to their campus. Mosby (2009) noted that Black males sense of belonging could be negatively impacted by their population size. Thus, when African American males were the only representatives of their racial/ethnic groups in class, they felt isolated. When this occurred, participants noted that they contemplated changing their academic and career goals and/or leaving college.

Overcoming barriers has also been associated with success. For example, Beckles (2008) noted that students perceived that a desire to prove others wrong, those who may not have faith in their ability to succeed, was believed to lead to academic success. In a similar vein, Hampton (2002) found that students who perceived that African Americans benefited from less support than other racial/ethnic groups had higher GPAs. Thus, a perceived need to overcome barriers may impact students' academic performance. Overall, a mindset of dedication to success was identified as leading to academic success (Beckles, 2008; Faison, 1993; Perrakis, 2008). For instance, Perrakis found that as students' dedication to persistence improved, their GPA also increased. Further, students with higher GPAs had statistically significant differences in their dedication to persistence than students with lower GPAs who experienced lower levels of dedication.

Several investigators have noted the importance of a supportive environment cultivated by institutional faculty, advisers, and other personnel (Beckles, 2008; Goins, 1995; Jordan, 2008). In particular, Jordan's (2008) study identified students' perceptions of factors associated with academic success. Jordan's research indicated that students believed they were more successful when faculty members facilitated interactive classrooms and listened to their concerns. Research also illustrates the importance of peers in positively and negatively impacting students' academic success (Beckles, 2008; Faison, 1993; Jordan, 2008). While Beckles (2008) noted that peers served as a source of support for academic success, Faison (1993) identified a negative correlation between peer group dependence and academic achievement. Jordan's (2008) research served to delineate a rationale for these incongruent findings. Jordan noted that while peer group relationships were identified by students as positively affecting their academic success, the nature of the relationship itself is an important indicator of student success. Relationships that are centered on academic-oriented activities (e.g., study groups, tutoring) were identified by students as positively affecting their success, while non-academic relationships, even with fellow collegians, could deter academic success.

While faculty and peer relationships have been identified as factors affecting academic success, several scholars noted that familial support and encouragement were also important (Beckles, 2008; Mosby, 2009; Hampton, 2002). Findings and themes from previous investigations indicated that students benefit from family support. For instance, Hampton (2002) noted that students with higher familial support benefited from higher grade point averages. Similarly, Mosby (2009) noted that parents and family influenced students' desire to attend college, their career goals in college, and their aspiration to continue toward identified career goals. However, Mosby also found that family members could also serve to detract from success if/when they conveyed negative messages about school or overemphasized athletic commitments over academic achievement.

Several investigators identified the importance of work and financial considerations in relation to academic success (Mosby, 2009; Hampton, 2002; Jordan, 2008). Mosby (2009) stated that financial instability was a concern to African American students. Jordan (2008) noted that when students struggled due to insufficient income, that they increased their hours of employment. Jordan also found that this negatively affected the amount of time Black males were able to dedicate and achieve successfully their collegiate coursework. However, as noted by Hampton (2002) greater levels of employment did not always serve to detract from collegiate success. Hampton found that students whose academic goals were aligned with their employment benefited from higher GPAs than those whose goals and employment was not aligned.

The aforementioned studies provided a conceptual lens for this study. These studies indicated the importance of the following factors in affecting Black male academic success: a) sense of belonging; b) desire to overcome real/perceived barriers; c) dedication to success; d) supportive institutional environment; e) peer relationships; f) familial support; g) financial considerations; and h) work-school balance and alignment. This study elicited recommendations from students for enhancing academic success. These recommendations are conceptualized within the framework of these above factors. The next section provides an overview of the methods employed in this study.

Method

According to Holloway (1997), qualitative research honors the voices, lives and sociocultural realities of participant's by affirming their role as providers of knowledge. In particular, it is an important approach for understanding the marginality and experience of marginalized groups (Flick, 2006). Given that the purpose of this study was to garner recommendations for enhancing academic success through the perspectives of African American male students, an often-marginalized group, this study elected to employ a qualitative research design. Thus, semi-structured interviews were conducted with twenty-eight Black male community college students.

Setting and Participants

Data included in this study was collected at Star Valley Community College (SVCC) (a pseudonym). SVCC is a mid-sized community college located in the Southwestern United States with an enrollment of approximately 13,000 students. SVCC is recognized by the federal government as a Minority Serving Institution (MSI), an institution which enrolls a high proportion of students of color (O'Brien and Zudak, 1998). As such, more than half of the students attending SVCC are students of color. The racial/ethnic breakdown of the student population is as follows: White, 39 percent; Hispanic/Latino, 32 percent; other, 16 percent; African American, 8 percent; Asian American, 4 percent; and Native American, 1 percent. Across racial/ethnic groups, female students are well-represented, accounting for 59 percent of the student population at this campus. Male students represent only 35 percent of the student population with 6 percent of students not reporting their gender. The gender imbalance between males and females is particularly evident among African American students where males account for only 148 of the nearly 1,100 Black students on campus. Given this circumstance, the 28 participants interviewed represent nearly 20 percent of the total Black male population at this institution.

All participants in this study were African American males. To participate in this study, participants had to be: a) at least eighteen years of age; and b) currently or formerly (within past two years) enrolled as student at SVCC. Participants were selected via a maximum variation sampling technique. This technique purposefully includes a diverse pool of participants in order to elicit themes which are relevant across a varied group of participants (Merriam, 1998). Thus, participants in the sample were representative of diverse ages, majors, and degree goals. Participants' ages ranged from 18 to 58 years of age, with a mean age of 24.5 years. While business was the most common major among participants, students were inclusive of numerous major fields including: criminal justice, culinary arts, biological sciences, psychology, liberal arts, architecture, nursing, political science, philosophy, music, computer science, physical therapy, and sociology. Student degree goals also varied as follows: five participants desired to earn an associate's degree; nine participants had the goal of earning an associate's degree and transferring to a four-year institution; and seven participants planned to transfer to a four-year institution without an associate's degree. In addition to maximum variation sampling, convenience sampling was also utilized. Convenience sampling served as the primary form of contact for the researchers to engage the maximum variation sampling technique. Convenience sampling allows the researcher to acquire participants who are readily available for study participation (Gay, 1996). In this study, the researchers attained participants by hosting a table in the campus quadrangle during lunch which served as a point of contact for participant recruitment.

Data Collection

Data in this study was collected through a semi-structured interview approach. As noted by DiCicco-Bloom and Crabtree (2006), semi-structured interviews are "generally organized around a set of predetermined open-ended questions, with other questions emerging from the dialogue between the interviewer and interviewee/s" (p. 315). Preplanned probes were employed in the interview protocol. Probes served to provide an additional set of sub-questions used to guide participants in better understanding and addressing the general questions in the interview protocol (Brenner, 2006; Johnson and Christensen, 2004). Open-ended concept mapping was employed in this study. Open-ended concept mapping is a technique where participants are given a blank template and asked to depict factors associated with a concept (Zanting, Verloop and Vermunt, 2003). Prior to each interview, students were given a blank sheet of paper and asked to depict factors they believed affected their academic success. Students employed varying forms of depictions including poetry, drawings, listings, and narratives. During the interviews, students were encouraged to employ their concept maps as a point of reference for discussing their collegiate experiences. After each interview, concept maps were collected by the researchers. These maps were utilized as a supplemental form of data in the coding, initial analysis, and final analysis processes.

Data Analysis

Interview transcripts and concept maps were coded and analyzed via a systematic data analysis technique. This approach allows researchers to identify predetermined research goals, areas of questioning, pre-hypothesized codes, and a conceptual framework prior to data collection (Huberman and Miles, 1994; Miles and Huberman, 1994). As noted earlier, the conceptual/theoretical lens of this study was based upon extant literature on African American male academic success. Thus, the factors identified in this literature guided the process of pre-hypothesizing codes. Throughout the data collection process, additional codes were identified beyond the pre-hypothesized codes and several pre-hypothesized codes were eliminated. After each interview, the researchers documented important points identified in the interview and concept mapping process (e.g., typing up observation notes). Further, contact summary and document summary forms were employed and used to organize, assemble themes, and support the data reduction process. Coding was implemented in a two stage process; first, the researchers employed basic codes. Basic codes were codes identified in the pre-hypothesizing stage and during the process of data collection. Second, more advanced interpretive and patterned codes were identified. Throughout the coding process, memoing was used to notate important points identified and to describe the relationship between identified codes. After coding was complete, the researchers engaged in an iterative analytic process where codes and visual displays were used to postulate and confirm study findings.

Validity Measures and Limitations

Two primary forms of validity were employed in this study, member-checks and inter-coder reliability. Lincoln and Guba (1985) stated that member checks is a validity measure used in qualitative research where input from participants is sought on preliminary findings. In this study, a focus group session was hosted to gain participants' input, correction, verification, and clarification of findings. Students' input from this stage was incorporated into the final study write-up. Inter-coder reliability was also utilized as a validity measure. The researchers selected portions of interview transcripts which were coded individually first, and then compared for similarities in emergent codes. This process was undertaken to ensure that a high degree of congruent coding was occurring between researchers. Validity measures were particularly important in this study for ensuring that pre-hypothesized codes did not dictate the researchers' ability to identify other important factors impacting Black male academic success in the community college.

As with all research, this study was not without limitations. Since data for this study was collected from the perspectives of students, it is likely participants were unable to discuss recommendations for academic success related to structural issues (e.g., inter-organizational communication, intra-campus politics). Further, given the focus of qualitative research is specificity as opposed to generalizability (see Auerbach and Silverstein, 2003), findings from this study are not generalizable to wider populations. However, findings may provide important insight to determine whether recommendations are applicable in other community college settings. The next section presents findings from this study derived from student recommendations.

Findings

Findings from this study revealed four primary areas of recommendations: 1) create awareness of campus resources; 2) bring role models to campus; 3) establish a Black Male academic success program; and 4) frame of mind. Three recommendations were provided for community college personnel (e.g., administrators, faculty, staff) while one was specific to African American male students themselves. Recommendations provided are interrelated, as many addressed the importance of utility. Utility refers to students' perceptions that their collegiate endeavors are worthwhile. This underlying concept indicates the importance of societal messages to Black males about the importance of education, for them. Recommendations from Black male students are presented.

Create Awareness of Campus Resources

A number of participants noted that Black males were often unaware of campus resources (e.g., tutoring, career counseling, mentoring, grants) available to them. Students stated that this served to impede Black male success, especially when they encountered barriers. Barriers identified by students in relation to this recommendation varied; however, they generally focused on academic performance issues as well as solidifying and establishing a plan of action to obtain one's career objective(s). Given this circumstance, students suggested that the campus could enhance awareness of campus resources. In particular, students recommended that the campus host events (e.g., expanded orientation session, one-day seminar) catering to African American male students. The most frequent event format recommended was an orientation format. For example, one student stated the following:

> So, like, so like you know, calling them [Black males] to come in and let them know, like an orientation, let them know the options that are available to them, here at the school and the resources that are there. Yeah, I think like, a lot of people, who like maybe, for the math thing, or who might be like lower in English or something, they feel like, oh well, let them know the options that are available to them, here at the school and the resources that are there.

This student went on to note that many students would be more motivated to enroll, persist, and succeed in college if they were aware of institutional mechanisms designed to support their academic success. Specifically, he stated that this was important for students who struggled in math and English, coursework which he believed were most likely to lead to poor academic performance.

Students believed that these academic awareness events could serve a wide variety of purposes, such as: a) increasing student involvement in campus organizations, thereby imbuing a sense of community among students at the college; (b) orientating students to academic services (e.g., tutoring centers, mentoring programs) designed to enhance their success; (c) serving as a platform for students to inform campus personnel of their awareness, or lack thereof, of institutional services; and (d) introducing students to key campus personnel who could serve to provide them with information needed to support their success. For example, one participant discussed the latter recommendation stating:

> And the counselors! Show your counselors too. I don't know, maybe they [campus staff] might want to put a couple of pictures up or encourage students to visit their counselors, because counselors are pretty up for [helping you] everything. So those types of things could help, not just young Black men, it could help a lot of people. . . showcase them and say hey, they are here to help you talk to you. Because, I know they are, because they have said it to me, anytime.

This participant noted that campus counselors served to connect students with individuals, services, and provided them with information to navigate campus organizational channels and processes. Students believe that this foreknowledge of resources would allow Black males to feel more confident: engaging in difficult coursework; planning for the future semesters; and believing that the institution was committed to their success. Confidence in academic pursuits serves to affect students perceptions of the utility (or worthiness) of college. Students who do not see success in college as a likely outcome may be less interested in pursuing college. Thus, creating awareness of campus services allows students to see that a system of support is in place which can help make their academic dreams a reality.

Bring Role Models to Campus

The vast majority of study participants noted that there were negative stereotypes about Black males in education. They believed that Black males were perceived as intellectually inferior, or more commonly stated 'stupid', by society as a whole. Several students noted that these perceptions often caused them to disengage, purposely avoiding class participation. Further, students noted that these perceptions impacted their own confidence in the utility of their educational pursuits. Their ability to succeed in college and the eventual translation of academic success to personal and financial success were questioned.

In order to counter academic inferiority stereotypes and to enhance the perceived utility of college, several students suggested that successful African American males be invited to serve as role models. Students noted that role models could come from many locales, including: (a) representatives of local Black community leaders from varied fields (e.g., dentists, accountants, CEO's, aeronauts); (b) Black males who have successfully transferred from the community college and graduated from a four-year institution; and (c) Black male leaders of campus, especially those in administrative roles. Participants stated that role models could serve as a source of inspiration for students; they could also provide internships, apprenticeships, career advice, financial advice, and suggestions for succeeding in college.

In particular, students noted that role models who enjoyed financial stability would serve to best motivate Black male students. For example, one student stated that the institution should invite role models:

> who have went here, or, who moved on or graduated, if they look at maybe their success, or how they might just have a house, they're able to make their payment every month, you know, they are living nice, they have a bank account, savings account, and you know, they might not be making as much as some other person not going to school, but they are probably working less, and they have the weekends to do what they want. So, people just coming back and giving an example and just kind of encouraging and motivating people to stick in there.

An important component of this student's statement is the notion that college may not always lead to higher paying jobs, but it may lead to more enjoyable career options. These career options could allow individuals to work fewer hours and have weekends off. This sentiment is echoed by a participant who suggested that the campus bring Black business executives who could discuss how education allowed them to reach their goals, he commented:

> Recruit black males like, the CFO, a black guy, Boeing, He became CFO of the world's biggest aeronautical firm, that's Boeing, and with only just a BS in accounting, actually science and accounting. Yeah, I think his name's James Bell, yeah James Bell. He was in, I shouldn't go like that, he was internal CFO of Boeing with just a BS and ran that whole accounting thing brilliant man with just only a BS. Imagine if I work hard, get that experience, and get a PhD! Work with people, speak different languages, travel the world, what do you think will happen?

As indicated by participants, role models can inspire students to aspire to greater academic and career horizons. They can also serve as a reminder that overcoming obstacles to academic success are possible and that the investment in doing so is worthwhile. Role models may be a visible reminder that students should place confidence in the utility of college.

Establish a Black Male Academic Success Program

A number of participants stated that relationships with other Black male collegians were important to their sense of belonging to the institution. However, they noted that the nature of their interactions delineated whether the relationships positively or negatively affected their academic success. Participants noted that when relationships were based on academic pursuits (e.g., intellectual conversations, studying, peer to peer tutoring) then the relationships positively affected their success. In contrast, interactions with campus peers that were focused on non-academic pursuits (e.g., 'hanging out', partying) served to negatively affected success. Thus, students suggested that a university sponsored/supported mechanism was needed to support positive peer-group connections.

As a result, the most common recommendation from students was the establishment of a Black male academic success program. Students suggested that the program have several components: (a) a peer mentoring program that allows more senior students to mentor incoming students; (b) workshops on challenges facing first-generation college students, including data on African American male success in education and in society; (c) creating awareness and usage of campus resources; (d) educating students on campus policies, such as how to understand which classes to take and when to take them; (e) establishing a strong self-determination component that provides open and honest dialogue with students on what is expected to succeed in college and in their future careers; and (f) proactively addressing students needs (e.g., transportation, housing, grades) by providing access to support services and resources.

While most students noted that the program could serve as a point of regular contact among Black males, the rationale for the program/organization varied. Some students suggested that the program focus on building students' self-esteem and confidence. For example one student suggested that this occur through hosting events with performances, he stated:

> Well I'd try to come up with certain activities, probably I wouldn't wanna really, I would wanna like have activities in the school, like to where I know a lotta guys here like to sing or rap or something. I think if you put 'em in a position to where like they could shine a little bit, they'll appreciate that little moment, and they'll feel like they're having success at the school.

In contrast to this perspective, several students recommended that the organization be dedicated to educating Black males on issues facing them in society and in education. The rationale for this mission was to encourage Black males to see the utility of college. For instance, one student discussed the following:

> Provide a program association, in this case for African-American males to have them to believe that what you win by choosing college. You know, in a sense it all depends on how you use, how you view about college. You know, how do you develop a program for minorities basically, so they can, how can I put this, bring ideas in, you know, develop multiple projects for them so they can have a different outlook about college. I mean. . . speaking to minorities out there, asking African-American males out there that, you know what, college is serious. You know, provide steps around, you know, just giving the African-American males numbers, ratios about, you know, why minority males is dropping out, why [they are] unsuccessful, and giving them steps to build and to change that.

In a similar vein, another participant suggested that the association host events which allowed students to see the utility of college. In particular, this student believed that an enhanced view of collegiate utility could lead to a greater focus (or goal commitment) to one's academic pursuits, he stated:

> Show the rewards of academic process and community college, and try and get like, several different individuals of power to talk about their experiences. And I'll try and get people that can relate, you know what I'm saying? I'll get like, a black man, who you know, started off kind of shaky but then started to focus and then really got rewarded. You know? Like he has everything he wants and you know. Just basically put together an event like that. And also, I'll—afterwards I'll, maybe I'll try and put together like, it's difficult. You know, like everybody could complain about something but when it comes to the solution it's like.

The structure of the organization described by participants ranged from a club to a campus-sponsored program. It should be noted that the campus in which this study was conducted had a university supported minority male club. This organization engaged in many of the activities described by students in this study. As such, this recommendation is based upon a ubiquitous affirmation of support for this campus organization, both from those who participated in it, as well as those who had heard of its operations.

Frame of Mind

A large number of students in this study discussed the importance of being 'focused'. For these students, being focused suggested that they were both committed to and engaged in academic work. Engagement was typified by studying, attending class, turning in homework, and completing assignments on time. Participants noted a simple relationship between focus and academic success; when they were focused on their academic pursuits they performed well in school, when they were not focused, they performed poorly. Having the right frame of mind for college was the only student recommendation specific to students. Underlying these comments was the need for Black males to have an ethic of self-determination, or as one student stated: "at the end of the day you responsible for your own self, I only tell you so much and you know, you got to find your own way". Another student noted that students had the 'tools' (e.g., resources, institutional support, networks) necessary to enable their success. He also noted the importance of self-determination:

> And it's up to the individual, you know. Definitely up to the individual because you can always make, you can put so much tools in somebody's hands, but it's up to the individual to use those tools. You can advertise it, you can get out, you can speeches and all this, I've heard a lot of good speeches and stuff like that. A lot of programs out there, but if people don't want to use the tool, what can you do?

By having the right frame of mind, participants noted that students should: a) create and maintain a successful environment conducive to studying; b) separate themselves from in-school (e.g., 'hanging out', skipping class) and out-of school (e.g., neighborhood, external peer discouragement) distractions; c) be emotionally committed to college); d) being resilient to barriers (e.g., poor relations with faculty, difficulty in a class) impeding academic success; and e) seeing the utility of college; in essence, believing that college was a commitment worthy of their effort. In particular, one student summarized many of the above points in his interview. He stated:

> The institut[ion] is giving you all the opportunities. It is put right there in front of you. I think the students need to put themselves in those areas of opportunity. They need to understand you need to be in the right frame of mind. You need to put yourself in the right kind of environment to study. I mean you need to separate yourself from a lot of things whether you want to do good or not. I mean you have to, you got to be focused and ready to go to college, not just wake up and say "I'm gonna go to college." There's a lot involved. There's a lot involved. Time! You know, education. I mean, you've gotta do a lot of things to go to college, and you can get past that, you know, and not be afraid of it. You'll succeed once you do cause there's something that you want . . . . you have to want to learn. . . . Like I said, you gotta have the right frame of mind to come to college before you come to college.

While this student provided a good overview of what was meant by being in the 'right frame of mind', another centered his comments on the importance of being emotionally committed to college. This student compared college to a job, using job performance as a metaphor for academic grades. He stated the following:

> So, we need to change that leisure mind frame, and like, when they start, go like . . . hey, this ain't playtime for you to eat or, you know, talk. This is for you to study. This is a job. And your performance is that report card. You keep on getting that low grade, you know, you gonna slip through the cracks. And those with that 'A' and getting the high grades going excel. You know what I mean, you open the door. You open the door. . . . And that's another reason. Like, people look forward to university, which is not bad, but it's a job. That's how I look at the university. It's a job.

When this student used the phrase 'open the door', he suggested that college was like an open door. He noted that individuals in one's life serve to create opportunities for students to pursue their goals. He suggested that when students avoided capitalizing on these opportunities, the 'door slams, and they're sealed'. The student stated that in the past, he failed to 'walk' through the educational doors that his father, mother and other family members had opened for him. This occurred early in his community college career where he had two consecutive semesters of poor grades. He noted that his poor grades were a result of him not being in the right frame of mind. Now, he said that he was committed to college, seeing it as one large door, noting that he would 'run' through the door by applying himself to college.

As evidenced by this theme, student academic success is both the responsibility of the institution and the student. While institutions are responsible for providing personnel, policies, procedures, programming, and a climate conducive to success, the student is responsible for maintaining the 'right frame of mind'. This mind frame allows them to capitalize on the opportunities afforded to them by the institution.

Discussion and Conclusion

Harper (2010) indicated that the vast majority of literature on Black males in education is concerned with problems facing this student population as opposed to solutions to their success. He further stated that "Much remains to be learned from those boys and men who, despite all that has been stacked against them, manage to thrive and persist through high school graduation, baccalaureate degree attainment, and even into graduate studies" (p. 2). With this in mind, this manuscript sought to learn from the insights of Black male students. Across the recommendations provided, it was clear that students were concerned with recommendations that reinforced the utility of college.

Overwhelmingly, students' recommendations suggest that seeing college (and other academic pursuits) as worthwhile are integral to Black male academic success. This notion correlates with foundational persistence research on college students from Bean and Metzner (1985) which suggested that utility was imperative to the persistence of nontraditional students (e.g., part-time students, minorities, older students) in higher education. This research has also been affirmed with specific attention to Black males in the community college (Mason, 1994; 1998). The relationship between scholarly findings and the voices of Black male students serves to further illustrate the importance of Harper's (2010) comments. Black males, at least in this study, do possess an understanding of factors impeding their success. Additionally, they are also aware of strategies which could potentially counteract the barriers they face.

While findings from this study are not necessarily generalizable to all community colleges, the recommendations provided may serve as an initial point of conversation on strategies to enhance the success of this population at other institutions. In particular, the recommendations provided may be applicable to institutions concerned with issues related to students' perceptions of the utility of college. Utility should be of concern to community college personnel as it is both directly and indirectly affirmed as an important component to Black male academic success throughout the literature (Beckles, 2008; Faison, 1993; Perrakis, 2008).

In closing, the recommendations provided by Black males proffered four recommendations. An underlying theme connecting all recommendations was the importance of utility. Three recommendations were provided for community college personnel (e.g., administrators, faculty, staff), they included: 1) creating awareness of campus resources; 2) bringing role models to campus; and 3) establishing a Black Male academic success program. One recommendation was specific to African American male students themselves. Participants noted the importance of having a 'right frame of mind', which is both committed to and engaged in academic work. It is the author's hope that further research will acknowledge the importance of Black male students as purveyors of knowledge and important contributors to strategies for enhancing their success in the community college, as well as in other education settings.

References

Auerbach, C. F., and Silverstein, L. B. (2003). *An introduction to coding and analysis: Qualitative data.* New York: New York University Press.

Baldwin, C. P., Fisler, J., and Patton, J. M. (2009). Who's afraid of the big bad wolf? Demystifying Black male college students. In H. T. Frierson (Ed.)., *Black American males in higher education: Diminishing proportions* (pp. 181-205). Sussex, United Kingdom: Emerald.

Bean, J. P., and Metzner, B. S. (1985). A conceptual model of nontraditional undergraduate student attrition. *Review of Educational Research, 55*(4), 485-540.

Beckles, W. A. (2008). *Redefining the dream: African American male voices on academic success.* Unpublished doctoral dissertation, Morgan State University.

Brenner, M. E. (2006). Interviewing in educational research. In J.L. Green G. Camilli and P. B. Elmore (Eds.), *Handbook of complementary methods in education research* (pp. 357-370). Mahwah, N.J: Lawrence Erlbaum and Associates.

Bush, E. C. and Bush, L. (2010). Calling out the elephant: An examination of African American male achievement in community colleges. *Journal of African American Males in Education, 1*(1), 40-62.

DiCicco-Bloom, B. and Crabtree. B. F. (2006). The qualitative research interview. *Medical Education, 40*(4), 314-321.

Faison, A. C. (1993). *The effect of autonomy and locus-of-control on the academic achievement of Black male community college students.* Unpublished doctoral dissertation, City University of New York.

Fashola, O. S. (2005). *Educating African American males: Voices from the field.* Thousand Oaks, CA: Corwin.

Flick, U. (2006). *An introduction to qualitative research.* Thousand Oaks, CA: Sage.

Flowers, L. A. (2006). *Effects of attending a 2-year institution on African American males' academic and social integration in the first year of college. Teachers College Record, 108*(2), 267-286.

Gay, L. R. (1996). *Educational research: Competencies for analysis and application.* (Fifth edition). Upper Saddle River, NJ: Prentice-Hall.

Goins, C. L. (1995). *Psychosocial and academic functioning of African-American college students: Social support, racial climate and racial identity.* Unpublished Doctoral Dissertation, University of Washington.

Hampton, P. (2002). *Academic success for African-American male community college students.* Unpublished doctoral dissertation, University of Southern California.

Harper, S. R. (2010). In his name: Rigor and relevance in research on African American males in education. *Journal of African American Males in Education, 1*(1), 1-6.

Holloway, I. (1997). *Basic concepts for qualitative research.* Malden, MA: Blackwell.

Huberman, A. M. and Miles, M. B. (1994). Data management and analysis. In N. K. Denzin and Lincoln Y. S. (Eds.), *Handbook of Qualitative Research* (pp. 428-444). London, UK: Sage Publications.

Johnson, B. and Christensen, L. B. (2004). *Educational research: Quantitative, qualitative, and mixed approaches.* Thousand Oaks, CA: Sage Publications.

Jordan, P. G. (2008). *African American male students' success in an urban community college: A case study.* Unpublished doctoral dissertation, University of Pennsylvania.

Lee, C. (2000). *The State of Knowledge About the Education of African Americans.* Washington, D.C.: American Educational Research Association, Commission on Black Education.

Lincoln, Y. S. and Guba, E. G. (1985). *Naturalistic inquiry.* Thousand Oaks, CA: Sage Publications.

Mason, H. P. (1994). *The relationships of academic, background, and environmental variables in the persistence of adult African American male students in an urban community college.* Unpublished doctoral dissertation, Northern Illinois University.

Mason, H. P. (1998). A persistence model for African American male urban community college students. *Community College Journal of Research and Practice, 22*(8), 751-760.

Merriam, S B. (1998). *Qualitative research and case study applications in education.* San Francisco: Jossey-Bass.

Miles, M., and Huberman, A. M. (1984). *Qualitative data analysis.* Thousand Oaks: Sage Publications.

Mosby, J. R. (2009). *From strain to success: A phenomenological study of the personal and academic pressures on African American male community college students.* Unpublished Doctoral Dissertation, University of San Diego.

O'Brien, E. M. and Zudak, C. (1998). Minority serving institutions: An Overview. *New Directions for Higher Education, 102,* 5-15.

Perrakis, A. I. (2008). Factor promoting academic success among African American and White male community college students. *New Directions for Community Colleges, 142,* 15-23.

Travis, R. L. (1994). *Noncognitive predictors of academic success for non-traditional students at a large, southeastern, urban community college.* Unpublished doctoral dissertation, Florida International University.

U.S. Department of Education, National Center for Education Statistics, 2003-04 Beginning Post-secondary Students Longitudinal Study, First Follow-up (BPS:04/06).

Wood, J. L. (2010). *African American males in the community college: Towards a model of academic success.* Unpublished Doctoral Dissertation, Arizona State University.

Wood, J. L. and Turner, C. S. V. (2011). Black males and the community college: Student perspectives on faculty and academic success. *Community College Journal of Research and Practice, 35,* 1-17. doi: 10.1080/10668926. 2010.526052

Zanting, A., Verloop, N., and Vermunt, J. D. (2003). Using interviews and concept maps to access mentor teachers' practical knowledge. *Higher Education, 46,* 195-214.

Chapter Four
Societal Perceptions of African American Males in Higher Education and the Adverse Impact It Has on Their Academic Achievement at Predominantly White Institutions

Ron Brown, Ph.D.,
Lone Star College System, Texas

Introduction

For the past decade the attainment gap in college admission and graduation rates between Black males and their White counterparts has continued to grow. A growing body of research has held that there is a negative correlation between educational attainment and the decline of the Black family structure. As the structure of the Black family has deteriorated due to the lack of a male presence, so have participation rates in higher education for African American males. It is established that environmental and cultural factors have a profound influence on human behaviors, including academic performance. What is less understood is how environmental and cultural factors influence the way in which Black males come to perceive education and how those perceptions influence not only their behavior but their performance in school. It is unknown why being African American and male causes this segment of the population to stand out in the most negative and disheartening ways, both in school and in society.

This study measures the perceived influence of three factors (societal dissonance, self efficacy, and institutional support) on the academic success of African American male students at a predominantly White institution of higher education. The purpose of this chapter is to discuss the perceived influence of racialized discrimination (societal dissonance), on the academic success of seven academically successful African American male undergraduate students at a predominantly White institution of higher education. This was done by examining students' self-efficacy, support structure, and academic background, guided by three research questions, one of which focused specifically on *Societal Dissonance*.

Through the experiences of the participants, the study provides insight into issues of societal perception, persistence, support, and access through the perspective of African American males. This chapter will provide a contextual understanding of African American males in higher education and provide those who work with the African American male populations in higher education, as well as in K-12 settings, insight to Black males from their perspective. The data and information contained within the body of this chapter may be used to assist institutions of higher education in the recruitment and retention of African American males by providing strategies and recommendations.

Societal Dissonance

Festinger's theory of cognitive dissonance deals with discrepancy between cognitions. Festinger (1957) defined these cognitions as "any knowledge, opinion, or belief about the environment, about oneself, or about one's behavior" (p. 62). The related concept of *societal dissonance* is based on the foundations of cognitive dissonance theory. Thus, societal cognitions are based on the beliefs and perceptions held by people (society) instead of the beliefs held by the individual concerning displayed behavior. According to cognitive dissonance theory, people have a tendency to seek consistency among their cognitions (i.e., beliefs, opinions); the same holds true for societal dissonance. When society perceives an inconsistency between attitudes or behaviors (dissonance), something must change to eliminate that dissonance. In the case of a discrepancy between attitudes and behavior, society most likely changes its attitude to accommodate the behavior.

Festinger (1957) identified two factors that affect the strength of dissonance: the number of dissonant beliefs and the importance attached to each belief. These factors apply to cognitive and societal dissonance alike. Festinger suggested three ways to eliminate dissonance: (a) reduce the importance of the dissonant beliefs, (b) add consonant beliefs that outweigh the dissonant beliefs, and (c) change the dissonant beliefs so that they are no longer inconsistent.

Based on Festinger's theory (1957), dissonance occurs most often in situations in which society must choose between two incompatible beliefs or actions. In the case of African American males, societal dissonance influences the way in which they are perceived. As with other subgroups, African American males can be praised or vilified; they are often viewed from a deficit perceptive. Societal dissonance is the inability to reconcile conflicting beliefs about a group with actions carried out by individuals from that group. Dissonance occurs when society cannot differentiate between stereotypical representations of Black males (which are generally negative), and the characteristics of individual Black males encountered in the real world.

Research Question One

What is the perceived influence of societal dissonance on the African American male's academic success?

The seven young men interviewed for this study had encountered many obstacles, in the form of low expectations, negative stereotypes, and unrealistic pressures to represent the entire Black race; yet, they had been successful in continuing their journey into and through higher education. Society sends out inconsistent and sometimes unjustified messages about perceptions and attitudes toward African American males. These young men, like many others, challenged societal stereotypes to achieve their academic success. A selection of their interview responses summarizes these challenges to the stereotypes and their solutions for societal dissonance.

Andrew recognized the general social stereotypes of the Black community, particularly young Black males. He saw it as his obligation to challenge that stereotype through his personal behavior.

> I think the Black community and a lot of the Black males here are perceived as being lazy. And to an extent we are. I think it ties back to the stereotypes of Black males and the Black community in general, that it's so much easier to sell drugs or to rap or to play basketball and be successful than to put your face in a book and work hard for four years in order to achieve that same goal. . . . I have always tried to be a noble person and tried to have some sense of integrity. You can't really *break* a stereotype, but you can be an *exception* to a stereotype.

Andrew recognized that, whether or not by choice, he was a representative of his race in everyday situations.

> I don't want the Black community to continue to be perceived as being lazy, which motivates me on a daily basis to make sure that I am noble and do not need to achieve for my personal success but for the success of the Black community. It is easy to stereotype a race, especially the Black race. When you are in the class and you are the only Black student there, when you say something in class, you are a representative of the Black race. For a lot of people, you are the only Black person that they interact with or may see. So if you say something out of turn or you act a certain way, you behave in a certain way, it only reinforces what they see on TV.

Damian pointed out that he was not the only representative of his race on the campus. He was sometimes reluctant to be identified with some peers, and sometimes he was embarrassed or at least uncomfortable about the way some other African American males represented his race.

> I think it would have an influence on anyone. Whether negatively or positively, if someone does not believe in you or has a negative perception of you, it can have an influence on how you perform in school. You hear about that kind of stuff all

the time on TV and in the news, about how some guy killed his mother and father because he was abused as a kid. The abuse doesn't always have to be physical for it to affect a person. I think it's the same for Black males in college. The teachers don't think you are smart, the students don't think you are smart, it's hard but you have to get over it.

When you see someone acting out, wearing baggie pants or just clowning, which you see too often on this campus, it's like, "There goes *my* reputation. That's how *I'm* going to be viewed." You hear someone coming down the sidewalk and talking really loud, and you turn around and it's a Black guy. Do you know how that is? It's embarrassing. . . . I'm not the only Black person on a predominantly White campus, it's [already] a lot of pressure to fight those stereotypes. And then it's frustrating when you have peers who don't care.

Jesse framed the social dissonance experienced by African American males on the campus of an institution of higher education in terms of competition with students of other races.

I spend so much time in the library trying to compete with the other cultures because I know that they are doing the same amount of work that I am doing, and that they are trying to compete with me for the same jobs . . . later on in life.

I think it [societal dissonance] plays a major part on how we interact with the other students and then, how it affects us in class. I often find myself taking time out to think about what I want to say in class. Instead of just speaking my mind, or blurting something out, I take time to think about it. So I guess it's good and bad. Good because I don't talk much, but when I do, it is usually of quality. The bad would be, no one should have to be that scared to share their thoughts. I think negative stereotypes and looking down on people plays a huge role in one's college experience, actually in life.

[In one class] instead of being the team leader (which I should have been) and instead of speaking my mind and my opinions, I was actually in the background. I was actually at the bottom of the totem pole, maybe because the people around me were so intelligent. I felt maybe ashamed to speak my mind. We had to present a project to our class, but working with this group, I felt [they were] smarter than I was. A little bit smarter than me. Can you feel sometimes when a person is smarter or has that intelligence level? It's kind of above you, sometimes by the way they present themselves.

Once I was placed in that group among the other smart business majors, I had to keep that image intact; but at the same time, it kind of defeated me. It is kind of hard to look upon that situation. Let's say we are both going in for the interview for the same job; the employer can't look on both of us and say, "Alright, I'm going to pick him because.. or I can't X you out because you weren't raised in the same environment."

Saviour presented one constructive solution to challenge negative stereotypes about the African American male held by people on the higher education campus in particular and in society in general. He saw his role as an "educator" of society regarding the image of the African American male. Inferred in his description is his assumption of role model as well as educator.

> My job is a job, but it's not a job. We put on programs . . . that promote awareness and spread information, because a lot of people come here, especially White people, and they don't know anything about other cultures. They say things like, "What's life's like being Black?" or "I've never seen a Black person before." It's like all they see is what they see on TV, so when they walk across the street, they don't know any other dimension. So we try to let them see another side. In that aspect I'm a leader because, when people see me and they see what I am all about, they see something different, something they've never seen before. So I try to teach them. It's just in small ways, I'm not going to go down my résumé or anything, it's just small things like that.
>
> I don't like to make excuses for anybody or make excuses for why I have not done well on a test or something like that. But truthfully, I think being negatively stereotyped or perceived as bad hurts. I always try to treat everyone with the same amount of respect and teach people whenever I have an opportunity, but when you walk in to class and you have already been judged, it is pretty hard to act normal. When you are constantly looked upon as bad or not able to do the work, sometimes you can't help but start to believe it. That is when you have to be strong and not let that stop you from being successful.

Without saying so directly, Wayne implied that African American males on campus may not be as different in their social roles as some have presumed. He described them as being categorized in much the same way as other males on campus.

> I would say Black males in this campus are divided into three categories: athletes, Greeks and regular folks. If you are not an athlete, you are nothing; if you are not a Greek, you are nothing; and then you fall into that category of "just so and so." That's the way we talk about each other here. . . . You [are defined] by a title or a role and you get lumped into one of the three.

Analysis for Research Question One

Although the participants in this study all alluded to the fact that negative stereotypes and perceptions of Black males on campus and in society *could* have a negative influence on their academic performance, the general consensus seemed to be that this particular group of young men used this deficit perception of Black males to their advantage. Jesse, Damian, and Saviour all stated directly that the negative pressures and stereotypes of societal dissonance would affect a Black male's academic matriculation into college in an adverse way. When asked whether he thought that dissonance on a societal level had an influence on a Black male's academic success, Jesse responded, "I think it plays a major part on how we interact with the other students and then, how it affects us in class." This clearly shows that the deficit perspective unjustly given to Black males at times has the potential to affect Black males, not only in life but in the classroom as well. This group of young men addressed the issue of negative stereotypes, feelings of isolation, and low academic expectations by performing well in the classroom. Saviour went a step further, stating that it was his "job to act as an educator," to teach others when confronted with issues of a deficit perception of Black males. He also said, "I don't like to make excuses for anybody or make excuses for why I have not done well on a test, or something like that. But truthfully, I think being negatively stereotyped or perceived as bad hurts." Andrew took it upon himself to address this obstacle by ensuring that his personal behavior did not match that of the stereotypical young Black male.

While the findings related to this question showed evidence of the participants doing exceedingly well academically despite obvious feelings of isolation and low expectations held by others, one participant expressed feelings of societal pressures affecting his academic performance. It was surprising to hear from Saviour that in 2007 students of the African American race were still receiving questions asking "what it is like to be Black." As stated earlier, these young men, like many others before them, have challenged societal stereotypes and social dissonance to achieve academic success. Andrew summarized the ultimate response to this research question best: "I have always tried to be a noble person and tried to have some sense of integrity. You can't really *break* a stereotype, but you can be an *exception* to a stereotype."

From this, one can assume a direct relationship between societal dissonance and African American male's academic performance, and successful matriculation into college. It is not the intention of the researcher to prove that negative stereotyping is exclusive to African American males or to excuse the poor academic performance of Black males in college. In agreement with Damian, it is the opinion of this researcher that negative stereotyping has the *possibility* of adversely affecting anyone. These data are offered for consideration to assist you in forming your own conclusions.

The findings seem to be consistent with research reported by Steele and Aronson (1995), who postulated that, when a person's social identity is attached to a negative stereotype, that person will tend to underperform in a manner consistent with the stereotype. Steele and Aronson attributed the underperformance to a person's anxiety that he or she will conform to the negative stereotype. The anxiety manifests itself in various ways, including distraction and increased body temperature, all of which diminish performance level.

Findings for Research Question One

What is the perceived influence of societal dissonance on the African American male's academic success?

1. There was a direct relationship between societal dissonance and these African American males' academic performance and successful matriculation into college.
2. This group of young men addressed the issue of negative stereotypes, feelings of isolation, and low academic expectations by performing well in the classroom.
3. Although these Black males were aware of the deficit perception of them they combated the negativity by doing well in the classroom, several stated that the negative perceptions affect them and hurts them emotionally.
4. These Black males addressed deficit stereotyping by ensuring that their personal behavior did not match that of the stereotypical young Black male.
5. These findings are consistent with research reported by Steele and Aronson (1995) postulating that, when a person's social identity is attached to a negative stereotype, that person will tend to underperform in a manner consistent with the stereotype.

According to the participants in the present study, perception of African American males is usually discussed from a deficit perspective. Many African American males with varied backgrounds, including doctors, lawyers, social workers, teachers, janitors, and construction workers, are confronted with stereotypes every day. Bill Cosby once stated, "If a White man falls off a chair drunk, it's just a drunk. If a Negro does, it's the whole damn Negro race." While some may find this statement a little farfetched, many African American males would agree wholeheartedly, as validated by the participants in this study.

Myriad issues emerged from this study. The participants all expressed feelings of isolation and negative stereotypes in both the classroom and in life. Faculty members at institutions of higher education can challenge the deficit perspective and stereotypes of Black males in their classrooms, thus helping address the issue of societal dissonance concerning Black males. As stated earlier, Festinger (1957) identified three ways to eliminate dissonance: (a) reduce the importance of the dissonant beliefs, (b) add consonant beliefs that outweigh the dissonant beliefs, and (c) change dissonant beliefs so they are no longer inconsistent. These goals can be achieved by integrating minority and racism-related content into the curriculum; for example, rather than concentrating on "African American month," the faculty could integrate into the curriculum an ongoing program that identifies the contributions, feelings, and lifestyles of minorities.

Aronson (1968) offered strategies for reducing dissonance on an individual level. Given the similarities between rectifying individual and societal misconceptions and inconsistencies, these strategies apply to societal dissonance as well: (a) changing behavior to match one's attitude, (b) changing attitude to match one's behavior, and (c) cognitively minimizing the degree of inconsistency or its importance. Participants in this study reported that non-Black students saw the Black students as intellectually inferior. Faculty can address this issue by interacting with all students at the same level, by treating all students the same way, and by holding all students to the same standards. Such practices acknowledge Black students as equals while at the same time not spotlighting anyone or openly showing emotion that could be misconstrued as favoritism. The first two strategies mentioned will not only acknowledge the contributions of other cultures but will relieve pressures that many of the participants described related to having to prove how smart they are in order to be accepted.

The faculty member who senses tension or isolation within the classroom can give those on the receiving end an opportunity to express their feelings and views. The opportunity may be in the form of forums, workshops, or general information sessions. Many of the participants in this study stated that, if an opportunity were presented, they would use it to educate those who are not familiar with other cultures. Aronson (1968) suggested that reducing dissonance might occur by acquiring new information that is consistent with attitudes or actions that seem inconsistent at first. Faculty can challenge stereotyped perceptions of the Black male through their interactions in the classroom. Instructors can minimize the importance of a negative attitude or behavior. This can be done by focusing on the positive aspects of African American culture instead of targeting negative aspects. Festinger (1957) stated that minimizing the emphasis on differences or acknowledging the differences from a positive aspect can reduce dissonant beliefs.

Demonstrations of racism are deeply rooted in the societal perceptions of African American males and the generalized stereotype of them being intellectually incompetent. This perception affects Black males not only internally but also externally through today's policies in higher education. While America has made progress in rectifying the devastating impact of discriminative practices both socially and politically, which were at one time not only common but accepted and viewed as norms, society has a long way before claiming meaningless victories of temporary change. The nation has not moved away from a discriminative mentality. Although laws have been reviewed and changed and some restrictions have been lifted, according to some of the findings about how Black males perceive themselves and their place in society and how they think others perceive them have not changed.

Self-Efficacy

According to Bandura (1994), *self-efficacy* can be defined as "people's beliefs about their capabilities to produce designated levels of performance that exercise influence over events that affect their lives" (p. 2). These beliefs help to determine how people think, feel, react, and behave. Bandura asserted that self-efficacy can be developed by four primary forces of influence: mastery experiences, vicarious experiences, social persuasion, and emotional/physical reactions.

Mastery experiences are the most effective way of creating a strong sense of efficacy in students (Bandura, 1994). Experiencing success adds to one's sense of value and confidence in one's abilities; in contrast, experiencing a series of failures undermines efficacy. Therefore, self-efficacy can be related to fear of failure. This fear can be responsible for inhibiting growth and development in students of all races, grades, or ability levels in academic settings. Fear of failure develops early in childhood and leads to anxiety during performance evaluation, a lack of effort and persistence, and overall poorer performance in achievement settings (Bandura, 1978; Steele and Aronson, 1995). Howard and Hammond (1985) asserted that everyone encounters failure but unexpected failure affects students differently from expected failure.

Positive social models are vital to establishing positive self-efficacy. Vicarious experiences provided by social models serve to create and strengthen self-beliefs of efficacy. As suggested by Bandura (1994), "Seeing people similar to oneself succeed by sustained effort raises observers' beliefs that they too possess the capabilities to master comparable activities to succeed" (p. 71). The reverse holds true as well. Observing others' failures, in lieu of great effort, lowers one's perceived efficacy. Moreover, the impact of the social model on efficacy is influenced by perceived similarity to the model. This point is especially important in mentor-mentee relationships: "The greater the assumed similarity, the more persuasive are the models' successes and failures" (p. 81).

Social persuasion, a deliberate attempt on the part of one party to influence the attitudes or behavior of another party so as to achieve some predetermined end on a societal level, serves as another way to strengthen beliefs of self-efficacy. "People who are persuaded verbally that they possess the capabilities to master given activities are likely to mobilize greater effort and sustain it than if they harbor self-doubts and dwell on personal deficiencies when problems arise" (Bandura, 1994, p. 74). In contrast, social persuasion can harness negative beliefs concerning efficacy. People who perceive that they lack competence in certain areas tend to avoid those areas as a means of avoiding failure. Emotions and reactions serve as the final influence on efficacy. According to Bandura (1988), people rely on their somatic and emotional states when examining their capabilities. Stress reactions, tension, and mood tend to affect one's judgment of self-efficacy. Therefore, "reducing people's stress reactions and altering their negative emotional proclivities and misinterpretations of their physical state" (p. 37) can modify self-efficacy.

Bandura (1997) observed that people live with psychic environments that are primarily of their own making. Often, people can gauge their confidence by the emotional state that they experience as they contemplate an action. Moreover, when people experience aversive thoughts and fears about their capabilities, those negative affective reactions can lower perceptions of capability and trigger the stress and agitation that ensure the inadequate performance that they fear. For example, when African American males go into a test-taking situation with expectations of not doing well, anxiety often occurs and can affect their performance. This is not to say that the typical anxiety experienced before an important endeavor is a sure sign of low self-efficacy; however, strong emotional reactions to a task can provide cues about the anticipated success or failure of the outcome.

Self-efficacy beliefs operate in concert with other sociocognitive factors, such as outcome expectations or goals, in the regulation of human behavior. Bandura (1984) argued that people's beliefs of personal competence "touch, at least to some extent, most everything they do" (p. 251). Likewise, self-efficacy beliefs mediate to a great extent the effects of other determinants of behavior. Therefore, when these determinants are controlled, self-efficacy judgments should prove to be excellent predictors of choice and direction of behavior.

Cokley (1998) acknowledged that racial and cultural identity models are important components of the psychosocial development of African American college students. Allen (2000) noted that education is considered to be a very important value within the African American community. For many African Americans, education has been the hope to obtain equality of opportunity and achieve a better standard of living. Yet, for many African American males, pursuing higher education has become increasingly problematic.

Self-efficacy beliefs may correspond to a decision to pursue certain life goals, including higher education. "A strong sense of efficacy enhances human accomplishment and personal well-being in many ways. People with high assurance in their capabilities approach difficult tasks as challenges to be mastered rather than as threats to be avoided" (Bandura, 1994, p. 202). Developing a positive self-image is especially important for African American males. According to Kunjufu (1984), developing positive self-images and self-discipline is a prerequisite for the effective education of African American males.

Certain factors can have particularly negative effects on the development of positive self-efficacy. According to Kunjufu (1984), the following factors have a negative influence on the development of young African American males: (a) chronic unemployment and underemployment, (b) the changing concept of childhood, (c) elitism, (e) low expectations, (e) lack of commitment to educate all children, and (f) misuse of achievement tests to label and place students. Nevertheless, institutions can be instrumental in assisting with the development of self-esteem in African American children. Kunjufu identified the following institutions as influential in the process: (a) the home, (b) the peer group, (c) television, (d) the school, and (e) the church. He asserted that these institutions should strive to emphasize positive African images to support self-esteem development in African American children.

Howard-Hamilton (1997) described four Africentric models that could be used to enhance African American males' development on college campuses. These models provide possible strategies for increasing self-efficacy and academic performance. The models are (a) Cross's (1991) Nigrescence model, (b) Robinson and Howard-Hamilton's (2000) Africentric resistance model, (c) Erikson's (1980) identity development model, and (d) Bandura's (1977) social learning model.

The is the theory of becoming Black (Cross, 1991). According to Cross, this theory consists of five stages. *Pre-encounter*, the first stage, occurs prior to an African American sensing a need to change his or her identity. Racial identity at this point is based on factors other than race, such as church and family. *Encounter*, the second stage, occurs when the African American experiences an event, usually racial in nature, that makes him or her begin to rethink his or her current identity. *Immersion-emersion*, the third stage, consists of two parts: a commitment to a personal change and a demolition of an old way of thinking. Immersion encompasses the person becoming deeply ingrained in any activity or organization associated with being "Black." This stage may be evidenced by changing one's name or attire to that of Africentricity or becoming involved in organizations of African Americans, regardless of their purposes. The decisions to select certain organizations and to engage in certain activities are classified as being irrational and often erratic. Emersion occurs as radical behavior begins to change. The person begins to realize the irrationality of his or her behavior and begins to focus on the nature and purpose of selected activities. In the fourth stage, *internalization,* the person begins to internalize his or her newly developed activity and is able to appreciate the identity and cultural views of others while feeling fine about his or her own identity and views. *Commitment*, the final stage, is described as the point at which the person becomes committed to others to help them develop their own identity. The final stage allows an opportunity "to translate their personal sense of Blackness into a plan of action or general sense of commitment" (as cited in Howard-Hamilton, 1997, p. 42).

The Africentric resistance paradigm is based on two concepts (Howard-Hamilton, 1997). This model fuses the Nguzo Saba value system, developed by Maulana Karenga, which "enables individuals to establish direction and meaning in their life" (p. 63) with the resistance modality model developed by Robinson and Ward. The resistance modality model is based on the philosophy that "there are healthy forms of psychological and personal resistance to negative and deleterious caricatures of one's race or culture that can promote personal growth and modify one's perception of the self and one's sense of community" (p. 64). This model is meant to promote personal growth through a strong sense of identity, resulting in a healthy resistance to negative messages that attempt to "demean, destroy, or detract from that culture" (p. 64).

By combining theories from the aforementioned models, the Africentric resistance model represents a "self-affirmation, reawakening, and rebirth of personal beliefs and behaviors. Africentricity represent a strong connection to one's spirituality and kinship via African culture" (Howard-Hamilton, 1997, p. 22). It culminates in a shared belief system whereby the self and others are seen as interconnected and results in a spirit of collective responsibility. According to Howard-Hamilton, the model "interweaves elements of the theoretical Nguzo Saba value systems with certain aspects of resistance that can initiate and promote psychological health and satisfying interpersonal relationships for African American men within and between cultures" (p. 23) The Africentric paradigm could serve as the framework for programs focused on the successful matriculation of African American men in institutions of higher education.

Identity development begins early in life and it is uncertain when, if ever, it ends. It is generally agreed that developing an identity is a life-long process, that a basic identity is solidified during adolescence and young adulthood but, as life progresses, it is continually refined. A positive resolution of the identity and repudiation versus identity diffusion crisis was classified by Erikson (1968) as "a sense of psychosocial well-being. Its most obvious concomitants are a feeling of being at home in one's body, a sense of 'knowing where one is going,' and an inner assuredness of anticipated recognition from those who count" (p. 165). Erikson's stage model has been used as a point of orientation for many other developmental theorists, such as Chickering (1969) in the development of his model of college student development and Phinney's (1989) model of cultural identity development incorporating appreciation for Erikson's original formulation of the construct.

Social learning theory is the behavior theory most relevant to criminology. Albert Bandura held that aggression is learned through a process called *behavior modeling*. He maintained that people do not actually inherit violent tendencies but model them after three principles (Bandura, 1976). He argued that people, especially children, learn aggressive responses from observing others, either personally or through the media and environment. He stated that many believe that aggression can produce reinforcements that can formulate into reduction of tension, gaining financial rewards, gaining the praise of others, or building self-esteem (Siegel, 1992). In Bandura's Bobo doll experiment children imitated the aggression of adults in order to gain a reward. Bandura was interested in child development because he maintained that, if aggression was diagnosed early, children could refrain from becoming adult criminals. Bandura (1976) argued that "aggression in children is influenced by the reinforcement of family members, the media, and the environment" (p. 206). Bandura stated that modeling influences do more than provide a social standard against which to judge one's own capabilities. People seek proficient models who possess the competencies to which they aspire. Through their behavior and expressed ways of thinking, competent models transmit knowledge and teach effective skills and strategies for managing environmental demands. Acquisition of better means raises perceived self-efficacy.

According to Loewen (1995), American history textbooks promote the belief that most important developments are traceable to Europeans. For example, most American history textbooks state that Hernando De Soto discovered the Mississippi River (of course, it had been discovered and named the Mississippi by ancestors of the original American Indians). De Soto's discovery had no larger significance and led to no trade or White settlement. Loewen stated, "His was merely the first White face to gaze on the Mississippi; therefore, he received credit." The Portuguese explorer Vasco da Gama is often credited with being the first to sail around Africa, in 1497 to 1499. There is evidence that Afro-Phoenicians actually preceded Da Gama on this route by more than 2,000 years. (White historians insist that a case for the Afro-Phoenicians has not been proven and that history should not be distorted merely to improve Black children's self-image.) In reading history recorded in this manner, Black students learn that Black feats are not considered as important as White ones (Loewen). This ideology does nothing for the psyche of young Black males looking for role models that would improve their self-image.

Research Question Two

What is the perceived influence of self-efficacy on the African American male's academic success?

Self-efficacy is an impression that one is capable of performing in a certain manner or attaining certain goals (Ormrod, 2006). It has been defined as a belief that one has of one's capabilities to execute courses of actions required to manage situations. Not to be mistaken with *efficacy*, which is the power to produce an effect, *self-efficacy* is the belief (whether or not that belief is valid) that one has the power to produce that effect. For example, a person with high self-efficacy may engage in a more health-related activity when an illness occurs, whereas a person with low self-efficacy would experience feelings of hopelessness (Sue, Sue, and Sue, 2005), related in some ways to the principle of locus of control.

One of the key issues in this study is the distinction between *self-esteem* and *self-efficacy*. Self-esteem relates to a person's sense of self-worth, whereas self-efficacy relates to a person's perception of his or her ability to reach a goal. This study focuses on self-efficacy because the lack of self-efficacy is one of the obstacles that Black males encounter in academia, often leading to low academic performance. Feelings of self-efficacy are influenced by home and school environments, both of which affect how a person relates to others in society. Since one's belief in one's abilities is largely formed through social interactions in the dominant home and school environments, low self-efficacy is difficult to overcome. The level of self-efficacy observed in the seven young men interviewed in this study was extremely high. The researcher found the young men to have a strong belief not only in themselves but also in their academic abilities. Generally, the young men's self-efficacy appeared to have been shaped through interactions with their support systems, particularly family, friends, and teachers. Excerpts from some of the interviews illustrate this high level of self-efficacy and some of the sources of that confidence.

Andrew's self-confidence and his strong sense of self-efficacy were expressed throughout his interview. He attributed his success to his "drive" and dedication and related it to his sense of honor.

> I am most proud of my drive and my dedication to my studies. My GPA is above
> 3.0. [Although] I would like it to be higher, I work hard on a daily basis and I have
> worked hard over the past year to achieve it. I have always tried to be a noble
> person and tried to have some sense of integrity.

Damian's strong sense of self-efficacy was expressed through his focus on making and achieving goals.

> I am extremely goal oriented. I have a very detailed plan for the next 10 or 15 years, at least. Before I came to college I said, of course, "I don't want to have to pay anything." I got that accomplished. I'm pre-med and so I don't want to spend my summers taking summer school and working at a crappy job.

The belief in yourself is very important. If you don't believe in yourself, why should anyone else? No one is going to just hand you anything in life, so you have to believe that you are capable and can do it. When you start doubting yourself is when you fail.

Jesse's goal was very specific, and his clear confidence that he would achieve it reflected a strong sense of self-efficacy.

> I want to achieve the best that I can achieve, so that I can possibly one day give back to my mother and my sister, who also raised her and me at the same time. I just like that driving force behind that. That's why I want to do great for my family, just the ability to do great one day for myself.
>
> While I believe in myself, I think the way you feel about yourself can be influenced by others. I think this kind of goes back to the first question. I have always had a great belief in myself and my abilities. I still think that I am very capable in doing whatever I put my mind to, but I still think society influences your self-belief.

Justin expressed his strong sense of self-efficacy through his dedication to high moral standards.

> I hold a lot of pride in upholding my principles of daily living . . . and shaping my own values. During the [elementary] school days and middle school [I was] pressured to compromise. But I think I've done a good job. I guess I give credit to my upbringing as far as sticking to those morals and being true to them daily. I would describe myself as personable, agreeable, and definitely dedicated.

While Saviour seemed to be more self-critical than the other interviewees, he still reflected his perception of a high degree of self-efficacy. He described his achievements in terms of competing with himself as well as with others to achieve his goals. His point about "slowing down" and "taking it as it is" can be interpreted as coming from his sense of overall self-efficacy, in which he can "afford" to ease up on the competitive nature from time to time.

> I think I am really hard on myself sometimes. . . . Not only am I hard on myself, I am a competitive person by nature. So I can be competitive with myself, I can be competitive with other people. I think sometimes there comes a point where you are a little bit too competitive and there's a point where you just need to slow down and take it as it is.

Self-efficacy is the key. You have to believe in yourself if you are going to be successful in life. When you look at successful business people, they all had a great belief in themselves. There have been times when I was unsure if I could pick up on something, but again, I have always been successful in the past, so that is when that belief in myself comes into play and I know I will do well.

Analysis for Research Question Two

As stated earlier, I found these young men to have a strong belief not only in themselves but also in their academic abilities, although at times their belief in their academic abilities did come into question. During the interviews, most of the participants stated that they were most proud of their GPA. It was obvious to the researcher that there was a direct relationship between self-efficacy and GPA, presumably the higher the GPA, the higher the level of self-efficacy. Based on several comments made during the interviews, it also seemed that the participants who had structured goals tended to have a higher level of self-efficacy as well. Some of the participants commented that their self-efficacy was derived from competition with other students. Others described achievements in terms of competing with oneself as well as with others to achieve goals. Saviour made a point about "slowing down" and "taking it as it is," which could be interpreted as coming from his sense of overall self-efficacy, in which he could "afford" to ease up on the competitive nature from time to time because of that belief.

According to Moore (2001, as cited in Thernstrom and Thernstrom, 2003, p. 5), "What separate African American male students from their Caucasian counterparts are the unmeasurable burdens of racism, discrimination, and negative stereotypes." These oppressive barriers are interpreted as messages of intellectual incompetence, which at times have negative effects on the academic identity and success of African American male students. "Success for African American males has less to do with academic capability and more to do with motivation, self-efficacy, commitment, and follow-through, which ultimately leads to success" (p. 36). For many young African American men, the ability to succeed in the education system depends on the ability to navigate through the barriers and constraints of society.

Findings for Research Question Two

What is the perceived influence of self-efficacy on the African American male's academic success?
1. The level of self-efficacy observed in the seven young men interviewed in this study was extremely high

2. The researcher found the young men to have a strong belief not only in themselves but also in their academic abilities, although at times their belief in their academic abilities came into question.
3. Generally, these young men's self-efficacy appeared to have been shaped through interactions with their support systems, particularly family, friends, and teachers.
4. The findings are consistent with research reported by Lee (2000), who contended that it is possible to educate all children, including Black males, at high levels.
5. Based on comments made during the interviews, it can be concluded that participants who had structured goals tended to have a higher level of self-efficacy.

The researcher found these young men to have a strong belief not only in themselves but also in their academic abilities, although at times the belief in their academic abilities came into question. Also, it seemed that the participants with structured goals tended to have higher levels of self-efficacy.

Self-efficacy is the belief in one's capabilities to organize and execute the courses of action required to achieve specified goals. By means of the self-system, individuals exercise control over their thoughts, feelings, and actions. Self-efficacy beliefs are most influential arbiters of human activity (Bandura, 1997). Institutions play a key role in reinforcing self-efficacy. The participants in this study showed very high levels of self-efficacy, wanting to be challenged, wanting to be successful, and wanting to be treated like everyone else on an equal playing field and to be held to the same standards as everyone else in the class. Faculty, administrators, and staff must hold all students to the same standards and expect all students to succeed.

Wayne revealed that, in selecting teams for projects in some of his classes, Black people were usually the last students selected or were not selected at all. Faculty or administrators could address this issue by selecting the teams, taking away from students the potential power to discriminate.

Saviour commented that being Black is perceived by some in a negative connotation, equating being Black to being unintelligent. Carey and Forsyth (2007) suggested teaching strategies that could assist administration and faculty efforts in reaching out to young Black males in the classroom. They stated that helping students to understand differences among the constructs of related social-cognitive theories, such as self-efficacy, outcome expectancies, behavioral intentions, self-esteem, and optimism, can provide a better understanding of the students' issues. This problem could also be addressed in the same way as the problem of negative stereotyping was addressed, by integrating minority and racism-related content into the curriculum. Such a strategy will not only acknowledge the contributions of other cultures, but will relieve some of the pressures that many of the participants described about having to prove that they are "smart" in order to be accepted.

Institutional Support

The relationship between the student and university is emblematic; neither can exist without the other. While providing students with personal and academic support for their educational and personal lives, the institution seeks to obtain stability of the student body until graduation. Thus far, predominantly White institutions of higher education have yet to effectively provide that support or find ways to retain African American males.

Negotiating the complexities of college applications, financial aid, payment options, choice of major/study, and scheduling is difficult for the inexperienced student, particularly for those who are neophytes to the college admission process. Combined with housing choices, meal plans, and newly acquired roommates, it is easy to understand why so many students have difficulty in acclimating to college life and the responsibilities that go with being a college student. Thus, it is sometimes necessary to add the very real possibility that the average new student may not be emotionally or academically prepared. Adding variables such as race to the equation can exacerbate the situation many fold.

Cryer-Sumler (1998) stated that an understanding of where undergraduate African American students at predominantly White institutions would refer other undergraduate African American students for assistance with stressful problems (and then trying to ensure that methods and other alternatives are accessible) is probably one of the most important issues faced when struggling to survive at a predominantly White institution. Diop (2004) found that Black students generally saw themselves as being treated fairly, neither being advantaged nor disadvantaged because of their race. This fairness of treatment is generally viewed as a very positive characteristic of an institution. Black students expressed that it would be helpful to design and implement programs to sensitize administrators, faculty, staff, and students to racial issues and concerns.

While integration theorists (e.g., Sedlacek and Brooks, 1976; Zusman, 1999) have argued that a lack of supportive ties on campus jeopardizes student persistence, research among Black students attending predominantly White institutions has revealed a countervailing pattern. According to Bryant (1998), Black students who were well integrated socially were often most likely to drop out, while those who appeared somewhat disconnected tended to persist. Black students are conflicted to be socially accepted, which often means that they find themselves at odds with student academic responsibility. In terms of network structure, the Black students most likely to be at risk academically were those reporting the largest number of strong ties on campus; this was not the case among their White counterparts. So the question remains: If Black males are generally treated fairly on campus and there seems to be some sort of institutional support for those students on predominantly White campuses, , then why do those institutions have difficulty in recruiting and retaining these students?

While the civil strife of the 1950s and 1960s was due to lack of access to equal opportunities both in life and in the nation's institutions of higher learning, students of color are still severely underrepresented in predominantly White institution, both as faculty and staff. Studies also reveal heavy pressure on Black students to be socially connected at levels that conflict with the student role. In terms of network structure, the Black students most likely to be at risk academically were those reporting the largest number of strong ties on campus (Bryant, 1998); this was not the case among their White counterparts.

The *Chronicle of Higher Education* reported an audit conducted at the University of Missouri at Kansas City (UMKC) that revealed "a miserable climate of race relations on the campus, particularly in the faculty ranks," according to an article in the *Kansas City Star* (Rosenberg, 2006). The audit also showed that Latino students, like Black students, felt no sense of community on campus. As a result, many of those students, especially Black and Latino males, struggled to graduate or left UMKC for another college. The audit, commissioned by the university, revealed that the most racist place on campus was the classroom. Black and Latino students told auditors that they often felt offended by faculty who seemed to hold low expectations regarding their abilities. If it is true that faculty have low expectations of minority students, is that because the students actually do not perform well, or do the students not perform well because of faculty's low expectations?

Minorities have experienced for decades the unequal distribution of education and question the quality, scope, and content of their higher education (Astin, 1985; Castellanos and Gloria, 2002; Gordon, 1999; Harris, 1996; Jackson and Moore, 2006; Kerr, 1991). The proportion of minority students participating in college has been rising but still lags behind attendance rates of the national norm. The changing demographics present a challenge to most college campuses, particularly in creating a climate that is conducive and reflective of the type of students needed to ethnically diversify higher education institutions. More specifically, institutions are confronted with a growing minority population that has a different value system, an intensified awareness of their minority status, and a need for climate inclusiveness, and who are the first in their families to attend college (Astone and Nunez-Wormack, 1990; Hurtado and Carter, 1997; Valverde and Castenell, 1998). These students are confronted with a challenge that requires managing and coping with psychological distress as they negotiate the complexities of campus culture at predominantly White institutions.

Research Question Three

What is the perceived influence of institutional support on the African American male's academic success?

Many of the participants discussed programs that targeted diversity issues during orientation activities. Several also mentioned groups on campus that provided an outlet to interact with a variety of people, as well as groups that specifically provided an opportunity to identify with other African American men. While acknowledging the value of these groups, most of the participants commented that most of the resistance that they had encountered on campus came in the form of preconceptions held by others on campus, not the University in particular. For example, Saviour stated:

> Higher administration does give us all these opportunities; they give us everything we need. There are basic amenities, tutoring sessions; we have like five mentor programs just in the Black community. We have facilities and we have so much at our disposal, but we choose not to educate ourselves. . . . At some point you have to take it upon yourself as an African American male student to quit putting the blame on everybody else. . . . No one is always going to give you the answer, sometimes you are going to have to go out there looking for the answer. If you are struggling in class, they have tips and ways and just anything at your disposal for you to deal with that. But I think we choose to not do that because the answer is not being fed to us through a spoon.

Several participants mentioned programs on campus that was particularly helpful upon their arrival to campus. One remarked, "I would love to see [organizations such as SAAB] grow more and influence more people." The participants stated that the programs that addressed stereotypes and racial issues openly and candidly were most effective.

Damian recognized the role of the university in providing services geared to minority groups, such as African American male students.

> Well, for one, orientation was incredible. There were a lot of things, a lot of little shows we had on stereotypes and stuff like that. I don't necessarily know if they talk to you about actually making better cultural decisions, but there's help there, but I don't even know if it's problematic. I'm not like a person who says it's our entire fault. We need to get together, you know.
>
> I think the school tries to make all of its students successful, because they have a reputation to uphold. I don't think they specifically target Black males, I think they try to help minorities. I think they still have a long way to go, but it's a start. If the university hired more Black professors, I think that would help with the success of Black males.

However, Damian recognized that the work of university organizations, as well as faculty, staff, and students, is far from finished.

> We still have mindsets of people here [on campus] that need to change, White people and other people. The thing I hate most about perceptions on campus is that they tend to report only bad things, and not really report good things that are happening in our community. That happens a lot here.

Others were less than enthusiastic about the institution's motivations for offering specialized services for the African American male student. Wayne stated:

> What I have seen here at the university is that the programs are being done just to say that they are providing a program, the programs don't really do anything.

In agreement, Jesse remarked:

> The institution has a certain responsibility to each of their students. I think the university tries to meet that responsibility with programs and things like that. Even though they offer programs like tutoring and some mentoring, I still feel as if I don't belong sometimes. I had a friend who graduated a couple of years ago, and he said he felt no loyalties to the university because he didn't feel like he was a part of the university, he didn't get that college experience that everyone else talks about. I never knew what he meant by that, I mean come on, we are at the university. As my time here went on, I started to understand what he meant, it's like we'll [the university] let you in the school, but you still are not a part of us. I don't know, I can't explain it. So I don't know if the school can have an influence, but I think it could definitely do a better job of making us feel wanted, or more accepted.

Saviour did not address the services of the institution directly. Instead, he focused on the perception widely held by students that being Black is equated to being not smart.

> When you first go into a class, . . . it is not the pressure from your teacher, [it's mostly] pressure from your peers. You walk in there and you know you have to be on your ground because, when they look at you, they see a Black person. . . . And they think immediately, "Oh! You must not be smart. You are not intelligent." . . . So you have to prove to them that you are a very smart person, that you know what you are talking about. So there is that pressure right there.

Saviour then described in interesting twist of perceptions: Being smart seems to translate to being "not Black." And then there is also that pressure:

"Okay, when I do prove to them that I am smart, that I know what I am doing, that I take my studies seriously, all of a sudden I'm not Black! It's just like, "Oh! But *you* are not Black." . . . People . . . are not trying to be actively racist. But these conceptions are stuck in your head, whether you know they are there, and they influence what they should do. . . . They do not analyze you as an individual. . . . It's really aggravating but I deal with it and I do what I can. Yeah! But not as a Black person because Black person can't be smart!

If the university addressed the negative stereotypes head-on, I think that would do wonders. As mentioned before, I try to teach whenever I can, but I am only one person. If the institution were to do something I think it would help. As far as learning what to do when you get into college, I think the university does a good job, all of the staff and counselors help as far as classes and stuff.

While most of the participants agreed that the institution provided satisfactory programs and/or facilities targeted toward diversification, there was a consensus that the institution did not adequately address issues of environmental change or campus climate. Many of the participants discussed programs that targeted diversity issues during orientation activities. Several also mentioned groups on campus that provided an outlet for interaction with a variety of people, as well as groups that specifically provided an opportunity to identify with other African American men. Even while acknowledging the value of these groups, most of the participants commented that most of the resistance that they had encountered on campus came in the form of preconceptions held by others on campus.

When an administrator or institution decides to change the campus climate and the deficit perception of African American males, several strategies must be used prior to embarking on that change. Unfortunately, utilizing the model for institutional change proposed by Sedlacek and Brooks (1976) 32 years later is still an appropriate option because the realm of higher education has not changed much in that period and is still not perceived as welcoming to all students. First, the organization must define its specific goals. Failure to do this has been the undoing of more than one cultural change. According to Sedlacek and Brooks, five key points are necessary to consider in defining organizational and institutional goals.

1. Goals must be stated to provide direction for change. Without stated goals, energy and action become misdirected and random and a change does not take place.

2. Goals should be as specific and operational as possible. Following this principle will help to avoid the "umbrella" goal, such as "eliminating racism in an institution," and substitute a series of subgoals, such as "increase the number of Black teachers" and "incorporate the contributions of minorities in the Chemistry 1 curriculum."

3. Strategies are separate from goals in that they are ways of accomplishing goals. Institutions must be able to separate means from ends.

4. Goals must be adjusted to the context of the times. For example, if compelling evidence should become available that African American men do better in society by attending all-Black schools, then goals and strategies should be shifted.
5. All goals must be evaluated and the extent of their accomplishment measured.

As the first key point states, goals must be stated not only to provide direction but also to provide consistency. As Sedlacek pointed out, if this goal is not met, energy and action become misdirected and random and change does not take place. A clear-cut direction also helps to avoid the "umbrella effect" to which Sedlacek referred in the second point. If true change is to take place, the university must create policies that will effect change for *all* students.

Examples of goals for institutions include the following (Sedlacek and Brooks, 1976):

1. Change the concept of teacher quotas and develop a fair policy.
2. Integrate minority and racism-related content into the curriculum; for examples, rather than institute African American month, integrate into the curriculum an ongoing program on the contributions, feelings, and lifestyles of minorities.
3. Change the use of standardized test scores for admissions and other alternatives rather than eliminating the tests.
4. Find ways to involve African American students' parents in school programs.
5. Develop proper techniques for teaching standard English to Black males, while making sure that their current speech style is denigrated in the process.
6. Find appropriate standards for judging and developing programs for African Americans in a positive way. Cultural and racial differences exist, and it is logical to use various techniques and criteria to judge success or failure.
7. Experience and understanding of racism and race relations should be required of all school personnel.
8. Black scholars should be included in the process of developing curricula. Not only does this have an important role in modeling applications for Black male students, it shows White and Black students that African Americans can and do perform many important roles in society and serves as an intermediate goal on the way to acquiring more full-time Black faculty members.

Several of the participants mentioned that they would welcome the opportunity to interact with faculty. Saviour commented that the faculty-student relationship might be stronger if the faculty member and student were of the same race. When Black males have an opportunity to interact with and observe faculty of color create programs and integrate materials into the curriculum, the role of scholar/professor becomes a reality for the students, indicating that the role of a scholar/professor is attainable by them as well.

The earlier the student knows about college and the concept of life-long learning, the better. All of the young men in this study stated that it had not been a question of *whether* they would go to college; rather, it was a question of *where* they would go to college. All of the participants reported that their familiar and extended support systems had played an integral part in ensuring that they received up-to-date college materials and scholarship information.

Early intervention programs have played a significant role in providing services, particularly for minority youth. As participation rates of African American students continue to increase, services that will guide them to successful entrance and transition to college life will be key determinants in student retention and graduation. Although there has been a significant increase in the higher education rates of minorities, this group is predominantly concentrated at community colleges, with few transferring to four-year institutions (Brewer, 1990). Most minority students (83.7 percent) are still enrolled in lower-cost public institutions (Wilds and Wilson, 1998). Therefore, programs to increase college and university participation by minorities must target public two-year and technical colleges.

If the goal is to increase participation of first-generation, low-income minority students at four-year institutions, early intervention programs should provide college preparation for more African American male students to meet the criteria of the more selective public flagship and private institutions. These initiatives can also decrease the gaps between the participation rates of White males and African American males, while addressing the lack of representation of minorities in certain career fields, including mathematics and science (Martin, 2007).

Early intervention programs such as the I Have A Dream Foundation (IHAD), National Early Intervention Scholarship Program (NEISP), and GEAR-UP provide a solid framework to increase the retention of first-generation, low-income minority students. African American male students are less likely than White male students to graduate from college and complete a four-year degree, especially at predominantly White institutions (Brewer, 1990; Wilds and Wilson, 1998). Therefore, the concern for students of color in higher education does not stop with access into the institution but continues with providing resources to retain these students. By implementing ongoing educational programs and student support services within the community and at post-secondary institutions, minority student concerns and issues in higher education are addressed at an early stage of college student development (Martin, 2007).

Faculty of Color

With the ever-changing demographics of the student population and the stagnant nature of faculty racial composition over the past twenty years, the retention of faculty of color at predominantly White institutions continues to be a significant issue in higher education. Knefelkamp (University of Michigan, 1998, p. 2), "In order for higher education to be more effective, we must have an accurate reflection of society represented within higher education." Faculty that resembles African American males will serve to increase the number of African American males on campuses of higher education. This requires an environment of equality and inclusion. Several participants mentioned that faculty of color (faculty who "looked like them") could possibly understand what the students had experienced in life, which would be an excellent addition to the campus experience. Bonner (2003) asserted that acclimating to the higher education environment has proven to be a formidable task for many minority faculty members. Particularly among the ranks of certain subcultures—women, cultural and ethnic minorities, gay and lesbian instructors— experiences with these environments have been described as "chilly."

To truly tap into the knowledge stores and intellectual reserves maintained by African American scholars, academe must first meet their most basic needs: Establish a safe and inclusive environment to successfully engage in critical discourse, create a forum to bond with peers, develop a means to foster viable connections with students and increase opportunities to interface with the institution. (p.4) Creating opportunities to network with other students and faculty of color is challenging because there are fewer students of color in graduate programs and fewer faculty of color in tenure track positions. Reaching out to those who are present and creating a welcoming environment for new students and faculty of color will promote the type of diversity that enhances the academic atmosphere (Venegas, 2001).

Teaching Strategies for Faculty

Carey and Forsyth (2007) suggested teaching strategies that could assist administration and faculty efforts in reaching out to young Black males in the classroom. They stated that helping students to understand differences among the constructs of related social-cognitive theories, such as self-efficacy, outcome expectancies, behavioral intentions, self-esteem, and optimism, can provide a better understanding of the students' own issues. This strategy is consistent with the responses given by the participants in this study, citing regular occurrences of feelings of isolation and negative stereotyping in the classroom. Encouraging students to develop a measure of self-efficacy for any academic-related behavior that avoids the confounding of self-efficacy with these other constructs is necessary. If academic behavior is socially stigmatized (e.g., low self-efficacy, low self-esteem) or if social norms suggest that one should engage frequently in a behavior (e.g., exercise), then social desirability response biases might inflate self-efficacy scores. Carey and Forsyth suggest that helping students to design an intervention program will enhance self-efficacy and possibly alter risky behaviors. This researcher contends that allowing the student to take part in self-diagnosis, in a sense assisting in his or her own treatment, will allows the student to have some sense of ownership concerning the issue.

If society is sincere in the attempt to address the issues that confront African American males and their troubled journey into higher education, it is important to enhance and reinforce not only their identities as students but also their identities as competent, intelligent, successful men. Societal perception and social messages are important factors in forming and maintaining high self-efficacy. "Just as Black males perceive themselves as superior in athletics and entertaining, they must also perceive themselves as superior and competent in the academic arena as well" (Whiting, 2006, p. 4). This means developing programs and strategies that improve their self-efficacy, target their self-efficacy, increase their willingness to make sacrifices, enhance their academic self-concept, improve their need for improvement, improve their need for achievement, increase their self-awareness, change their beliefs about the power of effort, enhance their concepts of masculinity, and nurture their racial pride (Whiting).

Many educators speculate that students of color learn best when they are actively involved in the process. Researchers (e.g., Chickering and Gamson, 1991) have reported that, regardless of the subject matter, students working in small groups tend to learn more of what is taught and retain it longer than when the same content is presented in other instructional formats. Students who work in collaborative groups also appear more satisfied with their classes (Beckman, 1990; Chickering and Gamson, 1991; Collier, 1980; Cooper, 1990; Goodsell, Maher, and Tinto, 1992; Johnson and Johnson, 1989; Johnson, Johnson, and Smith, 1991). This is consistent with the findings of this study. For example, Colin stated that he appreciated the support that he received from other Black students on campus. Various names have been given to this form of teaching, with some distinctions among them: cooperative learning, collaborative learning, collective learning, learning communities, peer teaching, peer learning, reciprocal learning, team learning, study circles, study groups, and work groups. But all in all, there are three general types of group work: informal learning groups, formal learning groups, and study teams (Johnson et al.). These intimate styles of learning strategies have shown tremendous results in academic growth among students of color (Lardner, 2003).

The institution in this study has taken great steps related to the recommendations presented above to address multicultural issues on campus. In 2005 the university announced a new position of Vice President for Diversity and Community Engagement. The responsibilities of the new position are to work with a broad range of student, faculty, staff, and community constituents to make the university a more inviting and inclusive environment and to develop strategies to connect intellectual resources of the university to various communities across in the state of Texas.

Moving Beyond the Deficit Perspective

With entrance to a new millennium, society is faced with new and challenging problems. Among them are economic constraints, educational restructuring, the ever-present challenge of diversity or lack thereof, and the continuing need for educational and racial equality. In this environment, higher education will not be able to ignore the demands and needs of society and will be called on to address these challenges, which include a major restructuring of society's institutional arrangements (Zusman, 1999). Educational policy makers will be challenged to create innovative approaches that will provide colleges and universities enough autonomy and flexibility to accomplish these challenges and goals, which have been created by a society that has not adjusted well to change or the deficit perspective of the African American male.

Recognizing that Black males are not merely victims but may also be active agents in their own failure means that interventions designed to help them must consider this notion as well. Changing policies, creating new programs, and opening new opportunities will accomplish little if such efforts are not accompanied by strategies to actively engage Black males and their families to take responsibility to improve their circumstances (Fashola, 2005). Institutionally, this may require programmatic interventions aimed at buffering and offsetting the various risks to which Black males are particularly vulnerable. Fashola stated that effective initiatives must also involve efforts to counter and transform cultural and environmental patterns and the attitude that Black males have adopted toward education. One of the best ways to learn how this can be done is to study those schools and programs that have been successful in accomplishing this goal.

Demonstrations of racism are deeply rooted in the societal perceptions of African American males and the generalized stereotype of them being intellectually incompetent. This perception affects Black males not only internally but also externally through today's policies in higher education. Researchers and policy-makers rarely include the individuals who are the focus of their studies in the development of solutions to their own problems. Although individuals or groups are often asked their opinions about their plight, they are seldom asked to participate in the development of programs or models that will improve their lives. The very persons who would be most affected and who should be the first to be consulted are not given a voice in the dialogue, as if they had no stake in these important decisions that determine the course of the policies that will affect their lives.

While America has made progress in rectifying the devastating impact of discriminative practices both socially and politically, which were at one time not only common but accepted and viewed as norms, society has a long way before claiming meaningless victories of temporary change. The nation has not moved away from a discriminative mentality. Although laws have been reviewed and changed and some restrictions have been lifted, according to some of the findings about how Black males perceive themselves and their place in society and how they think others perceive them have not changed.

References

Allen, X. M. (2000). *Family functioning and the academic self-efficacy and academic achievement of African American male freshman and sophomore college students*. Unpublished doctoral dissertation, The University of North Carolina at Greensboro.

Aronson, E. (1968). Dissonance theory: Progress and problems. In R. P. Abelson, E. Aronson, W. J. McGuire, T. M. Newcomb, M. J. Rosenberg, and P. H. Tannenbaum (Eds.), Theories of cognitive consistency: A sourcebook (pp. 5-27). Chicago: Rand-McNally.

Astin, A. W. (1985). Involvement: The cornerstone of excellence. *Change, 17*(4), 34-39.

Astone, B., and Nunez-Wormack, E. (1990). *Pursuing diversity: Recruiting college minority students*. Washington, DC: ERIC Clearinghouse on Higher Education.

Bandura, A. (1976). Social learning analysis of aggression. In E. Ribes-Inesta and A. Bandura (Eds.), *Analysis of delinquency and aggression* (pp. 203-231). Hillsdale, NJ: Erlbaum.

Bandura, A. (1977). Social learning theory. In B. B. Wolman and L. R. Pomroy (Eds.), *International encyclopedia of psychiatry, psychology, psychoanalysis, and neurology* (Vol. 10 pp. 126-129). New York: Van Nostrand Reinhold.

Bandura, A. (1978). Reflections on self-efficacy. *Advances in Behavioural Research and Therapy, 1,* 237-269.

Bandura, A. (1984). Recycling misconceptions of perceived self-efficacy. *Cognitive Therapy and Research, 8,* 231-255.

Bandura, A. (1988). Self-efficacy conception of anxiety. *Anxiety Research, 1,* 77-98.

Bandura, A. (1994). Self-efficacy. In V. S. Ramachaudran (Ed.), *Encyclopedia of human behavior* (Vol. 4, pp. 71-81). New York: Academic Press.

Bandura, A. (1997). *Self-efficacy: The exercise of control.* New York: Freeman.

Bandura, A. (Ed.). (1995). *Self-efficacy in changing societies.* New York: Cambridge University Press.

Beckman, M. (1990). Collaborative learning: Preparation for the workplace and democracy. *College Teaching, 38*(4), 128-133.

Bonner, F. A., II. (2003). The temple of my unfamiliar: Faculty of color at predominantly White institutions (last word). *Black Issues in Higher Education, 20,* 49-52.

Brewer, C. (1990). *Minority success in college: What works—The Minority Student Success Project.* Seattle: Washington State Board for Community College Education and the Washington Center for Improving the Quality of Undergraduate Education. (ERIC Document Reproduction Service No. ED 345 933)

Bryant, N. L. (1998). *Networks, net work, and the costs of social integration: A case study of Black students at a predominantly White university.* Unpublished doctoral dissertation, University of Virginia, Charlottesville.

Castellanos, J., and Gloria, A. M. (2002). *African American and Latino students at predominantly White institutions:* A socio-social perspective of educational interactions and academic persistence (Vol. 1, No. 1, pp. 19-39).

Carey, M., and Forsyth, A. D. (2007). *Teaching tip sheet: Self-efficacy.* Washington, DC: Public Interest Directorate.

Chickering A. W. (1969). *Education and Identity.* San Francisco: Josepy-Bass.

Chickering, A. W., and Gamson, Z. F. (Eds.). (1991). *Applying the seven principles for good practice in undergraduate education* (New Directions for Teaching and Learning, No. 47). San Francisco: Jossey-Bass.

Cokley, K. O. N. (1998). *A comparative study of African self-consciousness, racial identity, and academic self-concept among African American college students at historically Black and predominantly White colleges and universities.* Unpublished doctoral dissertation, Georgia State University, Atlanta.

Collier, K. G. (1980). Peer-group learning in higher education: The development of higher-order skills. *Studies in Higher Education, 5*(1), 55-62.

Cooper, J. (1990). *Cooperative learning and college instruction: Effective use of student learning teams.* California State University, Long Beach, Institute for Teaching and Learning.

Cross, W. E., Jr. (1991). *Shades of Black: Diversity in African American identity.* Philadelphia: Temple University Press.

Cryer-Sumler, A. (1998). *Resources recommended by African American students at predominately White universities to assist their peers: Retention-related issues.* Unpublished doctoral dissertation, The University of New Orleans.

Diop, M. C. (2004). *Assessing the perceptions and attitudes of Black students in a Midwestern predominantly White institution.* Unpublished doctoral dissertation, The University of North Dakota, Grand Forks.

Erikson, E. H. (1968). *Identity: Youth and crisis.* New York: Norton.

Erikson, E. H. (1980). *Identity and life cycle: A reissue.* New York: Norton.

Fashola, O. (2005). *Educating African American males.* Thousand Oaks, CA: Corwin Press.

Festinger, L. (1957). A theory of cognitive dissonance. Stanford, CA: Stanford University Press.

Goodsell, A., Maher, M., and Tinto, V. (Eds.). (1992). *Collaborative learning: A sourcebook for higher education.* University Park: The Pennsylvania State

University, National Center on Post-secondary Teaching, Learning, and Assessment.

Gordon, J. U. (1999). *The African American male: An annotated bibliography.* Westport, CT: Greenwood Press.

Harris, W. G. (1996). African American males in higher education: Reframing the issue. *Black Issues in Higher Education, 13,* 92.

Howard, J., and Hammond, R. (1985, September 9). Rumors of inferiority. *The New Republic,* 72.

Howard-Hamilton, M. (1997). Theory to practice: Applying developmental theories relevant to African American men. In M. Cuyjet (Ed.), *Helping African American men be successful in college* (pp. 17-30). San Francisco: Jossey-Bass.

Hurtado, S., and Carter, D. (1997). Effects of college transition and perceptions of the campus racial climate on Latino students' sense of belonging. *Sociology of Education, 70,* 324-345.

Jackson, J., and Moore, J. (2006). African American males in education: Endangered or ignored? *Teachers College Record, 108,* 201-205.

Johnson, D. W., and Johnson, R. T. (1989). *Cooperation and competition: Theory and research.* Edina, MN: Interaction Book Company.

Johnson, D. W., Johnson, R. T., and Smith, K. A. (1991). *Cooperative learning: Increasing college faculty instructional productivity* (ASHE-ERIC Higher Education Report No. 4). Washington, DC: George Washington University, School of Education and Human Development.

Kerr, C. (1991). *The great transformation in higher education: 1960-1980.* Albany: State University of New York Press.

Kunjufu, J. (1984). *Developing positive self-images and discipline in Black children.* Chicago: African American Images.

Lardner, E. (2003). *Approaching diversity through learning communities.* Washington, DC: Center for Improving the Quality of Undergraduate Education.

Lee, C. (2000). *The State of Knowledge About the Education of African Americans.* Washington, D.C.: American Educational Research Association, Commission on Black Education.

Loewen, J. (1995). *Lies my teacher told me: Everything your American history textbook got wrong.* New York: New Press.

Martin, S. (2007). *Early intervention program and college partnerships.* Washington, DC: ERIC Clearinghouse on Higher Education.

Ormrod, J. E. (2006). *Educational psychology: Developing learners* (Fifth edition). Upper Saddle River, NJ: Merrill.

Phinney, J. (1989). Stages of ethnic identity development in minority group adolescents, *Journal of Early Adolescence, 9,* 34-49.

Robinson, T. L., and Howard-Hamilton, M. F. (2000). *The intersections of race, ethnicity, and gender: Multiple identities in counseling.* New Jersey City, NJ: Merrill Prentice-Hall.

Rosenberg, J. (2006). *Discriminations: Always out on a limb—Minority Repre sentation: Solution or problem?* http:/www.discriminations.us/2006/04/minority_representation_soluti.html.

Sedlacek, W., and Brooks, G. (1976). *Racism in American education: A model for change.* Chicago: Nelson Hall.

Siegel, L. (1992). *Criminology.* St. Paul, MN: West.

Steele, C. M., and Aronson, J. (1995). Stereotype threat and the intellectual test performance of African Americans. *Journal of Personality and Social Psychology, 69,* 797-811.

Sue, D., Sue, D. W., and Sue, S. (2005). *Understanding abnormal behavior* (Eighth edition). New York: Houghton Mifflin College Division.

Thernstrom, A. M., and Thernstrom, S. (2003). *No excuses: Closing the racial gap in learning.* New York: Simon and Schuster.

University of Michigan. (1998). *Diversity is necessary for academic excellence, Knefelkamp says.* Retrieved February 20, 2008, from http://www.umich.edu/~urecord/9798/ Feb18_98/knef.htm.

Valverde, L. A., and Castenell, L. A. (1998). *Multicultural campus: Strategies for transforming higher education.* Walnut Creek, CA: AltaMira.

Venegas, K. (2001). Students and faculty of color. *Faculty Forum: The Newsletter of the USC Academic Senate, 2*(1). Retrieved February 20, 2008, from http://www. usc.edu/academe/acsen/resources/newsletter/0001v2n1/newsvol2 no1article4.shtml.

Whiting, G. (2006). *The overrepresentation of Black males in special education: A clarion call for action and change.* Nashville, TN: Vanderbilt University.

Wilds, D., and Wilson, R. (1998). *Minorities in higher education: 1997-98: Sixteenth annual status report.* Washington, DC: American Council on Education, Office of Minority Concerns.

Zusman, A. (1999). Issues facing higher education in the twenty-first century. In P. G. Altbach, R. O. Berdahl, and P. J. Gumport (Eds.), *American higher education in the twenty-first century: Social, political, and economic challenges* (pp. 109-148). Baltimore: Johns Hopkins University Press.

Quantitative and Qualitative Research Studies on the First-Generation College Student

Chapter Five
Engagement Practices and Study Abroad Participation of First-Generation American College Students

Bryan Andriano, Ed.D.,
The George Washington University

Undergraduate study abroad participation rates in the United States have steadily increased over the past ten years (Institute for International Education, 2009) and recent research shows that 55 percent of current high school students were absolutely certain or fairly certain that they would study abroad in college (American Council on Education, Art and Science Group, and College Board, 2008). In addition, there is overwhelming public support of international education with 90 percent of Americans believing it was important to prepare future generations for a global society and 77 percent valuing "educational experiences where time is spent abroad in other cultures" (NAFSA, 2006, p. 2). However, the high rate of student interest and public support is at odds with the reality of the actual undergraduate student participation rate of approximately 1 percent (Institute of International Education, 2009).

Although there is support for and interest in increasing participation, the current profile of students completing study abroad programs is heavily skewed toward a majority female, Caucasian student studying the humanities (Institute of International Education, 2009). Although the definition of an underrepresented student is inclusive of students from different academic disciplines, racial and ethnic backgrounds, and life experiences, first-generation (FG) students—as one such identified underrepresented group (NAFSA, 2002)—transcends all demographic categories that have been defined as underrepresented.

Demographically, FG students represent nearly a quarter of American college student enrollments (Chen and Carrol, 2005). However, higher education administrators have little practical guidance for how to increase FG study abroad participation on their own campuses. Scholars have also only recently begun to explore this issue with few published empirical studies to form a foundation of research on the topic. Additional practical recommendations and empirical data are needed if efforts to achieve parity between FG college enrollments and FG study abroad participation rates are to be successful.

The relevant literature presents preliminary results on factors that may compel or dissuade students from participation in study abroad, but makes only cursory reference—if at all—to their parental education level. In light of this gap in the literature, this study attempted to evaluate if campus-based student engagement practices in a student's first year of study may serve as predictive indicators of study abroad participation during their undergraduate program at a four-year college or university in the United States. A multiple logistic regression analysis yielded cautiously generalizable results demonstrating that a FG student's exposure to diversity as well as living in campus-affiliated housing, participation in foreign language coursework, and private institution attendance all predicted study abroad participation.

The First-Generation Student Context

First-generation students are a significant segment of the higher education population in the United States, representing 22 percent of all students in four-year institutions between 1992 and 2000 (Chen and Carrol, 2005). As Table 5.1 demonstrates, this population is also disproportionately low-income; with more than half of FG students coming from families with gross incomes at or below $25,000, and 84.6 percent of first-generation students coming from families whose income levels are at or under $49,000. In addition to facing financial situations that may make college attendance difficult, this student population is also disproportionately underprepared for college when they arrive and generally lack the family and social support that their peers experience, complicating their navigation of their new collegiate environment. These students also may lack an understanding of higher education institutions as complex bureaucracies (Wilt, 2006), and additionally may not understand the expectations of student-initiated assistance (Deil-Amen and Rosenbaum, 2003). In sum, FG students face many challenges on-campus that other populations may not. These experiences can be particularly detrimental if students do not anticipate experiencing a challenging transition to college (London, 1992), knowledge that they may lack either because they have not acquired information about college through formal instruction or social interactions with those who have attended college.

**Table 5.1. Demographic Characteristics of
First-Generation Students Between 1992 and 2000**

Demographic Characteristics	Total	First-Generation students	Students whose parent(s) attended some college	Students whose parent(s) had bachelor's degree or higher
Gender				
Male	46.5	39.8	45.4	51.5
Female	53.5	60.2	54.6	48.5
Race/ethnicity				
American Indian	0.5	0.6	0.6	0.4
Asian/Pacific Isl.	5.1	4.7	3.9	6.5
Black	10.5	13.7	13.6	5.3
White	75.5	64.0	73.6	84.0
Hispanic	8.4	16.9	8.3	3.8
Family income in 1991				
Less than $25,000	24.1	50.3	25.9	7.4
$25,000-49,000	35.0	34.3	44.7	24.8
$50,000-74,999	24.4	12.7	23.1	32.3
$75,000 or more	16.5	2.7	6.3	35.5

(Chen and Carrol, 2005)

London (1992) claims first-generation students are "on the margin of two cultures" (p.6) because they may not readily fit into life on campus, and also may not have family members at home who have experienced college. This marginality may make a student's interactions with faculty, administrators, and their peers more important than for other students whose parents have experienced college attendance (London, 1992; Richardson and Skinner, 1992; Wilt, 2006).

The Study Abroad Context

While institutions of higher education are serving an increasingly diverse body of students, there has also been a greater commitment to ensuring that the students attending these colleges and universities have exposure to international study. High school students themselves expect to participate in study abroad while in college (American Council on Education, Art and Science Group, and College Board, 2008) and have been participating in greater numbers and in more diverse locations

(Institute for International Education, 2007). At the same time, the United States government has placed greater emphasis on increasing study abroad participation (American Council on Education, 2008; Benjamin A. Gilman Scholarship Program, 2006; Commission on the Abraham Lincoln Study Abroad Fellowship Program, 2005; Durbin, 2006; Hughes, 2007; O'Meara, Mehlinger, and Newman, 2001; U.S. Department of Education, 2006), and there is overwhelming public support for study abroad (NAFSA, 2006). Unfortunately, while great student interest in study abroad exists, the profile of participating students does not match higher education enrollment demographics.

In their 2008 publication, NAFSA: Association of International Educators extolled study abroad as pivotal to "the ability of the United States to lead responsibly, collaborate abroad, and compete effectively in the global arena" (NAFSA, 2008, p. 1). This document also placed particular emphasis on the domestic benefit of study abroad determining that the national benefit can be broken into two categories, strengthening national security and preparing US leadership. Study abroad can play a role in preparing American linguists with skills in critical languages that are gravely needed given that over sixty-five federal agencies have more than 34,000 positions that require foreign language skills and must be filled annually (Commission on the Abraham Lincoln Study Abroad Fellowship Program, 2005), a need that has gained urgency in a post-9/11 America (American Council on Education, 2002). With this need in mind, a 2003 report from NAFSA calls for "a Sputnik moment" (NAFSA, 2003, p. 3) recognizing the need to allocate resources to develop a national effort focusing on international education. The report urges that "study abroad must become the norm, not the exception" (p. 3) in order to accomplish this goal. Study abroad has a direct impact on strengthening national security by developing critical language skills, and can assist in preparing American leaders for global engagement.

An intended byproduct of study abroad is the opportunity for international American citizen diplomacy. Citizen diplomacy involves "individual Americans as students, teachers, athletes, artists, business people, humanitarians, adventurers or tourists. . . (who are) motivated by a responsibility to engage with the rest of the world in a meaningful, mutually beneficial dialogue" (US Center for Citizen Diplomacy, 2008). Study abroad plays a role in national diplomatic efforts by "fostering mutual understanding between nations at the citizen-level" (Hughes, 2007, p. 1) because students are able to sustain dialogue at the individual level in a way that is not otherwise possible through traditional means. This is further emphasized by Karen Hughes (2007), former Under Secretary for Public Diplomacy and Public Affairs who notes that "our education and exchange programs have proven to be our single-most important public diplomacy tool over the past fifty years" (p. 1). In this regard, the benefit of sending students abroad transcends the skills, values, and knowledge that the individual student gains (Johnson and Mulholland, 2006). This statement may not come as a surprise considering her role as a federal voice for public diplomacy issues; however both Presidents Clinton and George W. Bush also have vocalized their support for study abroad as a mechanism for soft diplomacy (Williams, 2007). President Obama has also declared his support for educational exchange saying that we must "find new ways to connect young Americans to young people all around the world, by supporting opportunities to learn new languages, and serve and study, welcoming students from other countries to our shores" and saying that such initiatives are "a critical part of how America engages with the world" (Obama, 2009).

Though the initiatives above suggest awareness of the importance of study abroad at the federal level (Benjamin A. Gilman International Scholarship Program, 2006; Commission on the Abraham Lincoln Study Abroad Fellowship Program, 2005; Hughes, 2007; NAFSA, 2003; U.S. Department of Education, 2006; Williams, 2007), data also suggest strong national support for international study at the citizen-level (NAFSA, 2006). In a 2005 poll conducted by NAFSA: The Association of International Educators, 90 percent of Americans believed it was important to prepare future generations for a global society. In addition, 77 percent "value educational experiences where time is spent abroad in other cultures" (p. 2). This data suggests that although only 1 percent of American undergraduate students participate in study abroad (Institute of International Education, 2007), substantial public support exists for international study.

Students themselves have placed greater emphasis on study abroad and are consequently participating in incrementally greater numbers (Institute of International Education, 2009). A 2008 poll conducted by the American Council on Education indicated that 55 percent of high school students were absolutely certain or fairly certain that they would study abroad in college. Unfortunately, the high number of interested students represents a "frustrated ideal" (p. 1) for international educators because the high percentage of interest is at odds with the low participation rate of undergraduate students participating in study abroad. Although overall participation in study abroad has steadily increased over the past decade, the percentage of students who are interested in study abroad in high school still does not match the overall participation rates.

Even through the massification and diversification of higher education during the twentieth century, the majority participant demographics of study abroad programs have remained relatively unchanged (Norfles, 2003; Williams, 2007). Study abroad has been described as an opportunity for White, middle-class, females (Smiles, 2001). This profile represents the majority of students in American under-graduate international study (Institute of International Education, 2009).

Incremental progress has been made between the 2000-2001 and 2007-2008 academic years to increase underrepresented student participation in study abroad overall (Institute of International Education, 2009). However, there remain a disproportionate number of minority students studying abroad, and minority and FG students continue to be underrepresented. Table 5.2 illustrates the student partici-pation rates from the 2009 OpenDoors report (Institute of International Education) and empirically demonstrates varying participation rates in American study abroad across racial and ethnic student populations.

Table 5.2. Percent of US Study Abroad Students

Race/ Ethnicity	2000/ 2001	2001/ 2002	2002/ 2003	2003/ 2004	2004/ 2005	2005/ 2006	2006/ 2007	2007/ 2008
Caucasian	84.3	82.9	83.2	83.7	83.0	83.0	81.9	81.8
Asian-Amer	5.4	5.8	6.0	6.1	6.3	6.3	6.7	6.6
Hispanic-Amer	5.4	5.4	5.1	5.0	5.6	5.4	6.0	5.9
African-Amer	3.5	3.5	3.4	3.4	3.5	3.5	3.8	4.0
Multiracial	0.9	2.0	1.8	1.3	1.2	1.2	1.2	1.2
Native-Amer	0.5	0.4	0.5	0.5	0.4	0.6	0.5	0.5

(Institute of International Education, 2009)

This skewed participation comes at a time when employers are increasingly seeking students who have participated in study abroad (Chichester and Akomolafe, 2003). As the American economy increasingly globalizes, employers have come to view the value of cross-cultural competence and the foreign language skills that may be gained through an experience such as study abroad (Adeola and Perry, 1997; Commission on the Abraham Lincoln Study Abroad Fellowship Program, 2005). Students recognize this need and 43 percent have noted that international experience and education will help advance their career or give them a competitive edge (NAFSA, 2006). Unfortunately, students who do not participate in study abroad may not have the opportunity to develop skills demanded by employers and that will allow them to successfully operate in the changing marketplace (Chichester and Akomolafe, 2003).

In addition to career clarification and preparation, there are academic and psycho-social benefits of studying abroad. Students who participated in study abroad were found to have increased functional knowledge, a greater academic understanding of cultural relativism, and an increased knowledge of world geography when compared to their peers who lacked study abroad experience (Sutton and Rubin, 2004). Other practical academic benefits of participation are the opportunity for foreign language acquisition or study of a field not available at a student's home campus (Burn, 1980) and the opportunity for experiential learning that may not be an option on-campus (Steinberg, 2007). Beyond scholastic benefits, various psycho-social benefits such as increased self image and self esteem (Juhasz and Walker, 1987), values clarification, and intercultural conflict and coping skills (Ryan and Twibell, 2000), greater openness to diversity (Ismail, Morgan, and Hayes, 2006), and foundational changes in personality (Harrison, 2006) have also been documented.

First-generation students have been identified as one population of students that are underrepresented in study abroad (NAFSA, 2002) and as a result do not benefit as their majority peers may from the educational, social, and psycho-social outcomes of study abroad participation. For this reason, practitioners need better guidance about what actions that they can take at their own institutions that can affect an increase in participation rates within this student population.

Empirical Basis for Research

A limited number of empirical studies have begun to explore the role of different aspects of the campus environment on student participation in study abroad. This topic has been discussed specifically in terms of access and the process through which students gain entry to study abroad (Bakalis and Joiner, 2004; Booker, 2001; Hembroff and Rusz, 1993; King and Young, 1994; Washington, 1998; Williams, 2007). Research also has examined underrepresented students' differential perceptions of study abroad (Bowman, 1987; Cash 1993; Norfles, 2003; Shirley, 2006; Bolen, 2001). This literature provides a solid base from which to explore the complex issue of underrepresentation by examining access, knowledge acquisition and perceptions of the experience, but largely fails to provide data on how underrepresented students arrive at their decision to participate. The work of Booker (2001), Williams (2007), and Norfles (2003) are particularly relevant to this research as these studies explored the student choice process from both the institutional and the student perspective. Special attention is given to a 2003 study conducted by Norfles on TRIO center director's perceptions of barriers to their student's participation in study abroad as this work was identified as the only research available that included first-generation students and the role of institutional referents on their participation in study abroad programs.

Williams' (2007) dissertation explored the role of institutional initiatives in encouraging student participation in study abroad. By surveying large research universities nationally, Williams was able to attain composite data on programs aimed at preparing underrepresented students for international study. Foundational to this study is the assumption that a pressing need exists for research that informs institutional action to more successfully recruit underrepresented students for participation in study abroad. This research represents a step beyond merely identifying specific barriers that impact participation. Instead the aim is to incite informed action by providing a snapshot of current practices at institutions nationally. Most relevant to this study, Williams argues that there is a need for knowledge of the practices at the macro-level that aim to boost participation rates of US students. However, the recommendations put forth by Williams would be strengthened by additional empirical research examining the extent to which environmental factors play a role in the decision of underrepresented students to apply to study abroad. Such a study would then provide institutions with the knowledge of where to place scarce resources and maximize the efficacy of efforts that aim to increase student participation.

Booker's (2001) dissertation, *Differences between Applicants and Non-Applicants Relevant to the Decision to Study Abroad*, is the seminal study on the student choice process in study abroad. Using consumer decision process modeling,

Booker created a new theoretical framework for understanding how students arrive at the decision to study abroad. Using this model, Booker identified specific factors that contribute to a student's decision to participate consequently leading to the evaluation of over one hundred factors that weigh on a student's decision to apply or not apply to study abroad. He argues that with greater examination of factors that may contribute to involvement, institutions will be equipped with a greater ability to target students for participation. Booker's study examined study abroad participants as aggregates and did not take into consideration gender, socio-economic status, or race/ethnicity. To this end, Booker identifies a clear gap in study abroad research in stating that "the study could be expanded to explore why minority students apparently are less likely to be interested in study abroad than non-minority students are" (p. 152). This assertion both supports the need for such research and provides a framework to do so.

In an attempt to gain insight on the barriers to study abroad participation for typically underrepresented students, Norfles (2003) conducted a study surveying TRIO Program directors asking what they perceived to be the greatest barriers for participating students. The TRIO program is a series extracurricular events and activities that provide structure for disadvantaged youth with the aim of encouraging academic excellence. Institutions of higher education may opt to offer space for on-campus centers to support these programs. Norfles argues that such centers, and their staff, provide an opportunity for a researcher to gain greater understanding of underserved populations because the staff is in constant contact with this particular population.

In designing her study, Norfles (2003) chose to survey the center directors at universities across the United States to gauge their perception of barriers to TRIO student participation in study abroad. Funding was identified as a primary barrier for students. Norfles stated that "high costs and limited financial aid funding were barriers to TRIO college-level students" (p.14), suggesting that funding is important for this population of students. In open ended survey results one director expressed that because students are unable to afford such experiences they do not typically have the opportunity to explore other factors that relate to their participation. Such a response suggests that data collection on subsequent barriers may prove difficult for this population given that the financial barrier, even if a misperception, may preclude exposure to additional factors for low-income first-generation students.

Although the financial barrier was found to be the primary obstacle for students, this study used open ended responses and additional survey items to gather additional information that related to student barriers to study abroad (Norfles, 2003). This allowed the author to describe the financial impact by further specifying it in terms of overall indebtedness, overall cost, and loss of income. In addition to the financial barrier the surveyed directors cited family constraints, as well as lack of information about the opportunity to participate in study abroad and as a specific barrier to these students.

Finally, Norfles (2003) found that one of the major barriers to participation for the students in her study were those individuals working with the students directly.

The TRIO directors, according to Norfles, overwhelmingly held the belief that low-income students do not benefit from study abroad. Consequently, the directors indicated that pursuing such an opportunity is "not a priority concern" and "isn't necessary for them to reach their educational goals" (p.17). Given that TRIO students specifically do not attend schools where a large number of students study abroad, a lack of support for international education among center directors could have an effect on overall student participation. As a result, Norfles argued that "some individuals that work with these students may also be considered a barrier to students' ability to study abroad when they limit the information provided to TRIO students and staff" (p. 17) and that "how directors value a study abroad experience, in most cases, is directly related to the level of support and information that they provide their students" (23). Consequently, the author stressed the importance of support from professional staff for the purposes of boosting underrepresented student enrollment in study abroad.

As one of the few studies examining first-generation students directly, the work of Norfles (2003) is groundbreaking. The author was able to gain access to a group of individuals intimately involved in the educational experience of first-generation students, and was able to conclude that the individuals working with students were the key to engaging or disengaging underrepresented students in study abroad. This finding emphasizes the importance of institutional relationships in the student's decision to study abroad and provides a basis for the exploration of the institutional environment that is the focus of this study.

Focus of This Study

Given that a major finding of the Norfles study was that the institutional referents themselves can play a role in determining underrepresented student participation in study abroad, a greater examination of the role of the dimensions of the institutional environment on study abroad participation is merited. The relevant literature on barriers and catalysts to study abroad describes a variety of factors that may influence a student's decision. Although university administrators cannot control all of the variables discussed as impactful on participation, they do have control over some aspects of a student's first-year experience. Four such specific areas were identified for this study which was intentionally limited to exploring the impact of four domains of the college environment on first-generation students: (a) student experiences with diversity, (b) institutional support, (c) the quality of students' relationships with institutional referents (fellow students, faculty, and university administrators), and (d) involvement with faculty.

A number of college impact models have been developed to explain the role that the institution plays in effecting change on specific student outcomes. These models focus on the source of student transformation by examining specific environmental factors. Outcomes, such as participation in study abroad programs, can then be used to determine how students have changed developmentally while they are in college. What generally defines these models is their attempt to understand how the institution plays a role in developing a specific student outcome (Pascarella and Terenzini, 2005); e.g., learning (Pascarella, 1985) or retention (Tinto and Cullen, 1973).

Identifying that no study to date has examined how facets of the institutional environment may impact FG student participation in study abroad through the lens of student engagement, two college impact models, Pascarella's General Model for Assessing Change (1985) and Astin's Inputs Environment Outputs model (1970a, 1970b, 1993) provided the primary conceptual frameworks for this study. Astin's model broadly claims that change occurs due to a variety of experiences students confront while in college; this change is effected by traits that they bring with them to college (inputs) and results in a specific outcome (outputs). Astin's work was extended by Pascarella's General Model for Assessing Change (1985), which further specified the *environment* portion of Astin's model. Two particular sections of the model, *interactions with institutional referents* and the *institutional environment* were explicitly examined through the design of this study. The *output* in Astin's model, or the *learning and cognitive development* outcome in Pascarella's model are taken in this study to be a student's participation in a study abroad program.

The Seven Principles of Good Practice in Undergraduate Education developed by Chickering and Gamson in 1987 also reinforce the use of the four domains of the college environment identified for this study. This document outlined specific areas that are important not only to ensuring learning but also have an impact on other areas of student engagement. The four domains of diversity, institutional support, quality of relationships, and faculty involvement were all included among the Seven Principles as well as in the National Survey of Student Engagement (2006) a tool used to assess the role of environmental variables on student outcomes. That the four areas addressed in this study are all mentioned in the Chickering and Gamson foundational document as well as the National Survey of Student Engagement (NSSE) lends weight to the exploration of their influence on student participation in study abroad.

According to Pascarella and Terenzini (2005) college impact models are particularly important in that they emphasize "factors over which college faculty and administrators have some programmatic and policy control" (p. 530). As such, the four domains to be explored in this study are those that potentially could be manipulated by practitioners to affect the desired outcome of increased participation in study abroad by FG students. Each of these four variables and their role in shaping student outcomes are presented in succession through the relevant academic literature.

The Role of Institutional Support for Student Success in College

Institutional support includes aid or assistance provided to students to cope with social, academic, and family responsibilities. Generally speaking, this support is purported to assist with both the student transition to college (Tinto, 2008), as well as academic success (Gerardi, 2006; Lotkowski, Robbins, and Noeth, 2004) for students completing their undergraduate studies.

Institutional support may be particularly important for some subpopulations of undergraduate students. Research conducted on the national level has demonstrated that overall, low-income students are less academically prepared than their higher income peers (Chen and Carrol, 2005). Twice as many low-income students take remedial courses, earn fewer credits in the first year, have lower GPAs in the first year, and are less likely to earn four-year degrees when controlling for other background variables (Chen and Carrol). As FG students are also overwhelmingly low-income, this data suggests that academic preparation may be a factor impacting the first-generation student's experience in college and may necessitate different types of support than that provided to other groups of undergraduate students.

That low-income students are both disproportionately academically prepared for college and lower performing has an important impact on such a student's experience in college (Chen and Carrol, 2005). As a result of this inferior academic preparation these students may be required to take remedial coursework, stop out, or drop out (Chen and Carrol). Poor academic preparation for college-level work can also serve as an impediment for low-income student engagement while they are pursuing their tertiary education.

Poor academic preparation may require additional academic support for first-generation and low-income students while they are in college (Tinto, 2008). Tinto reinforces this point by arguing that "the success of academically underprepared students does not arise by chance" and that "without such support, the access to college we provide them does not provide meaningful opportunity for success" (p. 2). This argument places university administrators in the challenging position of providing the additional support for first-generation students while they are in college.

Beyond navigating the workings of a university, FG students may also have difficulty understanding their new academic expectations (Wilt, 2006). As such, counselors and mentors play a key role in the FG student's transition to the college environment. Wilt argues in his 2006 work that "given the complex life situations faced by low-income individuals, counseling can be a significant factor in their higher education success" (p. 2). Given the context of such complexity, Wilt argues that counseling can serve to compensate for a student's lack of experience with the college environment by assisting with their negotiation of the college bureaucracy.

The expectation of student autonomy in the academy may be problematic for students who do not have knowledge of how to function in such a bureaucracy.

Termed the "burden of student-initiated assistance" by Deil-Amen and Rosenbaum (2003, p. 586) students must be aware of the assistance available to them in order to seek it out. Once they are aware that help exists they must then take the initiative to do so. However, Deil-Amen and Rosenbaum argue that FG students "cannot easily get advice about how to succeed, what pitfalls to avoid, or how to plan their pathway through college" (p. 586). Problems associated with the expectation of student autonomy may be compounded if a student does not expect to experience a challenging transition to college (London, 1992).

The role of a college mentor also becomes increasingly important in light of the way that low-income students may view the transition to college. London (1992) argues that FG students can feel "on the margin of two cultures" (p. 6) because they may not readily identify with the majority population on campus and may not have a social support system that includes individuals who have experienced college attendance. This idea is further supported by the fact that middle-income first-generation students found the transition to college less difficult than their low-income counterparts (Richardson and Skinner, 1992). Because FG students may struggle with acclimating to a new culture on campus and may struggle with feelings of alienation institutional support is critical for these students in the first year and beyond.

Institutional support may be important for FG students because they may suffer from a lack of support from their family while they are in college (Billson and Terry, 1982; York-Anderson and Bowman, 1992). Family support for this population has been shown to impact their first year experience (Carter, 2006). In this study, Carter found that low-income students' functional, emotional, and attitudinal independence from their parents actually had a negative effect on their transition to college. This finding represents a reversal of the common assumption that it is beneficial for all students to gain independence from family. Given that first-generation students generally lack family support in college this finding may have a differential impact on this population.

The college environment is multifaceted and complex. For this reason the first-generation student's experience is actually a product of many different types of interactions with faculty, administrators and their peers. London (1992), Wilt (2006) and Richardson and Skinner (1992) argue that the classroom and the faculty, and the role of counseling and advising do impact a student's experience in college. Further, these types of interactions are more important for first-generation students as they may assist a student's transition to college (London, 1992; Richardson and Skinner, 1992) and the depth to which they are able to engage while in college (Tinto, 2008).

The Role of Quality of Institutional Relationships

Although it is important for first-generation students to have sufficient institutional support the *quality* of the relationship with peers, faculty, and administrators is also important to student success. The campus environment is really composed of a variety of overlapping experiences and relationships, for example relationships between students, faculty, and administrators may exist in-class and out-of-class, formally or informally. How students perceive these relationships has been shown to be impactful on decisions to attend, persist, and the level that they engage with their institutional environment (Tinto, 1993; Hazeur, 2007).

Overall a student's sense of belonging has been shown to be related to their decision to persist to graduation (Tinto, 1993). Student academic and social integration, partially the extent to which students engage with institutional referents, has been shown to impact retention positively (Astin and Oseguera, 2005; Pascarella and Terenzini, 1980; Tinto, 1982; 1999). Further it has been shown that a student's connection with their organization leads to greater integration. In short, the quality and depth of a student's relationships have a direct impact a student's decisions to continue enrollment.

Tinto (1988) found that both belonging and inclusion were important components of a successful transition to college. These findings have also been explored in specific underrepresented populations in higher education as Hurtado and Carter (1997) found that a sense of belonging is particularly important for Hispanic students attending college. As such the quality of student relationships with their peers can contribute to a sense of belonging which may impact the quality and success of their college transition.

As has been mentioned, college administrators may be important to first-generation students who may not understand how to navigate the institutional environment or their academic requirements while in college (Deil-Amen and Rosenbaum, 2003). However, if students have a negative perception of these administrators they may further distance themselves from these potentially critical resources. This issue described in the previous section may be resolved if students have a positive relationship or perception of administrators at their university.

Positive relationships with institutional referent groups such as peers, faculty, and administrators can be important because these relationships may impact how a student feels about the general fit of the culture within a university. It has been argued that "a student's sense of connection to a college or university community remains an essential element of engagement, retention, and success" in college (Hazeur, 2007, p.4). In sum, a student's perception of fit may have a concrete impact on a student's ability not only to be successfully retained and persist to graduation, but also may create hurdles that are obstacles to engagement while in college if it results in disengagement.

Low-income and FG students may have certain attitudinal characteristics that impact their college experience. Research by Lotkowsky, Robbins, and Noeth (2004) found that time management and study habits, academic self-confidence and academic goals were the three strongest factors impacting full-time student retention at four-year colleges. It can be postulated that for students who lack these preparatory skills, this may serve to further complicate student engagement and ultimately the success of a first-generation student while they are in college. FG students who are facing these hurdles may not seek out assistance if they perceive institutional referents to be hostile, unhelpful, or a barrier to their goals. Indeed, this thought is in line with group socialization theory suggesting that a student's peer group may impact their educational decisions including what is worthy of being learned (Austin, 2002). No research has evaluated the relationship between the quality of relationships with institutional referent groups on a student's decision to participate in study abroad.

The Role of Faculty Contact and Interaction

Faculty remains a critical referent group for first-generation students because they are at the center of the knowledge sharing that is a cornerstone of the collegiate experience. For many first-generation students who are also low-income the classroom may represent the only opportunity that they have to engage in learning and interact with faculty and their peers (Tinto, 2008). For this reason, Tinto argues that there is a "centrality of the classroom to student success" (p. 600) for this population of students.

University faculty also play a role in promoting positive engagement practices and learning for students (Umbach and Wawrzynski, 2005). Faculty and student contact has been shown by researchers to positively affect student learning (Astin, 1993; Ewell and Jones, 1996; Pascarella and Terenzini, 1991; Tinto, 1993). Additionally, increased faculty contact has also been shown to be the top indicator of student persistence in higher education (Braxton, Sullivan, and Johnson, 1997; Huratdo and Carter, 1997; Stage and Hossler, 2000).

Although much of the research on faculty contact and student learning relies on self-reported measures of student engagement, the work of Umback and Wawrzynski (2005) focused on faculty attitude and behaviors that may increase student learning. Using data from the 2003 National Survey of Student Engagement student survey (n= 22,033 first year students, 20,226 senior students) and faculty survey (n=14,336) the authors found that on "campuses where faculty report frequent course-related interactions both first-year and senior students were more challenged and engaged in active and collaborative learning activities" (p. 12). Student gains were also noted in the categories of social development, general education knowledge, and practical competencies. Although these in-class interactions showed a great effect on students, out-of-class contact with students proved less impactful. These types of interactions positively impacted the category of active and collaborative learning, however once the authors accounted for institutional control variables the impact was reduced substantially. Umback and Wawrzynski's study centralizes the role of faculty in overall student learning. In sum, they found that at institutions where faculty-student engagement was high students tended to feel more supported and were actively engaged in their own learning.

Faculty contact is one important aspect of overall student engagement. At present the relevant research has demonstrated that increased contact has a positive association with persistence to the second year of study (Braxton, Sullivan and Johnson, 1997; Hurtado and Carter, 1997; Stage and Hossler, 2000) and increased learning while in college (Astin, 1993; Ewell and Jones, 1996; Fries-Britt, 2000; Pascarella and Terenzini, 1991; Tinto, 1993). However, no study to date has examined if these interactions are impactful on student participation in study abroad as an educational outcome.

The Impact of Diversity Experiences in College

Diversity encompasses a variety of contexts—political, racial/ethnic, religious beliefs, and personal values—and in higher education can take the form of contact with students that are from different ethnic, racial, economic or social backgrounds (Pascarella, Edison, Nora, Hagedorn, and Braxton, 1996). Research has shown that students tend to build greater tolerance to difference during their time in college (Astin, 1993; Pascarella and Terenzini, 1991) and that values, beliefs, actions, and attitudes are impacted most by interactions with fellow classmates and faculty (Astin, 1993; Pascarella and Terenzini, 1991). The peer group plays a unique role in the way that students experience gains in openness to diversity as exposure to diversity experiences that specifically require interaction between students are positively related with a student's openness to diversity (Pascarella, Edison, Nora, Hagedorn, and Braxton, 1996; Whitt, Edison, Pascarella, Terenzini, and Nora, 2001). Research demonstrates that students experience both exposure to and benefit from an increased openness to diversity in college and that their peer group and university faculty play a role in encouraging openness.

Two studies have specifically evaluated what additional variables may impact student openness to diversity. One study by Pascarella, Edison, Nora, Hagedorn, and Braxton (1996) found that precollege openness to diversity and perception of a nondiscriminatory college environment were both important indicators of an openness to diversity at the end of students' first year of college. This study also identified several practices that limit student openness to diversity. These were identified as participation in intercollegiate athletics, inclusion in a social fraternity or sorority, and enrollment in mathematics coursework as they all had a negative impact on student openness to diversity (1996). In a subsequent study Whitt, Edison, Pascarella, Terenzini, and Nora in 2001 explored whether these patterns persist into the second and third years of study. They found that largely precollege openness to diversity persisted throughout a student's undergraduate career. The findings of Pascarella, et al. and Whitt, et al. further the work of Astin (1993) and Pascarella and Terenzini (2005) by suggesting that students' backgrounds and perceptions of the environment also play a role in student openness to diversity.

In addition to the factors that encourage openness to diversity, research has also been conducted on what direct benefits students receive from experiencing diversity in college. In one study curricular enhancements that increased the content of multicultural diversity in coursework resulted in an increase in greater critical and active thinking among students (MacPhee, Kreutzer, and Fritz, 1994).Although the level of impact differed by racial and ethnic group, overall students with exposure to a diverse student body tended to have higher incidences of intellectual engagement and motivation (Gurin, Dey, Hurtado, and Gurin, 2002). Overall, students with high exposure to diversity in during their undergraduate careers tended to report higher levels of satisfaction with their college experience.

Study abroad is fundamentally an experience that exposes students to diversity. However no research has been conducted exploring if high or low exposure to diversity is correlated with a student's decision to participate in a study abroad program. By including this factor in the analysis of this study the author will be able to expand research on the impact of diversity experiences by examining if a predictive relationship exists between diversity experience and study abroad participation.

Conclusion

Exposure to diversity, the quality of institutional relationships, experiencing a supportive institutional environment, and engagement with faculty have shown to be beneficial for other educational outcomes such as retention, persistence, and engagement (Astin and Oseguera, 2005; Bean, 1981; Lotkowski et al., 2004; Pascarella and Terenzini, 1980; Tinto and Cullen, 1973; Tinto, 1999), cognitive development (Gurin, Dey, Hurtado, and Gurin, 2002; Kuh, 1995; MacPhee et al., 1994), social development (Pascarella and Terenzini, 2005) and remain important indicators of effective engagement practices for students in general (Chickering and Gamson, 1987). Further, some of these engagement practices have been shown to impact populations of students, including first-generation college students, disproportionately both positively and negatively. These differential impacts occur while students make the transition to college and persist to graduation.

Although research is robust on the impact of engagement on many educational outcomes what has yet to be explored is whether or not these educational practices are also impactful for one specific type of educational outcome: participation in study abroad. Equipped with this gap in research, this study sought to identify if four specific types of engagement practices may serve as impactful predictors of American FG undergraduate student study abroad participation.

Research Questions, Dataset, and Methodology

In order to gain a greater understanding of the phenomenon of underrepresentation and how student engagement with the institutional environment impacts study abroad participation, this study evaluated four specific variables relating to a student's experience in college. To explore this present gap in the literature five research questions were developed that relate directly to four main composite variables evaluated in the study:

1. What are the demographic characteristics of first-generation college students who do and do not study abroad?
2. What is the relationship between a first-generation student's experience with diversity and their participation in study abroad programs?
3. What is the relationship between a first-generation student's perception of a supportive institutional environment and their participation in study abroad programs?
4. What is the relationship between a first-generation student's perceived quality of institutional relationships and their participation in study abroad programs?
5. What is the relationship between a first-generation student's involvement with faculty and participation in study abroad programs?

The data used for this study to answer the research questions were collected by the Center for Post-secondary Study (CPS) at Indiana University-Bloomington (IUB) through the National Survey of Student Engagement (NSSE) College Survey Report (CSR). With the affirmation that "what students do during college counts more in terms of desired outcomes than who they are or even where they go to college" (Kuh, 2001, p. 1) the National Survey of Student Engagement (NSSE) seeks to quantify how frequently students are involved in engagement behaviors on college campuses. The survey was founded with seed money from the Pew Charitable Trust in 1998, and is now self-supported through the use of direct-fees paid by institutional participants. The goal of this survey is to collect information about student engagement from colleges across the United States.

The survey instrument covers a variety of areas of engagement that are considered good practice in undergraduate education. Such areas include a student's background, their perception of the college environment, and an estimation of their own growth since they began college. As the NSSE is widely used in higher education to evaluate levels of student engagement on campuses, institutions may use this data to inform programmatic enhancements or changes that they believe will result in positive student learning outcomes.

The survey is distributed widely at universities in the United States. In 2003 (NSSE) the survey was used on 437 campuses and, in 2006, 557 campuses were surveyed (NSSE, 2006). The *College Student Report* survey is distributed to both freshman and seniors allowing for longitudinal comparisons of student engagement practices as well as snapshot analyses of students who are at different educational levels within an institution. The large size of the annual sample makes it unique in its reach in the field of higher education. Although strictly speaking the sample is not nationally representative, its results are generalizable to institutions that meet a similar profile to participating institutions. Annually, the results bear a strong resemblance to the general profile of institutions in the United States (NSSE, 2006). To illustrate this point, a table comparing NSSE and IPEDS 2003 data, adapted from the NSSE 2003 annual report, can be found in Table 5.3. Overall the NSSE, though the CSR, is a tool that can be used to evaluate engagement in a variety of practices on college campuses at the institutional or national level.

Table 5.3. NSSE and IPEDS National Comparison 2003

Carnegie Classification	NSSE 2003	IPEDS 2003
Doctoral/Research Ext	10%	11%
Doctoral/Research Int	9%	8%
Master's I and II	45%	43%
Baccalaureate—LA	19%	16%
Baccalaureate—General	17%	22%
Sector		
Public four-year	42%	37%
Private four-year	58%	63%
Region		
Far West	8%	10%
Great Lakes	18%	15%
Mid East	19%	19%
New England	8%	9%
Plains	11%	11%
Rocky Mountains	2%	3%
Southeast	24%	26%
Southwest	9%	7%
Location		
Large city (>250,000)	20%	19%
Mid-size city (<250,000)	30%	29%
Urban fringe large city	17%	17%
Urban fringe mid-size city	7%	8%
Large town (>25,000)	3%	4%
Small town (~5,000)	17%	17%
Rural	4%	6%

(NSSE, 2003)

The NSSE annual report describes the profile of participating institutions as being similar to the national profile through data reported through the IPEDS. As seen in Table 5.4., a comparison of the student characteristics of NSSE respondents,

NSSE schools and IPEDS data on national enrollments at four-year institutions reveals a similar pattern.

Table 5.4. NSSE 2003 and National Four-Year Demographic Information

	NSSE Respondents	All NSSE Schools	National
Gender			
Men	34%	45%	45%
Women	66%	55%	55%
Race/Ethnicity			
African American/Black	8%	10%	11%
Amer. Indian/Alaska Native	2%	1%	1%
Asian/Pacific Islander	6%	5%	6%
Caucasian/White	79%	70%	68%
Hispanic	8%	8%	8%
Other	1%	3%	4%
Multiple	6%	–	–
International	5%	3%	3%
Enrollment Status			
Full-Time	89%	83%	82%
Part-Time	11%	17%	18%

(NSSE, 2003)

Institutions of higher education often use their own NSSE data to compare their CSR scores against peer institutions or progress with institutional forecasts or strategic plans. However, academic researchers may also request data directly from the CPR to conduct analyses using NSSE annual CSR data sets. The later process was used for this study to examine how certain facets of the institutional environment may influence first-generation students and their decision to study abroad. This study examined first-generation American undergraduate college students who responded to the 2003 and 2006 distribution of the CSR instrument. This sample is comprised of 443 FG students, 97 study abroad participants and 337 non-participants.

Secondary data gathered through the CSR for the NSSE was used in this study. Using a secondary data set allows the researcher to rely on the strengths of the collection methodology as well as sources of additional variables that can be used as control variables in modeling data. However, using secondary data requires caution and critical review of the approaches followed when the data is collected as such processes occur beyond the supervision of the researcher. One of the strengths of relying on data collected through a frequently used instrument such as the CSR is that its repeated use can be used to establish the reliability of the data generated by the survey (Alreck and Settle, 2003). Having a series of data can assist with the decision that a survey instrument is reliable. However, instrument reliability can be equally beneficial or detrimental on the overall reliability of the study (Fraenkel and Wallen, 2009); poor instrument reliability has a negative effect, and good instrument reliability has a positive effect. In the case of the NSSE *College Student Report*, measures were taken to ensure instrument reliability and subsequent internal validity of the conclusions of the NSSE (Kuh, 2001) and the survey has been used extensively as the basis for empirical research on student engagement (Carini, Kuh, and Klein, 2006; Filkins and Doyle, 2002; Harper, Carini, Bridges, and Hayek, 2004; Laird and Kuh, 2005; Pike and Kuh, 2005; Pike, 2006; Umbach and Wawrzynski, 2005).

To answer the five research questions descriptive statistics and a binary multiple logistic regression analysis were employed. Composite variables were created using multiple survey items to create the four main variables of interest: (a) perception of institutional support, (b) quality of institutional relationships, (c) involvement with faculty, and (d) exposure to diversity. Factor scores were calculated for each composite variable using the Statistical Package for the Social Sciences (SPSS). These scores were then used to develop the final best-fit predictive model for study abroad participation of FG students.

Design Issues

Secondary data were used for all analyses in this study. As a result this work rests on any design flaws inherent in the data used for the analysis including those that may arise from self-reported student data. Also, lack of comparison data, be it nationally representative demographic information or other empirical research on the topic, should be considered when generalizing results.

The validity of self-reported data is generally affected by an inability to provide accurate information (Wentland and Smith, 1993), the intentional withholding of information believed to be true (Aaker, Kumar, and Day, 1998), and the inflation of experience (Pike, 1995). First, an individual may not be able to provide information if they do not fully understand what is being asked of them. Second, if an individual is uncomfortable about the topic they may avoid a truthful response. And third, when individuals provide self-reported data there is generally an inclination to inflate their experience. However this effect has been shown to be relatively constant across sampled populations (Pike, 1995). Student response bias is a concern for any data collected through direct administration, given these specific concerns the NSSE CSR was designed intentionally with these challenges in mind.

A significant limitation of this study is the lack of disaggregated data on study abroad participation. Students may have responded affirmatively to the item regarding study abroad participation indicating that they enrolled in some type of international study. However, not collected by the NSSE CSR, or consequently examined in this study, are the duration (short-term, semester, academic year), location (by region or country), or type (inclusion of: service learning component, internship or career preparation, foreign language instruction, direct enrollment at a foreign university, island program sponsored by their home institution). Additional analyses revealing this data are not possible without direct contact with the anonymous survey respondents and are a limitation of the survey construct. The consequence of this holistic definition of study abroad is that any results must be interpreted with the understanding that there are many different types of study abroad experiences that comprise the monolithic definition included in the survey instrument and that no researchers would be able to evaluate the role of duration, location, or type of program using CSR data.

The FG students included in this study were identified as having parents who have not enrolled in higher education. However, it is important to note that the demographics of this sample portray a first-generation student that more closely reflects the demographics of the traditional undergraduate student. The FG students were majority female, have overwhelmingly attended private institutions, were between the ages of 20-23 during their senior year of college, and overwhelmingly lived on-campus during full-time enrollment status. Barring the special considerations of the FG student population mentioned above, the NSSE CPR closely resembles the general profile of American four-year institutions of higher education with relation to Carnegie classification, sector, size, geographic region, and location. Such demographics should be taken into consideration when interpreting any results.

With final regard to generalizability, a limitation of the findings of this study is that the data lacks a comparison pool. No national dataset collects information on first-generation student participation in study abroad, and only anecdotal literature and practitioner experience suggests that underrepresentation is a problem for this population. As a result the findings, even by frequency distribution of population characteristics, currently have little basis for comparison. This research is exploratory in nature as there is a general lack of rigorous empirical study on this population with regards to their enrollment in international education programs. That the field of study is nascent, particularly with regards to the first-generation student population, should encourage cautious generalization of the results by practitioners and scholars.

Results

Results were found for each of the five research questions developed for this study. First, results for research question one is presented. Second and finally, results for research question two through five are reported.

First-Generation Participant and Non-Participant Demographics

Question one related to the overall demographic composition of the first-generation students that did and did not participate in study abroad and took the NSSE CSR survey in their freshman year in 2003 and again in their senior year in 2006. The results show that these students are overwhelmingly traditional but differed in many ways. Overall, they were majority female (67.3 percent), Caucasian (77.9 percent), between the ages of 20-23 (91.6 percent), full time students (98.2 percent), in a fraternity or sorority (88.5 percent), academically successful in their freshman year (85.9 percent), live on-campus or in fraternity or sorority housing (80.6 percent), have participated in foreign language coursework (52.6 percent), attend private institutions (84.9 percent), and attend baccalaureate colleges (56.7 percent). Study abroad participants were more likely to attend a private institution, attend an institution with a Baccalaureate College—Arts and Sciences Carnegie Classification, are generally more racially or ethnically diverse, belong to a fraternity or sorority, be an athlete, live in on-campus housing, be more traditionally aged, and be a full-time student. The two sub-populations were found to be similar with regards to gender composition.

Results Associated with Main Engagement Variables

Stepwise binary multiple logistic regression analyses were used for questions 2 through 5 to determine if experience with diversity, perception of a supportive institutional environment, perceived quality of institutional relationships, and involvement with faculty had a predictive relationship with study abroad participation in the first-generation undergraduate population. As seen in Table 5.5, the results of the analysis showed a non-significant relationship between perception of a supportive institutional environment, perceived quality of institutional relationships, and involvement with faculty suggesting that a relationship does not exist between these variables and study abroad participation within this population. However, a statistically significant result ($p<.05$) was found for a student's exposure to diversity indicating a relationship between this variable and a FG student's participation in study abroad; a one-point increase in the composite diversity scale indicates that a FG student is 1.32 times more likely to participate in study abroad.

Final, Best-Fit Model

Given the finding of a statistically significant relationship between one of the main variables of interest for the study, a best-fit model was developed that included demographic characteristics of the sample. The final, best-fit model included student exposure to diversity, participation in foreign language coursework, living in campus-based housing, and attending a private institution.

**Table 5.5. Final Logistic Regression Model
Predicting Study Abroad Participation**

Variable	B	SE	Odds ratio	Wald Statistic
Experience with diversity	0.28	0.124	1.32	5.067**
Foreign language coursework	0.32	0.16	1.38	4.235**
Campus-affiliated housing	1.39	0.45	4.01	9.657***
Private institution attendance	0.83	0.46	2.30	3.313*

*p < .1 **p < .05. ***p < .01.

Major Findings

Three major findings were identified from the results of this study. First, that a student's exposure to diversity is a significant, predictive variable for undergraduate FG students who study abroad. Second, that there were three significant demographic variables that were included in the final best-fit model; (a) participating in foreign language coursework, (b) living in campus-affiliated housing, (c) and attending a private institution. Third, and finally, that gender and race or ethnicity did not have a statistically significant effect on study abroad participation in this population and in this study. As the central major findings of this study, each are discussed first through their suggestions for future research and second through suggestions for campus-based practitioners working with first-generation college students at American four-year institutions.

Major Finding 1: Significant Diversity Effect

The result of the binary multiple logistic regression analysis indicated that a FG student's exposure to diversity was predictive of study abroad participation. A one-point increase in the diversity scale would increase a FG student's odds of participation by 1.32, meaning that the student is 1.32 times more likely to participate in study abroad than had that increase in exposure to diversity not taken place.

The composite variable used in this study to describe a student's exposure to diversity comprised three discrete items; (a) having serious conversations with students of different race or ethnicity than their own, (b) having similar conversations with those who have different religious beliefs, political opinions, or personal values; and (c) how often their institution encouraged contact among students from different economic, social, and racial or ethnic backgrounds. Suggestions for research and practice address these areas separately and together.

Suggestions for Research

Research has shown that a student's study abroad experience can impact their openness to diversity post-participation (Ismail, Morgan, and Hayes, 2006), however no previous research has determined if a relationship existed between general exposure to diversity and participation in study abroad for students in general or within the first-generation student population. This leaves open the possibility for additional research on the role that exposure to diversity plays in the study abroad decisions of college students in general, as well offers an opportunity to examine its role for the many underrepresented populations enrolled in American colleges. This relationship could also be explored in a confirmatory study that examines a similar population of FG students.

Although this study treated exposure to diversity as a composite experience, future research could narrow this focus, identifying if one component of meaningful diversity experiences as defined in this study increases the odds of participation for this population over and above the other composite variables. For instance, it may be that it is the institutional commitment to encouraging contact among these populations that plays a large role in defining student's perception of other types of experiences that incorporate exposure to diversity. Or, it may be that race or ethnicity or values-related exposure such as religious views, political opinions, or personal worldviews play independent and important roles in opening a student's eyes to study abroad. Finally, it could be the intersection of the three that is particularly important. Such questions were out of the bounds of the research in this study; however, the role of diversity experiences on study abroad completion is an open area for scholarly inquiry.

Suggestions for Practice

Many institutions have worked to create an environment on their campuses that is supportive of diversity in its many forms and have attempted to construct opportunities for meaningful exchange of ideas between different populations of students. With this in mind, the significant exposure to diversity finding suggests that these efforts should continue to try to increase meaningful exposure to diversity among those of differing racial and ethnic backgrounds as well as religious, political, and personal beliefs. These interactions are not only beneficial to other areas of a student's collegiate experience, but also have now been shown to have a positive and predictive effect on their participation in international education. As a result, such interactions should be encouraged whenever possible among students.

It is important to note the language of the survey items relating to diversity experiences. The exchanges are defined as *serious* conversations, not cursory or fleeting, and that the scale relates to frequency of such interactions. This suggests that programming on-campus must go beyond the surface-level. There may be other opportunities intended to build collegiality among different groups of students, but this research indicates that what is important are meaningful, frequent interactions. This leaves practitioners to establish what the ideal opportunities may be for such interactions to take place on their campuses, but suggests that to be effective they must extend beyond the superficial, and must be frequent.

Generally, this finding necessitates that practitioners identify new ways to bring diversity into the campus experience of students. International, multicultural, or foreign language themed campus-based housing may be one way to achieve greater diversity of student participation in study abroad. However, it is important to note that not all students have access to on-campus social or educational events or services. First-generation students are more likely to be low-income (Chen and Carrol, 2005), and many may have responsibilities to family or employment that may take them away from campus, even if they live in on-campus housing. As Tinto notes the classroom is central to the student experience because it is the only place where all students may come together. If this is the case, curricular integration of diversity concepts could be particularly important for those students who may not be able to engage in the traditionally designed, campus-based, undergraduate experience.

Increasing exposure to diversity can be acquired through partnerships with and support for other campus offices such as multicultural student services, faith organizations, and politically-affiliated student groups. However, this exposure must be frequent and meaningful in order to affect a change in study abroad participation.

Major Finding 2: Significant Demographic Variables

Having participated in foreign language coursework, attending a private institution, and living in campus-affiliated housing during a student's first year were all shown to be statistically significant predictors of international study for first-generation undergraduate students. As a result these variables were all included in the final best-fit regression model. Not all of these are malleable characteristics of a student's experience that could be easily manipulated by higher education administrators, however their predictive ability merits a discussion of implications for further research and practice.

Foreign Language Attendance

Attending a foreign language course was shown to be predictive of study abroad participation. Statistically significant at the .05 level, a first-generation student was 1.38 times more likely to participate in study abroad if they had enrolled in at least one foreign language course as a first year undergraduate.

Suggestions for Research

Identifying that there is a relationship between enrollment in foreign language coursework and study abroad is important in opening the door for additional research. The NSSE CPR survey only collects dichotomous data on participation in foreign language coursework and therefore limits the possibility for analysis. Future research using other sources of data could identify if this predictive relationship persists or changes based on level of study or duration of attendance in foreign language coursework; for example, such research could explore if the predictive ability increases for students who are taking advanced language courses in culture or literature versus introductory language learning. Another area that could be clarified is whether or not the predictive ability of foreign language coursework attendance changes by language or language grouping. It could be helpful for practitioners to know if those students studying non-traditional languages are more likely to study abroad than their counterpart that enroll in a more traditionally studied language, as well as if they are more likely to travel to a destination where they may use those language skills. Such research could be important not just for identifying an avenue to boost study abroad participation but also for diversifying destination of study.

Future research could also examine the frequency of enrollment in foreign language coursework to evaluate if the predictive ability changes if a student enrolls in more than one course. Such analysis would be out of the structural bounds of the NSSE CPR dataset, and would need to be conducted using data from one or more institutions where such information is collected and readily available.

Suggestions for Practice

Study abroad may be seen by students, faculty, and administrators as a way to acquire, use, or hone, foreign language skills (Booker, 2001). Therefore it makes sense intuitively that a student that has participated in foreign language coursework during their first year of college may be more interested in the opportunity to continue language study abroad. It may be also that the experience of studying a foreign language, even on campus, exposes them to international concepts or themes that open a student's mind to the opportunity of global study. That this experience has a relationship with study abroad participation should encourage administrators and faculty to encourage FG students to enroll in such coursework during their first year.

Given the statistically significant relationship between study abroad and foreign language coursework, the first step for campus leaders should be to ensure that such courses are offered as well as available to FG students on their campuses. This would include advocating for funding to support foreign language course offerings on-campus. When these courses are offered, care should be taken to make sure that introductory courses are available as first-generation students often attend college less prepared than their peers (Chen and Carrol, 2005) and may not have taken the required prerequisite courses for more advanced foreign language study. Given that these students also may not be aware that such courses are available to them or where to go to seek out information about such coursework (Diel-Amen and Rosenbaum, 2003), senior administrators should make sure that academic advising staff are proactive with this population and that they reach out early to them present foreign language coursework as recommended in their first year of study. Given that low-income first-generation students may have work or family commitments, offering coursework at varied times or in alternative formats may also increase access to these courses. Senior administrators may also want to consider requiring foreign language enrollment for all students due to its predictive relationship with participation in study abroad.

Although FG students may lack family support for college (London, 1992; Wilt, 2006), it is important for administrators to reach out to student's relatives when possible and practical to explain the benefit of enrolling in foreign language coursework as well as study abroad. Removing all barriers to access to foreign language coursework is an important step when encouraging enrollment, and bringing family into the conversation about why such classes may be beneficial could be a way to remove one important obstacle for FG students.

Living in Campus-affiliated Housing

Results from this study revealed that those first-generation students who lived in campus-affiliated housing were approximately 4.01 times more likely to participate in study abroad than those who were not, a finding that was significant at the .01 level. Campus-affiliated housing, defined as either a dormitory or sorority/fraternity building had the highest impact of all significant variables in the final regression model.

Suggestions for Research

This study has demonstrated the effect that living in campus-based housing while a freshman in college has on first-generation student enrollment in international education. However such a result does not explain what it is about this experience that would predict study abroad participation. It may be that those students who live in campus affiliated housing are higher income students who may also have access to other opportunities or life experiences that would encourage study abroad participation, or that those students who do not live in dormitories have additional obligations to family or work that would keep them from departing campus for an international experience. Living in university-affiliated housing could be a luxury to some students and may not be understood by parents who have not experienced college attendance. Future research should delve into these issues more deeply.

Living in campus-affiliated housing puts students in close contact with peers, potentially boosting their integration with the campus environment (Astin, 1993; Pascarella and Terenzini, 2005). Research on this topic could empirically explore if this plays a role in their choice to participate in study abroad. Conversely, for those students who do not fit into the campus environment, living in a dormitory may make that division all the more real and provide the additional incentive to leave campus and seek another campus experience abroad where may feel a better fit. Additional academic inquiry into whether or not institutional integration as well as student satisfaction with their college environment may reveal if these areas are also important for study abroad participation.

Suggestions for Practice

Simply, higher education administrators must encourage those that do not live in campus-affiliated housing to consider doing so if it is economically feasible. Senior administrators should set aside housing grants for first-generation or low-income students so that those who may struggle to afford to do so may be more likely. Such grants may also incentivize family members to support their child's decision to live in campus housing. Housing options for students should also be plentiful and generally attractive to students. Finally, just as with foreign language study, a policy change could be supported that would require all freshman to live in campus-affiliated housing.

With all of the constituents described here, study abroad professionals, senior administrators, residence life staff, and parents, it is important to stress that for some students living in campus-affiliated housing during their first year of college may not be an acceptable or appropriate option. However, given the effect this variable has on FG student participation in study abroad all barriers to student access to campus-based housing should be removed.

Private Institution Attendance

One variable was included in the final best-fit model that a higher education administrator can not explicitly control, private institution attendance. A first-generation student that attended a private institution was 2.30 times more likely to participate in study abroad than their FG peer at a public college, significant at the .10 level. This finding is particularly challenging because the majority of FG students attend public institutions of higher education (Chen and Carrol, 2005). For this reason, higher education scholars and administrators must address this disparity in research and practice.

Suggestions for Research and Practice

Given that this variable is so highly predictive of participation in study abroad necessitates further study. Such examination should identify why this relationship exists perhaps by looking at whether or not there are differences in institutional culture or support for international experiences, or differential student or administrator access to resources that may facilitate the recruitment and participation of this population of students in study abroad such as better informing FG students about study abroad opportunities through more effective marketing of study abroad, or that the institutions have additional staff to reach out to students and support them through the application process. However, all these possibilities are just conjectures without rigorous empirical research to establish whether or not a connection between the two is or is not present, and is statistically sound. Given that study abroad data is currently scarce nationally, institutional consortia or regional accrediting bodies may be possible avenues to approach and research these institutions.

That institutional type plays a role in predicting FG study abroad participation is supported by NSSE CPR demographics. This data indicates that the overwhelming majority of FG undergraduate students that study abroad attend private institutions. This finding is important for senior leaders at public institutions and should serve as a call to action to address rampant inequity in participation among first-generation students. That FG students only represent 6.2 percent of the FG study abroad participants is significant, considering that these students make up almost a quarter of higher education enrollments (Chen and Carrol, 2005). Senior leaders should use this finding to advocate for the appropriate methods to increase study abroad participation on their campuses. Other findings from this study suggest one way to accomplish this goal would be through increased efforts at encouraging meaningful and frequent dialogue between students of different political or religious beliefs and race or ethnicities, encouraging enrollment in foreign language coursework, and living in campus-affiliated housing.

Conclusion

Enrollment in foreign language coursework, living in campus-affiliated housing and private institution attendance were all shown in this study to have varying but predictive effects on FG student enrollment in study abroad. This section has discussed specific ways to employ these findings in the areas of research and practice.

Major Finding: Null Findings of Gender, Race and Ethnicity

The results of the regression analysis on demographic variables indicated no statistically significant relationship between study abroad participation and student gender, or race or ethnicity. Gender and race or ethnicity were both treated as dichotomous variables with gender divided by male and female and race or ethnicity grouped by majority/minority populations, indicating Caucasian students as the majority and all other racial and ethnic groups categorized as minority. This null finding runs against anecdotal and empirical literature that describes gender and race or ethnicity as being important factors skewing study abroad participation rates (Dessoff, 2006; Shirley, 2006; Slind, 2004; Washington, 1998).

Suggestions for Research and Practice

That race/ethnicity and gender do not play a role in study abroad participation for first-generation students implies that further research must be done to understand why these populations may differ from all other students in higher education. Returning to the demographic characteristics of the sample, the percentage frequency of Caucasian students is smaller for those who study abroad than those who do not (78.9 percent, and 72.2 percent respectively). This suggests that overall there is greater racial or ethnic diversity of first-generation students who have chosen study abroad. Demographically, there was little difference in gender across first-generation student groups with approximately a 1 percent difference between participation and non-participation favoring male participants in the study abroad pool. In addition, the regression analysis did not indicate a statistically significant relationship between race or ethnicity and study abroad. The demographic data and null finding on gender, and race and ethnicity has important ramifications for research on this population and topic; although this finding describes the phenomenon it does not explore why first-generation males as well as racial and ethnic minorities may have an increased interest in study abroad participation.

Future research should identify if the null effect of gender on study abroad in the FG population holds across program type and perception of fit on-campus. First, King and Young's research (1994) which found that shorter programs are more attractive for male participants suggests that grouping all program types together may actually mask gender difference that occurs within program types. Second, although one non-significant variable examined in this study was a student's perception of a supportive institutional environment, this is different from a student's overall feeling of fit on-campus. It could be that some FG students feel so marginalized on their campuses that they seek to escape to another academic environment abroad. Such conjectures could not be answered by this study, but must be examined in subsequent research.

Although overall participation of FG students is low, necessitating their inclusion in the definition of underrepresented students by NAFSA: Association of International Educators (2002), this research suggests that the racial or ethnic profile of those that attend is more diverse than those who do not and represents relative parity with regards to gender. With this finding, practitioners should look to the FG student returnees from study abroad programs to serve as ambassadors for other students on campus, a practice that could be particularly important for racial and ethnic minority students.

Conclusion

FG students do not fit the national trend of decreased participation among males and minority students. Specifically the results of this study have shown a null-effect of their gender and race or ethnicity on their study abroad participation. This information necessitates additional research to understand why this phenomenon may be taking place and provides recommendations to those administrators working with this population on campuses across the United States.

Conclusions of the Major Findings

The results of this study demonstrate three major findings regarding FG student participation in study abroad; (a) that student exposure to diversity plays a role in their enrollment; (b) that select demographic variables including enrollment in foreign language coursework, living in campus-affiliated housing, and attendance at a private institution all meaningfully contribute to the final, best-fit regression model predicting participation; and finally, (c) that neither student race or ethnicity nor a FG student's gender have a statistically significant relationship with participation. This section has detailed suggestions for research and practice for higher education scholars, practitioners, and policy makers as they relate to the three major findings of the study.

Composite Suggestions for Future Research and Practice

To facilitate the use of the findings of this study, all suggestions for research and practice are presented comprehensively in this section. First, recommendations for research are detailed, second, suggestions for practice are provided. Additional areas of exploration in research and practice that relate thematically to the topic of first-generation student participation in study abroad, but not to the findings of the study, are included at the conclusion of each section.

Composite Suggestions for Future Research

This study was exploratory given that no previous studies of student engagement and study abroad participation in the population were identified. As a result of this dearth of research there are many areas that should be explored in future research.

1.   The role of general exposure to diversity on college students, as well as other underrepresented populations in the US should be explored. Confirmatory study of the findings of this study on other FG students would bolster or refute the conclusions and make for stronger assertions regarding institutional practice or take the literature in a new direction.

2.   Student exposure to diversity in its disaggregated form; institutional commitment to encouraging diverse conversations and experiences, meaningful discussions with students of another race/ethnicity; meaningful discussions with students of another socioeconomic status, and political viewpoint or religion, could reveal important information for those diversifying study abroad. This would identify if the diversity effect is a function of the combination of these experiences or if efforts should be focused in one area or another.

3.   Establish if freshman enrollment in a foreign language continues to be predictive of study abroad participation for first-generation students by looking at level or duration of study, language, or language grouping in other FG student groups. In addition, whether or not this plays a role in diversification of destination of study should be explored.

4.   Assessment of what it is about living in campus-affiliated housing during the first year of college that impacts study abroad participation would further our understanding of FG students' participation in study abroad. This could be accomplished through a review of social integration generally to see if there is a relationship between the social integration that happens in dormitories or in sorority and fraternity houses and the decision to study abroad.

5.   A study could be designed that examines student perception of fit or if student satisfaction of their campus environment encourages or discourages participation in study abroad.

6.   That private institution attendees are so overrepresented in FG study abroad merits a thorough review of this phenomenon exploring what it may be about private institution attendance that makes this possible. Determining if it is what feeds into private institution attendance in terms of student background variables or what happens within private institutions would be an important area to begin such an evaluation.

7.   Research should be conducted that uncovers if grouping all program types together alters the variables included in the final regression model and determines if a null effect of gender and race or ethnicity hold across program type and perception of fit on campus.

8.   Finally, a qualitative study of FG students who feel marginalized on their campuses who did and did not participate in study abroad could reveal if disengagement with social integration plays a role in FG student participation.

The results of this quantitative study have shown a statistically significant, predictive relationship of student exposure to diversity, living in campus affiliated housing, participating in foreign language coursework, and private institution attendance on FG student participation in study abroad. Although this relationship has been empirically proven no explanation about why this relationship exists is possible; only inference using the support of previous research. For this reason additional quantitative or qualitative research that examines why there is a relationship between each of these significant variables would assist in understanding the phenomenon of underrepresentation of first-generation students. Specifically, qualitative research could assist in describing how the socialization of students, the role of peer influence, and level family support—all variables not considered in this study—contribute to an FG student's participation in study abroad.

Composite Suggestions for Practice

On American campuses there are many involved in the practical implementation of study abroad programs. Senior administrators, faculty, front-line staff, and students all play a role in either ensuring diversity in the pool of students that seek international education or maintaining stratified participation. Although it is challenging to speak to all populations, comprehensive suggestions for practice are discussed here along with suggestions that relate to the larger issue of under-representation in study abroad programs.

1.   Institutions should continue to create an environment where meaningful and frequent interactions among different populations of students can flourish. Those institutions that have not intentionally encouraged such practice should begin to do so immediately. One way of encouraging a climate where such interactions can take place is to be transparent about the institution's intent to do so by highlighting in advertising campus events that offer the opportunity for these interactions.

2.   When implementing programming or policy decisions aimed at encouraging contact between different student populations institutions should bear in mind that it is serious and frequent interactions, not cursory or fleeting, that encourage study abroad participation among FG students. A natural fit for such discussions is in the classroom. Structured, guided discussions and thematic inclusion of diversity in curricula could be one way to achieve this goal.

3.   Practitioners should consistently seek out new ways to bring diversity into the campus experience of students. This could be through campus-based development of international, multicultural, or foreign language themed housing, but should not ignore that some FG students will not have access to much of the social and academic programming offered on-campus. As a result,

practitioners should partner with faculty to ensure that such dialogue can prosper within the walls of the classroom.

4. Senior administrators should make sure that foreign language coursework is open and available to first-year students. This may necessitate coursework being offered at non-traditional times to accommodate FG students and their additional life commitments.

5. Academic advisors should be made aware of this research and coached to discuss the option of foreign language coursework with FG students. Subsequently the benefit of foreign language coursework should be explained to FG student's family as well so that both students and family are informed about the opportunity.

6. Senior leaders should advocate for funding for foreign language offerings to ensure that such opportunities persist for consecutive years and may even consider requiring foreign language coursework for all students in their freshman year.

7. Higher education administrators should encourage all students to live in campus-affiliated housing during their first year of study if it is economically feasible. Senior leaders should also create housing grants to offer to those students who may not be able to afford campus housing. This funding may provide an additional incentive for nonsupportive family to permit students to live at college. Administrators may want to consider a policy change that would require that all students live in institution-sponsored housing during students' freshman year.

8. Finally, study abroad staff should continue to use FG study abroad returnees as ambassadors for the experience. Practically, this can involve hiring returned FG students to work in the study abroad office, by asking them to lead information sessions on study abroad opportunities, or by asking them to participate in mentor programs for FG students considering participation.

Changing the demographic characteristics of undergraduate study abroad cannot occur without intentionality on the part of higher education administrators. Just as Jane Knight (1994) suggests that successful internationalization cannot come without first developing intentional planning, successful diversification of study abroad cannot occur without diligent and thoughtful preparation. Institutions that do not currently have established efforts to diversify the student profile participating in study abroad should work to ensure that such efforts receive the support needed to succeed on their campuses and that such efforts are localized in their relevance to the type of students that enroll in their institution.

Discussion

As Knight claimed in 2004 "the international dimension of higher education is becoming increasingly important, complex, and confusing" (p. 5). Knight here was referencing the expansion of international efforts at universities world-wide, but her point can be taken and applied at a more micro level with regards to campus-based international education initiatives in the United States. As study abroad becomes more complex in type, duration, topic, and, of course, in the demographics of participating students, and efforts are made to ensure representative diversity of those students that enroll and complete global study programs, it may also become more challenging for researchers studying this population and practitioners working with these students. This is all the more reason why greater attention must be paid to this topic in research and through the identification of best practices for administrators serving this population.

A key component to internationalization of a university are the students that participate in international study programs. However, ignoring who the students are that are participating falls short of equity goals that are set in other areas of institutional practice. Higher education is a nexus of social reproduction; if campus leaders continue to provide stratified opportunities for students, a cycle of inequity will continue that does not prepare students to function in a global workplace, and world that continues to globalize. It may be challenging to intentionally diversify any portion of higher education participation, particularly among a group of students that are seemingly invisible on campus. However, this is precisely why it is critical to do so.

Although first-generation students are often pooled together because they share one important characteristic—that their parents have not attended college—they are also a group of students who have many different backgrounds, experiences, and life stories. It is with this in mind that the results from this study should be taken as only a step in the direction of a greater understanding of these students; the results cannot and should not be blindly applied to all first-generation students in all areas of higher education.

That the population demographics may favor a first-generation student with more traditional student characteristics, should not devalue the results of this study. Instead, this finding only focuses the applicability of the results. As previously stated, FG students are hard to typify, something that makes studying and serving this student population a challenge. However, this should remind those who research and/or administer educational programs for this population that they are indeed dynamic individuals united by one important characteristic. Future work will need to deconstruct the first-generation student population to examine if, and perhaps by consequence how, subsets of this highly diverse group may be similar or different with regard to their interactions with and engagement in the institutional environment as well as how these interactions may play a role in their decision to participate in study abroad.

Conclusion

The purpose of this study was to establish if a predictive relationship existed between four student engagement factors and participation in study abroad. Relevant empirical studies and literature of practice on study abroad participation and student engagement were explored through and supported by two models of college impact; Astin's Inputs Environment Outputs model (1970a, 1970b, and 1993) and Pascarella's General Model for Assessing Change (1985). Using secondary data from the 2003 and 2006 administration of the NSSE CSR a binary multiple logistic regression analysis was conducted to create the final best-fit model for first-generation student participation in study abroad.

Although no relationship was found for a student's perception of institutional support, quality of institutional relationships, or involvement with faculty and participation in study abroad, this research found that a student's exposure to diversity was impactful on their decision to seek and complete international study. In addition to the core composite variables examined in this study, three specific background or demographic variables were also found to have a predictive relationship with a student's decision to study abroad. Living in campus-affiliated housing, enrolling in foreign language coursework, and attending a private institution were all found to be statistically significant, predictive, and practically important variables for this population of students.

Through three major findings this study has provided specific suggestions for research and practice. It is perhaps through these findings, cautiously generalizable across four-year American undergraduate institutions, that institutions may begin to address the issue of low participation rates of first-generation undergraduate students in study abroad programs.

References

Aaker, D.A., Kumar, V., Day, G. (1998). *Essentials of marketing research.* New York, NY: Wiley and Sons.

Adeola, F.O., and Perry, J.A. (1997). Global study: Smooth or bumpy ride: Global study is to diversity as internship is to job experience. *The Black Collegian Online*, 10. Retrieved from: http://www.black-collegian.com/issues/1997-10/bumpy.shtml.

Alreck, P. and Settle, R. (2003). *The survey research handbook.* New York, NY: McGraw Hill.

American Council on Education, Art and Science Group LLC, and College Board. (2008). *College-Bound students' interests in study abroad and other international learning initiatives.*

Astin, A. (1970a). The methodology of research on college impact, part one. *Sociology of Education, 43*(3), 223-254.

Astin, A. (1970b). The methodology of research on college impact, part two. *Sociology of Education, 43*(4), 437-450.

Astin, A. (1993). *What matters in college.* Jossey Bass: San Francisco.

Astin, A., and Oseguera, L. (2005). Pre-college and institutional influences on degree attainment. In A. Seidman, and V. Tinto (Eds.), *College student retention: Formula for student success* (pp. 245-276). Westport, CT: Praeger Publishers.

Austin, Z. (2002). What is learnworthy? Lessons from group socialization theory for professional education and continuing professional development. *Pharmacy education. 2*(4), 161-166.

Balakis, S. and Joiner, T.A. (2004). Participation in tertiary study abroad programs: The role of personality. *International Journal of Education Management, 18*, 286-291.

Bean, J. P. (1981). Proceedings from The Association for Institutional Research 2005: *The application of a model of turnover in work organizations to the student attrition process.* Minneapolis, Minnesota.

Benjamin A. Gilman International Scholarship Program. (2006). Gilman Alumni Representative Program 2005-2006. Houston, TX: Institute of International Education.

Billson, J.M. and Terry, B.T. (1982). In search of the silken purse: Factors in attrition among first-generation students. *College and University, 58*(1), 57-75.

Bolen, M. (Fall 2001). Consumerism and U.S. study abroad. *Journal of Studies in International Education, 5*, 182-200.

Booker, R. (2001). *Differences between applicants and non-applicants relevant to the decision to apply to study abroad.* (Unpublished doctoral dissertation). University of Missouri, Columbia, MO.

Bowman, J.E. (1987). *Educating American undergraduates abroad: The development of study abroad programs by American colleges and universities.* CIEE Occasional Paper Series. New York. Council on International Educational Exchange.

Braxton, J.M, Sullivan, A.V., and Johnson, R.M. (1997). Appraising Tinto's theory of college student departure. In John C. Smart (Ed.), *Higher Education: Handbook of Theory and Research*, Vol. 12. New York, NY: Agathon Press.

Burn, B. (1980). Study abroad and international exchanges. *The Annals of the American Academy of Political and Social Science. 449*(1), 129-140.

Cash, R.W. (1993). Assessment of study abroad programs using survey of student participation. Paper presented at the Annual Forum of the Association for Institutional Research, Chicago, IL. (ERIC Document Reproduction Service No. ED 360 925).

Carini, R. M., Kuh, G. D., and Klein, S. P. (2006). Student engagement and student learning: Testing the linkages. *Research in Higher Education, 47*(1), 1-32.

Carter, E. (2006). *Parental assistance and first-year college student independence and adjustment.* (Unpublished doctoral dissertation). Syracuse University, Syracuse, New York.

Chen, X., and Carrol, C. D. (2005). *First-generation students in post-secondary education: A look at their college transcripts.* Washington, DC: U.S. Department of Education, National Center for Education Statistics.

Chichester, M., and Akomolafe, S. (2003). Minorities and underrepresented groups in international affairs and the foreign policy establishment. Paper presented at the Global Challenges and U.S. Higher Education Conference, Duke University. Retrieved from: http://www.duke.edu/web/cis/globalchallenges/research_papers.html.

Chickering, A., and Gamison, Z. (1987 March). Seven principles for good practice in undergraduate education. *The American Association for Higher Education Bulletin.*

Commission on the Abraham Lincoln Study Abroad Fellowship, Program. (2005, November). *Global competence and national needs.* Washington, DC.

Deil-Amen, R. and Rosenbaum, J. E. (2003). The social prerequisites of success: Can college structure reduce the need for social know-how? *Annals of the American Academy of Political and Social Science. 586,* 120-143.

Dessoff, A. (2006). Who's not going abroad. *International Educator. 15*(2), 20-27.

Ewell, P. and Jones, D. (1996). *Indicators of "good practice" in undergraduate education: A handbook for development and implementation.* Boulder, CO: National Center for Higher Education Management Systems.

Filkins, J.W., and Doyle, S. K. (2002, June). *First-generation and low income students: using the NSSE data to study effective educational practices and students' self-reported gains.* Paper presented at the annual forum of the Association for Institutional Research, Toronto.

Fraenkel, J. R., and Wallen, N. E. (2009). *How to design and evaluate research in education.* Boston, MA: McGraw-Hill.

Gerardi, S. (2006). Positive college attitudes among minority and low-income students as an indicator of academic success. *The Social Science Journal, 43*(1), 185-190. doi:10.1016/j.soscij.2005.12.016

Gurin, P., Dey, E. L., Hurtado, S., and Gurin, G. (2002 Fall). Diversity and higher education: Theory and impact on educational outcomes. *Harvard Educational Review, 72*(3), 330-366.

Harper, S. R., Carini, R. M., Bridges, B. K., and Hayek, J. C. (2004). Gender differences in student engagement among African American undergraduates at historically Black colleges and universities. *Journal of College Student Development, 45*(3), 271-284.

Harrison, J. K. (2006). The relationship between international study tour effects and the personality variables of self-monitoring and core self-evaluations. *Frontiers: The International Journal of Study Abroad, 8,* 1-22.

Hazeur, C. (2007). *Purposeful co-curricular activities designed to increase engagement: A practice brief based on BEAMS project outcomes.* Institute for Higher Education Policy. Washington, DC.

Hembroff, L., and Rusz, D. (1993). Minorities and overseas studies programs: Correlates of differential participation, Occasional Paper No. 30. New York:

Council of International Educational Exchange (CIEE). (ERIC Document Reproduction Service No ED 368 283). Retrieved from: http://www.ciee.org/ images/uploaded/pdf/occasional30.pdf.

Hughes, K. (2007, November 16). Remarks by undersecretary of state for public diplomacy and public affairs Karen Hughes to the Institute of International Education. Federal News Service. Retrieved from: http://www6.lexisnexis. com/publisher/EndUser?Action=UserDisplayFullDocumentandorgId=574an dtopicId=25104anddocId=1:702597051andstart=8.

Hurtado, S., and Carter, D.F. (1997). Effects of college transition and perceptions of the campus racial climate on Latino students' sense of belonging. *Sociology of Education, 70,* 324-345.

Institute of International Education. (2007). *International Scholarship Program: August 2005 Program accomplishments and summary.* Houston, Texas.

Institute of International Education. (2009). *OpenDoors Report.* Washington, D.C.

Ismail, B., Morgan, M., and Hayes, K. (2006). Effect of short study abroad course on student openness to diversity. *Journal of Food Science Education, 1,* 15-18.

Johnson, V. and Mulholland, J. (May/June, 2006). Open doors, secure borders: Advantages of education abroad for public policy. *International Educator, 15*(3), 4-7.

Juhasz, A. M. and Walker, A. M. (1987). The impact of study abroad on university students' perceptions of self. *Resources in Education, 27*(7), 1-37.

King, L. J., and Young, J. A. (1994). Study abroad: Education for the 21st century. *Die Unterrichtspraxis, 27*(1), 77-87.

Knight, J. (1994). Internationalization: Elements and checkpoints. *Canadian Bureau for International Education Research. 7,* 1-15.

Knight, J. (2004). Internationalization remodeled: Definitions, approaches and rationales. *Journal of Studies in International Education. 8,* 5-31.

Kuh, G.D. (2001). The National Survey of Student Engagement: Conceptual framework and overview of psychometric properties. Indiana University Center for Post-secondary Research and Planning: Bloomington, IN.

Kuh, G. D. (1995). The other curriculum: Out-of-class experiences associated with student learning and personal development. *Journal of Higher Education, 66,* 123-155.

Laird, T. F. N., and Kuh, G. D. (2005). Student experiences with information technology and their relationship to other aspects of student engagement. *Research in Higher Education, 46*(2), 211-233.

London, H.B. (1992). Transformations: Cultural challenges faced by first-generation students. In L.S. Zwerling and H.B. London (Eds.), *First-generation students: Confronting the cultural issues* (5-11). New Directions for Community Colleges, 80 (4). San Francisco, CA: Jossey Bass.

Lotkowski, V. A., Robbins, S. B., and Noeth, R. J. (2004). *The role of academic and non-academic factors in improving college retention.* Iowa City, IA: ACT.

MacPhee D., Kreutzer JC, and Fritz JJ. (1994). Infusing a diversity perspective into human development courses. *Child Development, 65*(2), 699-715.

NAFSA, (2002). *Subcommittee on underrepresentation in education abroad newsletter.* NAFSA: Association of International Educators.

NAFSA. (2003, November). *Securing America's future: Global education for a global age.* Washington, DC.

NAFSA. (2006). *Americans call for leadership on international education.* Washington, DC.

NAFSA. (2008, January). *Strengthening study abroad: Recommendations for effective institutional management for presidents, senior administrators, and study abroad professionals.* Washington, DC.

National Survey of Student Engagement. (2003). *College student report questionnaire.* Bloomington, IN: Indiana University Bloomington Center for Post-secondary Research.

National Survey of Student Engagement. (2006). College student report questionnaire. Bloomington, IN: Indiana University Bloomington Center for Post-secondary Research.

Norfles, N. (2003). Toward equal and equitable access: Obstacles and opportunities in international education. *Global Challenges and U.S. Higher Education Research Conference,* Duke University Durham, North Carolina.

Obama, B. (2009). *Remarks of President Barak Obama at student roundtable.* Retrieved from: http://www.whitehouse.gov/the_press_office/Remarks-Of-President-Barack-Obama-At-Student-Roundtable-In-Istanbul/.

O'Meara, P., Mehlinger, H., and Newman, R. (2001). *Changing perspectives on international education.* Bloomington, IN: Indiana University Press.

Pascarella, E. T. (1985). College environmental influences on learning and cognitive development: A critical review and synthesis. In J. Smart (Ed.), *Higher education: Handbook of theory and research* (pp. 1-61). New York, NY: Agathon Press.

Pascarella, E. T., Edison, M. I., Nora, A., Hagedorn, L. S., and Braxton, J. M. (1996). Effects of teacher organization/preparation and teacher skill/clarity on general cognitive skills in college. *Journal of College Student Development,* *37*(1), 7-19.

Pascarella, E. T., and Terenzini, P. T. (1980). Predicting freshman persistence and voluntary dropout decisions from a theoretical model. *Journal of Higher Education, 51*(1), 60-75.

Pascarella, E. T., and Terenzini, P. T. (2005). *How college affects students: A third decade of research* (First edition). San Francisco, CA: Jossey-Bass.

Pascarella, E. T. and Terenzini, P. T. (1991) *How college affects students: Findings from twenty years of research.* San Francisco: Jossey-Bass.

Pike, G. R. (2006). The convergent and discriminant validity of NSSE scarlet scores. *Journal of College Student Development, 47*(5), 550-563.

Pike, G.R. (1995). The relationships between self-reports of college experiences and achievement test scores. *Research in Higher Education, 36,* 1-22.

Pike, G. R., and Kuh, G. D. (2005). A typology of student engagement for American colleges and universities. *Research in Higher Education, 46*(2), 185-209.

Richardson, R.C., Jr., and Skinner, E.F. (1992). Helping first-generation minority students achieve degrees. In L.S. Zwerling, and H.B. London (Eds.), *First-generation students: Confronting the cultural issues* (pp. 29-43). New Directions for Community Colleges, *80*(4). San Francisco, CA: Jossey Bass.

Ryan, M. and Twibell, R. (2000). Concerns, values, stress, coping, health and educational outcomes of college students who studied abroad. *International Journal of Intercultural Relations, 24*, 409-435.

Shirley, S. (2006). *The gender gap in post-secondary study abroad: Understanding and marketing to males.* (Unpublished doctoral dissertation). University of North Dakota, Grand Forks. ND.

Slind, M. (May 2004). Barriers to diversifying education abroad. *Under representation in Education Abroad Newsletter, 1*(1), 2-3.

Smiles, R., (2001, August 2). A world-class education: Rewards abound for those who dare to teach or study abroad. *Black Issues in Higher Education.* Retrieved from: http://www.findarticles.com/cf_0/m0DXK/12_18/77398870/print.jhtml.

Stage, F.K., and Hossler, G. (2000). Where is the student? Linking student behaviors, college choice and college persistence. In J. Braxton (Ed.). *Rethinking the departure puzzle: New theory and research on college student retention.* Vanderbilt University Press.

Steinberg, M. (2007). The place of outcomes assessment in higher education today and the implications for education abroad. In M. Bolen (Eds.), *A guide to outcomes and assessment in study abroad*, Carlisle, PA: Forum on Education Abroad.

Sutton, R.C., and Rubin, D.L. (2004, Fall). The GLOSSARI project: Initial findings from a system-wide research initiative on study abroad learning outcomes. *Frontiers: The Interdisciplinary Journal of Study Abroad, 10*, 65-82.

Tinto, V., and Cullen, J. (1973). *Dropout in higher education: A review and theoretical synthesis of recent research.* Washington, DC: Office of Planning, Budgeting, and Evaluation.

Tinto, V. (1982). Limits of theory and practice in student attrition. *The Journal of Higher Education, 53*(6), 687-700.

Tinto, V. (1988). Stages of student departure: Reflections on the longitudinal character of student leaving. *The Journal of Higher Education, 59*(4), 438-455.

Tinto, V. (1993). *Leaving University: Rethinking the causes and cures of student attrition* (Second Edition). Chicago: University of Chicago Press.

Tinto, V. (1999). Taking student retention seriously: Rethinking the first year of college. *NACADA Journal, 19*(2), 5-9.

Tinto, V. (2008). *When access is not enough.* The Carnegie Foundation for the Advancement of Teaching. Retrieved from: http://www.carnegiefoundation. org/perspectives.

Umbach, P., and Wawrzynski, M. (2005, March). Faculty do matter: The role of college faculty in student learning and engagement. *Research in Higher Education, 46*(2), 153-184.

U.S. Center for Citizen Diplomacy. (2008). *Every citizen a diplomat.* Washington, DC.

U.S. Department of Education. (2006). *A test of leadership: Charting the future of U.S. higher education.* Washington, DC.

Washington, D.D. (1998). *African-American undergraduates' perceptions of an attitudes toward study abroad programs.* (Unpublished doctoral dissertation), George Mason University. Vienna, VA.

Wentland, E.J., Smith, K.W. (1993). *Survey responses: An evaluation of their validity.* San Diego, CA: Academic Press.

Whitt, E.J., Edison, M.I., Pascarella, E.T., Terenxini, P.T., and Nora, A. (2001). Influences on students' openness to diversity and challenge in the second and third years of college. *Journal of Higher Education, 72,* 172-204.

Wilt, R. (2006, Spring). A success model for low-income students. *Inquiry, 11*(1), 65-73.

Williams, F. (2007). *Study abroad and Carnegie doctoral/research extensive universities: Preparing students from Underrepresented racial groups to live in a global environment.* (Unpublished doctoral dissertation). Virginia Commonwealth University, Richmond, VA.

York-Anderson, D., C. and Bowman, S., L. (1992). Assessing the college knowledge of first-generation and second-generation college students. *Journal of College Student Development, 32,* 116-122.

Chapter Six
"I Thought I Was So Dumb. . . ":
Low-Income First-Generation College Students, Inequities in Academic Preparation and Reference Group Theory

Ashley C. Rondini, Ph.D.,
Transylvania University

Introduction

Reference group identity is developed in relation to the collectivities with which an individual perceives him or herself as having the most similarities in structural position (see Merton 1957). For students from low-income families with limited parental educational attainment, the achievement of academic success at elite universities is complicated by a number of structurally-based obstacles which differentiate their experiences from students who comprise the majority of their peer reference group on campus. Students from low-income families with limited parental educational attainment—particularly if they are students of color—are disproportionately likely to have attended under-resourced public high schools, due to the effects of pervasive, de facto class- and race-based residential segregation (Massey and Denton 1993; Oliver and Shapiro 1997; Conley 1999; Fine 2003). The lower quality of education experienced by students who attend under-resourced public high schools often compromises the degrees to which they can be realistically prepared for the academic rigor of elite university coursework, irrespective of the efforts that they devote to their studies. Since relatively few low-income first-generation college students attend elite schools, those who do attend are likely to have been distinguished as the highest academic achievers among their pre-collegiate peer reference group. Students from low income families are also less likely than the more privileged members of their peer reference group on campus to have had access to extracurricular resources and opportunities with which to acquire the cultural and human capital that would enhance their academic performance. The transition to an elite university from a low-income community, therefore typically involves a shift in the immediate peer reference group against which low-income first-generation college students compare their academic preparedness. Parents of these students are unlikely to have first-hand knowledge of higher educational institutions generally, and elite universities specifically. Subsequently, the extent to which they can directly relate to the academic challenges that their children encounter in comparison to their peer reference group in an elite university setting is likely to be limited.

The purpose of this chapter is to elucidate the processes through which low-income first-generation college students typically recognized, and attempted to reconcile, the implications of structural constraints surrounding their efforts to comfortably adjust to, and academically succeed in, an elite university environment. As the students in this study compared their own academic adjustment processes to those of their more privileged peers, they experienced disillusionment with previously held assumptions regarding their preparedness for college. Some students clearly described initial tendencies to internalize their difficulties. In so doing, these students questioned the extent to which they were "capable" of academic success. This chapter also examines how these students navigated recognition of their parents' limitations to provide them with the kinds of financial, social, and cultural capital to which their wealthier peers, with college-educated parents, often had unmitigated access. Although many of the students eventually developed structural analyses of these inequities, the majority reflected on having struggled, at some point, with the idea that they "did not belong" at an elite institution.

Review of Literature

A number of factors comprise the structural barriers against which low-income first-generation college students contend in the pursuit of success at elite universities, before and after they commence their undergraduate careers. De facto residential segregation, in the analysis of Massey and Denton, as well as other scholars, translates into racialized segregation of access to many other types of resources typically correlated with family wealth, including educational and occupational opportunities, and corresponding access to social, human, and cultural capital (Massey and Denton 1993; Oliver and Shapiro 1997; Conley 1999). Whether in terms of social network connections, access to community resources, or access to educational and occupational resource distribution and opportunity structures, families with wealth are better positioned to bolster their children's academic success than are families with fewer assets. Residential segregation on the basis of race and class has historically reproduced the disparate distribution of financial and educational resources in ways which impede the likelihood that children of color in urban environments will attain social mobility (Fainstein 1993; Zhou 1997). The social and, subsequently, educational benefits, of wealth are thereby reproduced intergenerationally within families, as well as in communities (Keister 2000). Consequently, by any measure of school quality, non-white children typically begin their schooling in significantly lower-quality, overcrowded, under-resourced schools than those attended by white children (Shapiro 2005), based upon the tax-base-determined public school funding of the community in which they live.

Research has demonstrated that immigrant parents tend to hold higher educational aspirations for their children than do non-immigrant parents, at all socio-economic levels (Ogbu 1978; Kao and Tienda 1998; Cheng and Starks 2002; Kao 2004; Feliciano 2006; Kim 2008). Particularly in low-income immigrant families of color, the children of these parents are faced with the prospect of attempting to fulfill their parents' high aspirations for them without access to the same kinds of resources and opportunities enjoyed by their white, middle class, American-born peers with which to do so (Louie 2004; Feliciano 2006). Scholars have also found that racial minority students are generally likely to have higher educational aspirations than their white counterparts when socioeconomic status is taken into account (Feliciano 2006; Cheng and Starks 2002; Kao 2004; Kao and Tienda 1998; Qian and Blair 1999; Goyette and Xie 1999; Kim 2008). For low income, recent immigrant, and/or racial minority students, high educational aspirations are often mismatched to resources and opportunities available with which to realize them, due to the structural inequalities embedded within racially and socioeconomically segregated residential neighborhoods and public educational systems (Portes, McLeod, and Parker 1978; Oliver and Shapiro 1997; Conley 1999; Shapiro 2005).

The U.S. Department of Education reports that students who are the first in their families to pursue an undergraduate education comprise a minority of the student population at public four-year educational institutions, and an even smaller percentage at elite, private four-year institutions (Engle, Bermeo, and O'Brien 2006). Similarly, students from families in the lowest-income quartile are significantly less likely to participate in higher education than are their more privileged peers (Swail 2002: 19). Even when admitted, first-generation college students are less likely than their peers with college-educated parents to remain enrolled in four-year institutions and successfully attain a baccalaureate degree (Choy 2001; Pike and Kuh 2005). Among the low-income students who do enroll in four year institutions, a disproportionate percentage will leave school prior to earning a bachelor's degree (Hebel 2007; McSwain and Davis 2007). The U.S. Department of Education estimates that 43 percent of first-generation college students leave college without a degree, as opposed to 20 percent of those students whose parents had earned degrees (Engle, Bermeo, and O'Brien 2006). Risks associated with underrepresentation and attrition are exacerbated even further for low income and/or first-generation college students of color (Pike and Kuh 2005; Swail 2002; Carnevale and Fry 2000; Terenzini, Springer, Yeager, Pascarella, and Nora 1996).

Reference Group Theory

Merton advanced a general concept of "reference groups" (1957) to refer to the collectivities with which individuals most closely identify themselves. Reference groups are comprised of the people with whom an individual is most likely to compare him or herself, and as such they play a crucial role in the process of shaping one's identity. When an individual's structural circumstances drastically change, it is likely that the normative expectations that influenced the formation of his or her reference group identity in the previous context may need to be adjusted in some respects to integrate the expectations and social norms of the new environment. In the process of transitioning from one structural setting to another, fissures may develop between the individual and the reference group with which she or he had formed a sense of identification in the first context. The salience of a peer group identity may undergo dissolution as a result of these changes, risking an experience of disruption to the individual's sense of self.

The high school peer reference groups of low-income first-generation college students' are likely to have had consistently limited means and degrees of access to educational resources and opportunities, as was structurally determined by their circumstances. These students in the study, who had graduated at the top of their high school classes, were inclined to believe that they were well-equipped for academic success at college. For students whose family members were not generally college-educated, their acceptance to an elite university had provided them with a privileged status relative to the reference group of their extended families. It was not until these students' were surrounded by the reference group of their campus community that they came to recognize the shortcomings of their educational experiences in high school, relative to the high school experiences of their more privileged peers. In a dynamic described by Merton in his theory of "relative deprivation", students' academic experiences were recontextualized on campus, catalyzing a new process of social comparisons in which their own positions were found to be "unfavorable" (see Merton 1957). The experience of "normlessness" that this process brought about for students was difficult for them to explain to their parents and family members, who had not had similar experiences at elite institutions from which to develop a comparative frame of reference regarding the impact of pre-collegiate educational disparities on academic success.

Research Design and Method

This chapter represents one section of findings drawn from a broader qualitative, inductive study of the experiences of educational mobility for low income first-generation college students on an elite campus, conducted between 2008 and 2010. Data for the study was gathered through in-depth interviews with low-income first-generation college students enrolled at an elite private university, and parents of those students. I have employed a grounded theory analytical approach to this project, wherein the dominant themes and insights gleaned from the data itself have become the subsequent foci of my analysis (Strauss 1998; Charmaz 2006).

Research Site

"The University of the Northeast" is the pseudonym for a small, private, northeastern research university with a full-time undergraduate student body of approximately 3,300. The university has elite admissions standards, accepting only 32 percent of the students who apply. The university's website reports that 82 percent of entering first year students had been in the top 10 percent of their graduating high school class. The combined cost of tuition, room, and board for the 2009-2010 academic year was $48,468. Approximately 14-15 percent of students on campus are members of the first-generation of their families to pursue a baccalaureate degree, and the percentage of students of color[1] has varied between 14 percent and 18 percent in recent years. There are a number of programs in place through the university's Academic Services program to support students from underrepresented backgrounds. The university's Trio Student Support Services Program is funded through the U.S. Department of Education. The percentage of SSSP students that has successfully graduated from the university has ranged between 90-96 percent over the past four years. On average, the SSSP office reports that 90 percent of the students that participate in its program are students of color. To be eligible for the services offered through SSSP, a student must be a U.S. citizen or permanent resident. Department of Education guidelines require that of the students served by the SSSP program, two-thirds must be low-income first-generation students, and the other one-third must be either low-income, *or* first-generation, *or* diagnosed with a disability. Students who participate in the program have access to the benefits of professional academic advising, individual tutoring services, academic skills workshops, peer mentoring, and interactive programming and events throughout their time at the university. At any given time, campus-wide membership in the SSSP program at the University of the Northeast is capped at 135 students. In the year 2009-2010, there were 300 members of the incoming first year class who would have been eligible to participate in SSSP. This means that the majority of the population of eligible students on campus did not have access to the SSSP's services.

Sampling

The student participants in this study were recruited from the undergraduate student body of the University of the Northeast during the 2008-2009 academic year. My own past employment in multiple positions within the office of Academic Services enabled me to supplement interview data for this study with insights gleaned from informal ethnographic observations, as well as from interactions with students and co-workers over the six years previous to the start of this project. Student participants in the study were identified through a broad snowball sampling approach, utilizing three primary recruitment techniques. First, I hung recruitment posters in and near the Academic Services Offices where programs and services targeting the needs of low-income first-generation college students on campus are centrally housed. Secondly, I extended informal outreach to students with whom I had teaching and mentoring relationships to encourage them to talk to friends who might be interested in participating.[2] Finally, I informally enlisted the support and assistance of professional staff in the Academic Services office as referral sources for students who might be interested in participating. Because I utilized the programs offered by the Academic Services Offices as venues for recruiting my sample, the students in the study are disproportionately representative of the population of low income first-generation college students on campus that is actively connected to these services.

My sample criteria was designed to cultivate what Frankenberg calls "a purposive rather than random strategy for gathering interviews" (Frankenberg 1997: 26), wherein certain kinds of experiences are over-represented for the purpose of gaining specific insights into the range of perceptions constructed by individuals who share those experiences. This sample reflects the qualitative research goal of investigating nuanced processes of "meaning-making", rather than determining statistically representative measurements of experiences or outcomes (Denzin and Lincoln 1994). Participants in this study:(a) were over the age of 18; (b) were graduates of public high schools; (c) were the first of their families to pursue a baccalaureate degree, and (d) were eligible for federal Pell Grant financial aid funding (meaning that the student is from a family which has an income level of less than 150 percent of the poverty line); or (e) were the parent/guardian of a student who met the aforementioned criteria and was participating in the study. I collected data through a total of 30 in-depth interviews, yielding a total of nearly 800 pages of transcribed data. Sixteen of the interviews were with students, and fourteen of the interviews were with the parents of those students. On average, each interview lasted between 2 and 3 hours. I was unable to interview a parent for three of the students. The mismatch of numbers here reflects the fact that there was one family in which both parents requested the opportunity to participate.

Within the sample, fifteen participants (six of the students and nine of the parents) were women, and fifteen participants (ten of the students and five of the parents) were men. I interviewed a racially diverse sample, while remaining attentive to how racialization and racism informed students' and families' creations and articulations of social meanings. I situated the micro-level experiences of racialization processes within the broader intersections of race, class, and gender as they pertained to educational access, socioeconomic mobility, and identity formation. In total, the racial breakdown (as self identified) of the sample was as follows: ten participants (six students and four parents) identified as Black, African American, African, or Afro-Caribbean; eleven participants (six students and five parents) identified as Latino/a, Hispanic, Mexican, or Mexican American; one student participant identified as Asian/Asian American; two participants (one student and one parent) identified as Arab/Arab American; two participants (one student, and one parent) identified as white; and three participants (one student and two parents) chose to identify as Guyanese.

Study Design

For the first stage of my research, I conducted semi-structured, in-depth interviews with first-generation college students from low income families. The student interviews were conducted on campus, in the same building that houses the offices of the aforementioned programs supporting low income and first-generation students. Student interviews were conducted in English. My interview guide was designed to elicit open-ended responses about perceived educational opportunities, achievements, and challenges. I invited participants to share their impressions of the processes through which they have (or have not) acclimated to the norms of their respective campus environments. I also invited participants to describe the ways they connected their experiences as students at private universities to their membership in their families and communities of origin.

For the second stage of my research, I conducted similarly semi-structured, in-depth interviews with the parents or guardians of these students. This data provided information regarding the interpretative schema through which parents understood their children's educational opportunities, achievements, and challenges. I also invited these participants to describe how they interpreted the connection between their child's pursuit of higher education and their family or community member-ship. For many of the parents that participated in the study, English was a second language. I had asked the students in advance what their parents' first language was, and arranged for the assistance of translators for the interviews wherein students had indicated that their parents would likely feel more comfortably speaking in their first language. For interviews with five of the parents in the study, I employed the services of Spanish-speaking translators, who alternately conveyed my questions and the respondents' answers. The translators also assisted in the later transcription of these interviews.

All student and parent participants signed informed consent forms which detailed the purposes, structure, and intended distribution of the study, along with information regarding their rights to decline questions, stop the interviews, and opt not to have their interview sessions recorded. All of the participants agreed to have interviews digitally recorded for transcribing purposes. In all cases, I compensated participants for their time with a modest stipend. After the interviews were transcribed, I utilized the Atlas.ti qualitative data management software to initially code the transcripts for broad themes[3], and then again in accordance to the more specific themes that emerged from the data. The data, analysis, and findings presented in this paper were developed from one of these emergent themes, related to the intersecting implications of being from a low-income family with limited parental educational attainment, and having had secondary schooling experiences in an under-resourced public school setting, on a campus wherein the majority population does not share these experiences.

Grounded Theory Analysis

I analyzed the data from the semi-structured interviews in this study using a grounded theory approach, whereby I continually compared transcripts between interviews as my data collection process continued. In so doing, I was able to identify emerging themes in the research, while remaining data-driven. Glaser (1965) advocated qualitative research involving the constant comparison of data to enhance our understandings of social issues impacting individuals on a personal level. My approach is in keeping with the methodological recommendations of Glaser and Strauss, who argued that theoretical framings of sociological insights should be developed during the course of the researcher's data collection process (Glaser and Strauss 1967). Charmaz proposed that grounded theory research could produce "constructions of reality", reflecting "research participants' implicit meanings [and] experiential views" (Charmaz 2006: 10). To this end, my ongoing grounded theory analysis of data collected throughout the course of my research has enabled me to critically engage with the "constructions of reality" with which participants contended within the context of their own experiences.

Findings

A central dimension of inequality on campus unfolded when students became conscious of the discrepancies between the limited academic preparation for college that they received through their secondary schooling, and the significantly more comprehensive preparation received by their more privileged peers on campus. The first-generation students who came to college at the top of their high school classes, celebrated for having received the highest accolades in their families and communities, were then faced with the need to reconcile these images of themselves with their new-found recognition of deficits in academic skills and knowledge. For many students, gaining awareness of these inequities caused their confidence in their capacities for academic success to falter. Students' anecdotal accounts described their adjustment to the rigorous academic expectations and standards of their elite university environment as a struggle.

'I wasn't as prepared as I thought I would be':
Recognizing Past Educational Deficits

In the earliest stage of the academic adjustment process, students began to critically question whether they were equipped with the knowledge and academic skills necessary for success in college. Katrina, a twenty-two year old Black student, shared that her sense of this imbalance remains with her still, even several years into her undergraduate experience:

> for the educational issues, compared to being here and compared to where I *had* been, there is clearly an inequality. I am in my junior year, and I am just starting to get the hang of college, and that is pretty sad.

Relative to the expectations of their previous educational environments, Katrina and other students described feeling caught "off guard" by the challenges posed to their academic performance at the University of the Northeast. These students found that their college courses presupposed knowledge and/or mastery of material, concepts, and skills to which they had either not received substantial instruction—or in some cases, had not even been exposed—during their secondary schooling. Upon being confronted with this reality, Isabella, a twenty-one year old Latina student of Salvadoran descent, described her retrospective understanding of this dynamic:

> My high school was OK, but it lacked resources and I was at a dis-advantage . . . they just gave out grades, [and] they didn't really care. Even though I had a high GPA, my SATs were really bad.

Given the statistical odds that are stacked against the likelihood that low-income first-generation college students will matriculate at elite institutions at all, it is perhaps unsurprising that those who do were often among the most distinguished scholars at their respective high schools. The consequence is that these students may enter into the university environment with a false sense of mastery of skills in which, unbeknownst to them, they have not received adequate education. In another example, when asked what changes he has seen in himself since beginning his college experience, David, a nineteen year old Black student, referred to his academic performance as he replied:

> I became more humble in the sense of thinking that 'I'm the man'. . . in certain situations I realized that you just got to work a little harder, [rather] than do like I did in high school, where I kind of relaxed all the time.

David had encountered a challenge to the construction of his identity which he had previously based on an ease with academic success. While the "narrative biography" of his academic trajectory to this point was characterized by the distinctive prestige associated with his high academic achievement, the shift in context to an elite private university created a disruption to his sense of scholastic efficacy. He was forced, in this sense, to re-conceptualize the ease with which he had previously succeeded. David's previous experiences had led him to believe that his accomplishments had been solely a reflection of his own innate talent, intelligence, and effort. However, he now had to reconcile this understanding of his past experiences with the realization that he had received the majority of his education in environments that were shaped by constraints on the resources with which to sufficiently challenge him. Irrespective of David's readily apparent intellectual prowess, his intelligence and capacities for the acquisitions of academic skills had not been pushed to the realization of their fullest potential during high school. As a result, David's perception of his own aptitude had gradually become skewed, because the academic expectations and standards that he had always exceeded had not been commensurate to those of his peers in wealthier schools and communities. Subsequently, when faced with the challenges of rigorous coursework that presupposed degrees of preparation that he had not received, he began to doubt himself.

A sense of "loss" was experienced as these students began to understand the implications of their high schools' shortcomings for their experiences in an environment which implicitly rewarded the academic spoils of socioeconomic privilege. They described feelings of surprise and resentment in relation to their new understandings of the limited extent to which the internal resources of intelligence and talent could predict their academic success. To this effect, Roberto, a nineteen year old Latino student of Dominican descent, recalled:

> It felt very unfair. I was unprepared, and I didn't hate my school, but I couldn't believe that they didn't prepare me for a lot of other things. It's frustrating, because I try not to regret my high school. . . . But they were too small to offer AP classes. The classes, to be honest—like chemistry— were very like. . . [pause] . . . well, what I learned in one year in chemistry in high school was gone in a month here.

Students like Roberto and Isabella had previously received the message from their respective educational environments that their capabilities were developed to a level which surpassed the utmost standards of academic rigor and achievement. The repercussions of this dynamic are compounded by the pervasiveness of the meritocracy paradigm which propagates the disproportionate attribution of success or failure to individual level efforts, while rendering structural constraints invisible. For many low-income first-generation students, their parents' steadfast belief in American meritocracy had fueled the urgency with which they had purposely cultivated high educational aspirations in their children. With strong socialization into this ideology, these students frequently endured an experience akin to the idea of having the proverbial "rug pulled out from under" them. They are forced to recognize the deficiencies in their previous schooling, and, subsequently, in their own academic skills and knowledge base, despite their hard work and the previous accolades that it had afforded them. This is evident in the following commentary by Alejandro, a nineteen year old student of Mexican descent:

> I had a teacher tell me that my writing was not up to par with college writing. I failed my papers. She said that I failed the class. . . . That hurt, because I took AP and I was at the top of my class. Since elementary, I

was top of my class. In elementary school I was salutatorian. In middle school, top 20 percent. In high school the same thing: top twenty. I graduated with honors. Then come here, and have a teacher tell me that my writing wasn't up to par and that I'm not a good writer or that I'm not a good analyzer or that I am not a good 'whatever'? It kind of hurt, but then you also see the reality, and I wasn't as prepared as I thought I would be. It was definitely a big change in terms of, in high school not to be cocky or bragging, things just came naturally to me. I could just skim a book, or read a book, and take a test, and get an A on it. Some of the kids really had to put work into it, so I kind of got a little confident in the things that I felt came naturally. In mathematics, for example, I got a merit award. I would teach kids, and feel like the kids didn't understand the simplest things, because it just came naturally to me. . . . I got a little too confident in thinking that things came naturally. . . . It was a big jump.

The disjuncture in academic standards often resulted in lower initial grades on papers and exams than these students had ever previously received. Alejandro's account demonstrates the extent to which he realized his own concept of academic rigor would need to be re-calibrated to fit the expectations of his new environment, but also suggests that he questioned whether his sense of himself as a competent and capable student, also suddenly required readjustment. This initial stage of the adjustment process often led students to internalize the cause of their academic difficulties, and ultimately begin to doubt that they were "cut out" for an elite university education. Students had to adjust to the fact that the academic achievements that had seemed to "come naturally," as Alejandro said, would be far more hard-won for them in their new environment.

'I thought I was SO dumb': The Comparative Implications of Broader Inequities in Secondary Schooling Resources and Opportunities

Students vacillated between framing their academic difficulties in terms of individual-level "deficits", and the consequences of structural inequities. They expressed self-doubt and frustration in relation to both explanatory frameworks, and often conflated the two when they described their experiences. As demonstrated by the previous examples, recognition of past educational deficits introduced doubts for students about their likelihood of success. These doubts posed a disruption to the self-identities that had been shaped by the sense of academic efficacy that the students had developed throughout their secondary schooling. In Giddens' (1991) terms, the experience posed a potential contradiction to the "narrative biography" within which students had constructed their identities as exceptional scholars. Overlapping with this experience of dissonance, an additional layer of doubt entered into these students' self-concepts, when they began to recognize the extent to which their more privileged peers had been "buffered" from similar experiences by their disproportionate degrees of access to pre-collegiate educational resources and opportunities.

In other words, the students described beginning to understand that the mismatch between their own levels of preparedness and those demanded of them were not simply a function of the high school-to-college-level academic transition. Rather, they began to recognize that many of their peers, who constituted the predominantly white, middle-to-upper-class student body at the University of the Northeast, had been substantially *better* prepared for college-level academic work upon arrival. In some ways, the development of structural understandings could function to "spare" students the burden of attributing their academic difficulties to deficits in their own intelligence and capabilities. At the same time, the sense that so much of their educational experience was being shaped by structural factors over which they had no control was also a source of frustration, discouragement, and feelings of disempowerment. Similarly, in an account of how he viewed the peers on campus with whom he had come into contact, Alejandro described feelings of uncertainty and insecurity regarding how his own academic performance would compare to theirs:

> You . . . meet people who—I don't want to say are better than you but definitely know a lot more and are a lot more prepared than you are. . . I am not going to lie, I definitely was not prepared.

Most students described the recognition of this inequity as a source of even more profound self-doubt, combined with increased degrees of separateness from their environment, and a burgeoning sense of indignant disappointment. Lydia, a twenty-two year old, Dominican-born Latina student, recalled clearly how the comparisons that she drew between herself and classmates left her feeling academically inadequate.

> When I first got here especially in my classes, I thought I was *so* dumb. Seriously, all these people know so much and they speak so eloquently. They sound like they know so much about the world. I didn't consider myself smart enough to be here. . . In comparison to my peers I felt that I didn't belong here academically. I felt that I was not prepared enough to be here. In high school the longest paper that I ever wrote was *maybe* 5 pages. So, to have someone here tell me you need to write a 10-13 page paper, I was like, "What? What am I going to write about?" I came from such a different—I guess academic background. . . I wasn't exposed to a lot of things that people here knew, like every Shakespeare book, or any of that. I wasn't familiar with that. To me, hearing people talk about certain topics that I didn't know about, or certain books that I never had the chance to read. . . I felt *very* out of place.

A number of students described feelings of insecurity, anxiety, or—with the conflation of individual and structural explanatory frameworks—inadequacy, upon realizing that their peers had experienced academic preparation for college-level coursework far beyond that to which they had access. In a similar narrative of feeling like "the only one" in a classroom who was not engaging with the material as quickly or easily as it seemed her classmates were, Tara, a nineteen year old Jamaican-born Black student, described her experience of this stage as follows:

> In classes everyone seems so well prepared. . . . So this is routine for a lot of people; it's not anything *new*. It's new to *me* a little bit so it's harder for me. I am just now getting into the groove of the class at the end of the semester. That's funny huh? For some they were at the point that I am at, at the beginning. . . . I [came here] as prepared as I could be, because I took the best that I was offered at my school. . . . But I just feel that some people are more confident in raising their hands and discussing the readings because they know it better, while I am kind of learning. They have already been taught it.

Tara felt alienated from her classmates as she began to perceive the differences between their previous exposure to materials germane to the course, and her own lack of such exposure. For others, more pronounced feelings of resentment emerged in response to their awareness of the extent to which these relative degrees of advantage (or disadvantage) in the classroom hinged upon structural factors to which individual level effort and intelligence were not centrally relevant. Gabriel, a twenty year old Ghanaian-born Black student, recounted his frustration during his adjustment process to the demands of college coursework, and the study skills that he had to rapidly acquire in face of these new challenges:

> I guess my freshman year what frustrated me the most was [that] I remember after I got my grades back, from like my first two chemistry exams. I didn't do as well as I wanted. I remember writing this down: 'this is really unfair coming from the Bronx I haven't had the same amount of education as some of these other students coming from really good high schools.' I was really frustrated and I felt I wasn't really prepared enough to be where I am and I was struggling just trying to get over that. . . . It was very frustrating because coming in as a freshman there is a large spectrum on the plane that each student is in. There are some students who are very prepared and there are some students that haven't been as prepared. . . . Initially, I felt the education I was receiving there was good. But coming here, there are some students that have been prepared way above the level of education that we have received. I thought "I don't belong here. This is out of my league.

Gabriel's comparison between his own educational background and that of his peers destabilized his confidence, and left him with a sense of disempowerment regarding his capacity to determine his own educational outcomes through effort alone. The prospect of having to reconcile his newly acute understanding of educational inequities in secondary schooling with his high academic aspirations was daunting. Like many of his peers, his understanding of the extent to which structural factors had left him ill-prepared for his coursework led him to question how he could possibly succeed to the extent for which he had hoped.

'She has no idea what this feels like. . . ': Acute "Crises of Confidence" and The Limits of Familial Support

Most of the students in the study described having entered into a point of "crisis" in their confidence regarding the extent to which they could realistically see themselves succeeding at college, given these disparities of previous access to educational resources and opportunities. The term "crisis" is appropriate here, because it denotes the sense of acute panic that several students described, in not knowing where to turn to address the obstacles that they were only beginning to understand that they would confront. While students contended with degrees of differentiation and disconnection from families and peers at home, they also developed a sense of disconnection and differentiation from their new environment. Similarly, they perceived significant differences between themselves and the peers who were *not* struggling with the same adjustment challenges, or to the same extent, that they were. The cumulative impact of these fissures confounded their difficulty in reconciling their college experiences into their existing identity, because initial attempts to fit one into the other often seemed "mismatched".

Students with parents who were highly supportive of their educational pursuits struggled with the previously unfamiliar fear of falling short of their families' high expectations of them. For students who attempted to explain to their parents how the unanticipated pressures of their new environment were weighing upon them, the well-intended reassurances of unwavering faith in their abilities that parents offered in response sometimes had the ironic effect of increasing students' anxieties about their current struggles. Reflecting on her attempts to convey the degree of difficulty she was initially having at school to her mother, Tara recalled:

> I never really thought about it until now, but she didn't go through this so it's not like I was reaching her. . . . She didn't do this at all. She just has these expectations, even though she has no idea what this feels like or what this is about. She just assumes that I should just be able to be the best or something. I am really not here. There are people who have been doing college level things all their lives, I think.

Tara's mother, Corina, while deeply desiring to support Tara's happiness and success at school, was not able to relate to her experiences closely enough to provide the kind of validation that her daughter would have wanted to receive. Consistent with Tara's assessment, my interview with Corina provided insight into her unconditional faith in Tara's capacities to succeed. Corina framed her unwavering confidence in Tara's success as the logical reflection of what she thought of as her daughter's "natural" intelligence. When I asked Corina about her communication with Tara regarding her coursework, she gave the following reply:

> She talked to me about the classes. . . [pause]. . . . Mostly I leave it up to her because I don't know much about those classes, so all I can do is leave it up to her. 'Try and do the best that you can'. I couldn't advise her, and say do this or do that, because I don't know. I don't say; I leave it up to her. She was always brilliant, and always doing things on her own since she was little.

For Tara, her mother's absolute confidence in her capacities to succeed simultaneously provides her with comfort and tremendous frustration. While Tara has undoubtedly benefitted from her mother's ongoing encouragement and support over the course of her lifetime, she is confronted by the limitations of this form of support in the face of the structural inequities that inform her current academic challenges, irrespective of her own intelligence and efforts. Corina, who knows that her own limited education has not prepared her to assist Tara in the management of her coursework content, relies upon reiteration of her confidence in Tara's "brilliance", as the strategy of support to which she has access. In times of the most acute academic self-doubt for Tara, when Corina hopes to support her the most, these strategies actually result in the unintended consequence of heightening Tara's anxieties. Tara is caught between her strong desire to affirm her mother's faith in her, and her fear that the deficits in her secondary schooling may have created constraints on her ability to do so that are too significant to overcome.

The circumstance of Corina's limited educational attainment positions Tara at a comparative disadvantage to her peers who have access to readily applicable support and guidance from their college-educated parents and family members. Other students described feeling burdened by their parents' assumptions of their abilities to successfully "figure out" how to succeed at college, even as they are unable to provide concrete suggestions as to how he might go about doing so. When asked what aspect of his experience of being the first member of his family to go to college was most difficult for him, Romeo, a twenty year old Arab student of Egyptian descent, paused for several moments, and then replied:

> I am walking in a dark tunnel. You don't know what is going to happen at the end of the tunnel. I have thought, "If I was second or third, I would have a light to guide me". But everyone in my family—they can't help me, because none of them ever went to college. . . . I am *still* confused about college. *Am* I still missing something? What *can* I do to improve my GPA?

The imagery of the "dark tunnel" that Romeo uses to describe his experience conveys associations with apprehension and vulnerability. With the statement "You don't know what is going to happen at the end of the tunnel," Romeo betrays some of the doubt, insecurity, and fear that he carries with him regarding the possibility of failure in his academic endeavors. At the same time, he is acutely aware that his family is unable to provide more guidance for him, and that part of his experience as "the first" in his family to go to college will inevitably entail feeling directionless at times. Like Tara, Romeo also reflected on the limited extent to which his father, Akil, was able to offer useful guidance pertaining to his college education, apart from the reiteration of its importance. Romeo recalled:

> He left everything to me. He did not say too much. He trusts me a lot. My eighteen year old sister is a problem and is always deviating from that college system. So he is right on top of her; "stop cutting classes and go to school". But he couldn't do much for me. He could try to give me money for books, but he didn't really know too much about the credits and stuff. I told him "I am taking four and a half classes," and he was like, "aren't you supposed to be taking eight?" I said, "Dad what are you talking about? This is college, not high school."

In the commentary above, Romeo buffers the difficulties posed by his father's limited capacity to advise him by framing the absence of assistance as a reflection of his father's "trust" in him. Like Corina framing her confidence that Tara will succeed in terms of Tara's inherent capabilities (e.g., her "brilliance"), Akil's blanket faith in Romeo's inherent ability to do well in any circumstances is framed here as a compliment. He contrasts this dynamic with his father's continual attempts to encourage his younger siblings to achieve scholastically. However, Romeo then goes on to describe a past attempt by his father to make inquiries regarding his academic pursuits, which Romeo had dismissively rebuked as uninformed. The use of both anecdotes, side-by-side, demonstrates a level of ambivalence described by several of the students. On one hand, Romeo takes pride in his independence, and regards his father's acceptance of it as a mark of faith in him. On the other hand, he is also aware that there is no viable alternative for him; he could not elect to accept more guidance from his father, because he is aware that his father lacks the resources and knowledge with which to provide more.

In a different manifestation of this kind of disconnection, Lydia, a twenty-two year old Latina student of Dominican descent, described her own exasperation with what she perceives to be her family's unwillingness to concede that her academic pursuits are, in fact, challenging enough to require "hard work" and create stress for her. In the following extended account, she recalled a conversation with her mother which was illustrative of this sentiment, and then went on to place her mother's comments in the broader context of her family's perceptions of higher education:

> I pulled an all-nighter [sic] writing a paper. [My mother] didn't understand that. I called her at 1:00 a.m. because I was walking home alone, and I was really nervous. She said, "What are you doing up at this time of

night? Why would you spend the whole night writing a paper? Why would you ever spend so much time writing an assignment?" She doesn't understand. She has no knowledge of my assignments. She doesn't understand the time they require. She doesn't understand why a library would be open all night. She doesn't understand that. . . . For [my family], going to school is not like having a job. For them going to school is not that difficult. Like, "what do you *do*? You sit there, and that's it.". . . . They don't understand. They compare the jobs that they have, and that is why they don't have any time. They think that I have all the time in the world, because all I do is go to classes and then go home. . . . When I go home, they say, "*How* many classes are you taking? Four? *Four* classes and you think you don't have any time? *Why*?" They don't get it. They don't get that this is like a job. Because they do a lot of physical work, they think that sitting down in a classroom is really not that difficult. We have a lot of issues with that; "How do *you* not have time? You don't *do* anything all day!" That is what they tell me.

While Lydia's family had encouraged her to pursue an education, their limited understanding of the challenges involved in doing so made it impossible for her to receive the kind of encouragement and validation from them that she desired. The academic accolades that Lydia received in high school, as well as the English language fluency that her American schooling had facilitated, had led her predominantly first-generation immigrant family to believe that her life (including her college education) would be "easy" in comparison to their lives. In combination with the need to battle painful fears of inferiority to her peers, the perception that her efforts to persevere and succeed were being minimized by her family weighed particularly heavily upon her. Because she is the first member of her entire extended family to undertake a four-year degree, she struggles to translate the expectations of her educational environment into a frame of reference to which any of her family members can relate. Her family's lack of understanding regarding her college experiences is an ongoing source of frustration for Lydia.

"Lifelines": The Necessity of Non-Familial Support

In characterizing her academic difficulties, Katrina, a twenty-two year-old Black student, described being depressed, exhausted, and overwhelmed at times. While Katrina recognized that the deficits in her high school education have placed her at a disadvantage in comparison to her peers, she is constrained, by her financial obligations, in her capacities to devote as much extra time to her studies as she would need to feel "caught up" with other students. She recounts:

I went through stages where I felt I didn't belong here. That is really hard too. I wouldn't get bad grades but I noticed on a lot of my papers, a lot of the professors were saying the same thing about my writing style. It was depressing. I didn't get what I was doing wrong. Now I am at a point where I understand what the university expects of me, and that papers are structured this way. But I wasn't taught that in high school, so I am *constantly* trying to catch up. I am learning a lot, and I have learned a lot, but I am also overwhelmed and sometimes work is a factor as well.

Katrina does seek out additional assistance within the support structures available to her. However, she is not able to do so to an extent which effectively alleviates the pressure and self-doubt with which she contends in her attempts to navigate the coursework for which her high school experiences did not prepare her. When I asked how she coped with the intense pressures that she had described, she replied:

> I just do it. I have no other option. I use my friends to help me a lot more. I go to the writing center more, whenever I am not working. I try to use the resources available to me.

For Katrina and other students, campus support resources, staff members and peer networks became crucially important means for "intervention" in what might have otherwise resulted in a downward spiraling of students' educational experiences. The experience of "crisis" was, to some degree, mitigated through establishing connections with support resources, whether peers with like experiences, or staff members who were sensitive to the particular dilemmas faced by low income first-generation college students. In almost every instance wherein students named specific persons on campus who had significantly assisted them in times of great crisis, the staff person identified was affiliated with the Office of Academic Services, or the Student Support Services Program, both of which are sites oriented towards the needs of this specific population. Describing the critical role of an academic advisor and mentor employed through the Academic Services Office, Lydia reflected:

> He has been a mentor in every sense of the word. He has really, really helped me a lot. I would speak to him about my family. He heard me and understood where I was coming from, which was very important for me. He just went above and beyond his role as a mentor. Every time I had an issue I felt that I could call him up and tell him that "I am having a tough time with this", or "I need your advice." He was definitely one of the people that helped me stay at [the University of the Northeast], and graduate, and *survive*. If it wasn't for him it would have been so much more difficult, and I don't know if I would still be here.

While it could be argued that many college students, irrespective of their background, benefit from the guidance of mentors and academic advisors, institutionally based supports like these are of pronounced necessity to low-income first-generation college students. When students in the study spoke about the college personnel to whom they turned for advice and assistance in navigating their academic pursuits, the language of "survival" used here by Lydia was repeatedly employed. A number of students describe the support and guidance of academic advisors and mentors as the "saving grace" which brought them through these profound doubts as to their potential for success. In addition, interviews with parents often revealed a sense of indebtedness and relief with regard to knowledge of students' interactions with college personnel. Despite never having met students' mentors and advisors on campus in most cases, several parents knew of these individuals by name, based on students' accounts of their guidance and support. For some students, commonalities of experience were identified through contact with friends from home who, like them, were among the few who had gone on to attend competitive universities and were suffering from similar doubts, insecurities, and feelings of isolation. Gabriel recalled his early communication with another friend of his from high school, who had also gone on to attend an elite university:

> I remember talking to one of my friends in high school who felt the same way . . . he was really getting discouraged. His thoughts were: why was he even there at that school? I remember him saying, "There is no reason for me, a kid from the Bronx, to even be here"; "I shouldn't even be here". I remember saying "If you made it this far, you just have to put in the hard work and once you graduate we should all be on the same plane". . . . But it was discouraging; I felt similar to the way he felt, coming from the Bronx.

Gabriel invokes structurally based commonalities of experience regarding educational inequities as a way to engender feelings of solidarity, even as he solicits his friend's individual level resolve to combat the implications of their shared experiences. At the same time, Gabriel's dialogue with his friend from home helped him to refocus on the aspects of his experience over which he could still exercise some degree of control. The knowledge that his friend was struggling similarly provided a sense of validation for Gabriel, in that it reaffirmed that his own difficulties were informed by his prior lack of access to high-quality educational opportunities, rather than his own individual-level failings. Gabriel's connection to a friend from home who was also feeling displaced at an elite university recon-nected him to a reference group identity, wherein he was able to conceptualize his own experience in a more readily "normalized" way. Both Gabriel and his friend confronted structural constraints to high achievement in coming from a public high school in the Bronx to an elite university; however, Gabriel explained that just tapping into the commonality of that experience mitigated some of the feelings of alienation and isolation from which he had been suffering. In this sense, students sought out ways to establish new "reference groups" for themselves, specific not only to shared past or present contexts for their experiences, but also to the shared experience of having to reconcile the two, in needing to navigate college without solid secondary school preparation or parental guidance. This reference group identification process constitutes a variation on Merton's original concept; the markers of "in-group" commonality that Gabriel and his friend share are not those that define the majority group within the structural contexts of their respective environments. Rather, the basis of shared identification that these students have with each other is exactly those experiences and challenges which set them apart from majority group members within their respective structural contexts.

Discussion

For students who go from living in low-income communities to being immersed in an elite educational environment, a shift in reference groups occurs. Their families and peers at home are no longer the only groups against whom they compare themselves in terms of academic proficiency and achievement. The comparisons that these students draw between themselves and their more privileged peers call attention to the deficits in their knowledge and skills, owing to their comparatively poor secondary educational opportunities and lack of access to financial, social, and cultural capital. Further, because the academic accomplishments which set these students apart from their classmates in high school may have given them confidence about their future academic success, it is particularly disconcerting for them to discover that their secondary schooling may not have provided with a particularly remarkable degree of preparation for college. However, when the parents in the study spoke about their children's academic capacities, they had only themselves, or youth from their home communities, as the comparative frame of reference regarding educational attainment. By virtue of their matriculation in college, these students often already had attained a higher level of education than most of the people in their reference groups at home. In such a comparison, these students occupied a highly elevated status, and thus "earned" the unconditional faith that their parents held in them. Their parents' ideas about their inherent abilities to achieve in school were antithetical to the deep misgivings that some students developed regarding their likelihood of college success.

While students also understood the tremendous difference between their opportunities and those of their parents, they were also positioned to develop a more distinct understanding of differences in access to resources and opportunities between themselves and their more privileged peers than their parents were likely to perceive. Parents' previous frames of reference for the institutional contexts in which students had achieved academic distinctions were those of the public high schools in which many of the students *had* succeeded with relative ease, in comparison to their peer reference group. In the absence of comparative structural perspective which allowed for analysis of structural disparities, parents had largely constructed their children's previous successes as solely attributable to innate capacities, which made school "easy" for them. Students, on the other hand, were in the process of understanding the significance of contextual factors in measuring relative degrees of academic rigor and success. Even as they surpassed their parents' levels of educational attainment and, as such, prospects for socio-economic mobility, they become more cognizant of the ways in which the structural dynamics of class- and race-based inequities constrained their achievements. The students became acutely aware of the considerable contrast between the educational resources and opportunities to which their more privileged peers had been exposed within their households, communities, and school systems, and the lack of such exposure within their own experiences. This disconnection, between parents' and students' frames of reference was often difficult to overcome in their conversations with each other.

When students from low income families pursue higher educational opportunities, they do so in the context of the "narrative biographies" which frame their evolving identities. By threading analyses of family dynamics throughout the examination of students' narratives, this study demonstrates that students do not experience the academic or social aspects of their campus environments in ways that are decontextualized from their familial relationships, even as they are physically separated from their families. Low income first-generation students must reconcile the aspects of their identities as members of these collectivities, which would seem to put them at outsider status both in relation to those at home and in relation to those within their campus communities. Institutional dynamics can then magnify the resulting experiences of isolation and alienation on campus, in that the overall context of under-representation for low income, first-generation college students leaves those that are enrolled feeling more separate from the rest of the majority middle- to upper-class, predominantly white student body, with college-educated parents.

The shift in reference groups that low-income first-generation college students must undertake presents formidable challenges to the continuity with which they experience the intersecting of their identities shaped by academic aspirations, peer group interactions, and familial dynamics. While the students had all described various forms of encouragement to pursue and attain a college degree from parents and family members, all had also described the difficulty of actualizing the goals set for them in the face of their families' lack of financial, social, and human capital, as well as lack of familiarity with higher education. Students who are the first members of their families to attend college must independently find the resources and information needed to bridge the gap between college aspirations and college access. Unlike their parents, the students had first-hand experiences of these challenges, which had yielded an acute awareness of the comparative implications of their more privileged peers' disproportionate access to resources and oppor-tunities with which to bolster their academic efforts.

Directions for Further Study

The size of this sample is not large enough to offer statistically representative generalizations, nor was the study designed with this goal in mind. The purpose of this inductive, qualitative study was neither to disprove hypothesis regarding existing data about the challenges facing low-income first-generation college students, nor to generate monolithic assertions of facts with which to categorize these students' experiences. As David Karp argues, "One does not need huge sample sizes to discover underlying and repeating forms of social life, that, once described, offer new levels of insight for people" (Karp 1997: 202). The findings presented here, therefore, are useful in the extent to which they provide depth and nuance to the well-established quantitative data regarding academic difficulty for low-income first-generation college students.

The themes explored within this paper only represent a portion of those which emerged in the course of analyzing the interview transcripts. For example, beyond grappling with the ways in which structural inequities fueled their own self-doubt, students in the study also described experiences of marginalization on campus based on interactions with other students, or, in some cases, faculty members, who questioned or expressed doubt as to whether these students "belonged" at the university. In instances varying from subtle to unmistakably overt, many of the students described being tokenized in class discussions pertaining to race or socioeconomic class dynamics, by being asked to "speak for" the underrepresented population in question to the classroom of their predominantly white, middle- to upper-class peers. In other cases, students described being forced to confront questions as to whether they "deserved" to be at the university, with the underlying racist and classist implication that students "like them" (i.e.; students of color and/or from low-income families and communities) could not have earned admission on the basis of own hard work and merit. Students were repeatedly called upon to "defend" their work ethic, intelligence, and capacities to make valuable contributions to the campus community. In this way, they were forced to contend with prejudices of others, even as they simultaneously battled against both the structural obstacles surrounding academic adjustments to college, and the feelings of isolation that accompanied their status as "othered" outsiders in their classrooms. Exploration of how these dynamics interacted with those detailed in this paper would constitute rich grounds for further research, and provide a fuller, more multi-dimensional picture of the intersecting and overlapping inequities and pressures that low-income first-generation college students must endure in their educational pursuits.

Implications for Policy and Program Design

The findings of this study demonstrate the necessity of developing and enhancing programs and resources which take into account the micro-level experiences of self-doubt and familial disconnection which are likely to emerge as result of these students' experiences of intersecting macro-level disparities along lines of educational opportunity, class, race, and parental educational attainment level. Even for those parents who were demonstrably invested and involved in their children's pre-collegiate educational careers, their opportunities to meaningfully engage with students regarding their collegiate experiences may be limited by their own lack of experience with, or knowledge of, higher education. For immigrant parents, who may have spent the majority of their own lives living in countries outside of the United States, these barriers may also be compounded by lack of experience with the American educational system more generally. The students in the study who were experiencing academic difficulties found it difficult to bridge the disconnections between their own experiences with the stress of challenging coursework, and their parents' limited understandings of what their challenges actually entailed.

Programs aimed at supporting the success of low-income first-generation college students would benefit by taking the salience of shifting familial dynamics and intergenerational disconnections into account as important aspects of students' educational experiences. Because these intergenerational disconnections across experience are structurally based upon the differences between students' and parents' respective degrees of access to educational resources and opportunities, it is reasonable to predict that manifestations of these dynamics are likely to emerge within most families of low-income first-generation college students. Institutions should consider developing resources that these students can draw from in their efforts to reconcile these differences through shared understanding. Outreach materials should be made available by institutions, to help students to explain to their parents what their educational pursuits will entail, in languages and formats that are varied enough to be accessible to individuals across a broad range of backgrounds and educational attainment levels.

Similarly, students' experiences of peer reference group identities are likely to involve significant transformations as a result of transitioning from the academic contexts of under-resourced public high school settings to those of elite university classrooms. It is reasonable to predict that the students in this study are not alone in their experiences of grappling with the profound self-doubt that arises from these shifts and the academic implications that they bear. Given the feelings of isolation described in relation to peer reference group dynamics in college classrooms, the alienation and disconnection from the campus community to which low income first-generation college students may be particularly vulnerable should be addressed at the institutional level. My findings suggest that low-income first-generation students would benefit from participating in programs that facilitate networking with peers who are undergoing similar transitions and challenges. Such opportunities could foster the creation of informal support systems for students, with which to combat fears of not "belonging" at their educational institutions. Established institutional structures, such as the University of the Northeast's Academic Services Office, may offer a possible venue for the development of such initiatives.

Despite the various support structures that are in place to assist low-income first-generation college students, the institutional resources allotted for these purposes are inarguably insufficient to meet the demands posed by the number of students who fit this demographic profile. This may in part be attributable to the fact that the low-income first-generation student population on campus is approached through the implementation of intermediary programs and services, rather than the prioritization developing more inclusive overall structural processes and systems at the institutional level. While the efficacy of programs like the TRIO-funded Student Support Services office has been well-established, the program's funding allows for a small number of the eligible student population on campus to take advantage of its resources. Thus while great efforts are made to implement the provision of resources that students need, institutional budget constraints limit the extent to which these programs can realistically serve the population of students on campus that would most directly benefit from their services. It should be noted that, since the interviews for this study were conducted in 2009, 100 percent of the students in the sample have either persisted in their educational pursuits (albeit despite significant challenges, and with varying degrees of difficulty), or have graduated from the university. It is not a coincidence that the sample in the study both over-represents students who are connected to programs and resources on campus aimed at fostering success for low-income first-generation students, *and* over-represents-low income first-generation college students who are experiencing success. For students who cannot draw insights from family and community members that are applicable to their experiences at an elite university, these programs can provide a "lifeline" with which to anchor their educational experiences and maximize their likelihood of success.

It is easy to fall into the trap of conceptualizing the struggles and achievements of low-income first-generation college students solely in terms of their relevance to individual educational attainment and social mobility. Within such a framing, the interconnectedness of individual educational trajectories and intergenerational, collective family histories and identities can become obscured. While academic institutions understandably position students as individuals at the center of efforts that pertain to developing academic support services, it is also important that they not lose sight of the myriad of ways in which student's memberships in the collectivities of their families and communities of origin inform both their motivations to succeed and the parameters of the support that they need in order to do so. As a result, if we limit programmatic foci to students' interactions with formal institutional structures, the insights we glean regarding the meanings of their educational experiences are likely to be "only the tip of the iceberg" (Millman and Kantor 1975:32). A more nuanced approach to supporting the success of low income first-generation college students requires that the informal structures of their family systems must be taken into account as well. To conceptualize these students' accomplishments, struggles, and processes in navigating their academic pursuits without investigating the dimensions of identity connected to the collectivities through which they experience them is to miss a critically significant aspect of the meanings attached to their educational attainment.

Lastly, it should be noted the "elephant in the room" of this chapter is the issue of educational disparities in public secondary schooling for students in low-income communities within which both children of color and children of parents with limited educational attainment are disproportionately over-represented. Even when these students find ways to overcome the formidable structural barriers that would otherwise prevent them from gaining admission to an elite university, they continue to be academically and personally impacted by deficiencies in their secondary schooling throughout their college careers. While college access programs and support services programs provide some mechanisms for increasing the likelihood that low-income first-generation college students can realize their educational goals, they do so in the context of persistently racialized and socioeconomically stratified inequities throughout the U.S. educational system.

Notes

1. The number of students on campus is tracked by student's self report of identifying as Asian-, Latino/a-, African-, or Native-American.
2. Although I drew upon my personal associations with this population of students on campus, I limited eligibility for participation to students with whom I did not have a present or former teaching, advising, or mentoring relationship.
3. At the outset of my study, the four broad research questions that I aimed to address were as follows: (1) How do low-income, first-generation college students reconcile and negotiate their identities in relation to their families and communities of origin and the culture of an elite private educational institution during their academic tenure?; (2) In what ways do parental and familial/communal expectations shape and inform the social meanings of post-secondary education for these students?; (3) How does identification as being the first in their families to attend college shape and inform the approaches and strategies that these students employ to confront the structural inequalities embedded in the social and cultural milieu of elite university environments?; and (4) In what ways do racial and ethnic/cultural identities intersect with socioeconomic factors (e.g., parental education) to shape and inform meanings of higher education for low income first-generation college students amidst a mostly white and upper-middle or upper-class campus?

References

Carnevale, A. P., and Fry, R. A. (2000). *Crossing the great divide: Can we achieve equity when generation Y goes to college?* Princeton, NJ: Educational Testing Service.

Charmaz, K. (2006). *Constructing Grounded Theory: Practical Guide Through Qualitative Data Analysis.* Thousand Oaks, CA: Sage Publications.

Cheng, S. and Starks, B. (2002). Racial Differences in the Effects of Significant Other on Students' Educational Expectations, in *Sociology of Education.* Vol. 75. No. 4 (Oct.), 306-327.

Choy, S. (2001). *Students Whose Parents Did Not Go To College: Postsecondary Access, Persistence, and Attainment.* Washington D.C.: U.S. Department of Education, National Center for Education Statistics.

Conley, D. (1999). *Being Black, Living in the Red: Race, Wealth, and Social Policy in America.* Berkeley: University of California Press.

Denzin, N. K. and Lincoln, Y.S. (Eds.). 1994 (2005, 2007). *The Sage Handbook of Qualitative Research.* New York: Sage Publications.

Engle, J., Bermeo, A., and O'Brien, C. (2006). *Straight from the source: What works for first-generation college students.* The Pell Institute for the Study of Opportunity in Higher Education.

Fainstein, N. I. (1993). Race, Class and Segregation, *International Journal of Urban and Regional Research.* Vol. 17, 384-403.

Feliciano, C. (2006). Beyond the Family: The Influence of Premigration Group Status on the Educational Expectations of Immigrants' Children, *Sociology of Education,* Vol. 79, No.4 (October), 281-303.

Fine, M. (2003). Witnessing Whiteness, Gathering Intelligence, in Wong, L. M., Fine, M., Powell, L., and Weiss, L. (eds). *Off-White: Readings on Race, Power and Society.* New York: Routledge.

Frankenberg, R. (1997). *White Women, Race Matters.* Minneapolis: University of Minnesota Press.

Glaser, Barney. 1965. The Constant Comparative Method of Qualitative Analysis, in *Social Problems,* Vol. 12, No 4.

Glaser, B. and Strauss, A. (1967). *The Discovery of Grounded Theory.* Chicago: Aldine Publishing.

Giddens, A., (1991). *Modernity and Self-Identity.* Stanford: Stanford University Press.

Goyette, K. and Xie, Y (1999). The Racial Identification of Biracial Children with One Asian Parent: Evidence from the 1990 Census, in *Social Forces.* Vol. 76. No. 2 (Dec.), 547-570.

Hebel, S. (2007). The Graduation Gap, *The Chronicle of Higher Education.* March 23, 2007.

Kao, G. (2004). Parental Influence on the Educational Outcomes of Immigrant Youth, in *International Migration Review.* Vol. 38. No.2, (Summer), 427-449.

Kao, G. and Tienda, M. (1998). Educational Aspirations and Minority Youth, in *American Journal of Education.* Vol. 106. No. 3(May), 349-384.

Karp, D. (1997). *Speaking of Sadness.* Oxford: Oxford University Press.

Keister, L. A. (2000). *Wealth in America: Trends in Wealth Inequality.* Cambridge: Cambridge University Press.

Kim, N. (2008). *Imperial Citizens: Koreans and Race from Seoul to LA.* Stanford: Stanford University Press.

Louie, V. S. (2004). *Compelled to Excel: Immigration, education, and opportunity among Chinese Americans.* Stanford: Stanford University Press.

Massey, D. and Denton, N. A. (1993). *American Apartheid: Segregation and the Making of the Underclass.* Cambridge: Harvard University Press.

McSwain, C. and Davis, R. (2007). *College Access for the Working Poor: Overcoming Burdens to Succeed in Higher Education.* Washington D.C.: The Institute for Higher Education Policy.

Merton, R. K. (1957). *Social Theory and Social Structure.* New York: The Free Press.

Millman, M. and Kanter, R. M. (1975). *Another Voice: Feminist Perspectives on Social Life.* New York: Anchor Books.

Ogbu, J. (1978). *Minority Education and Caste: The American System in Cross-Cultural Perspective.* New York: Academic Press.

Oliver, M. and Shapiro, T. (1997). *Black Wealth/White Wealth: A New Perspective on Racial Inequality.* New York: Routledge.

Pike, G. and Kuh, G. D. (2005). First- and second-generation college students: a comparison of their engagement and intellectual development. *Journal of Higher Education* 76.3 (May-June 2005): 276 (25).

Portes, A., McLeod, S. A. and Parker, R. N. (1978). Immigrant Aspirations, *Sociology of Education.* Vol. 51. No. 4 (October), 241-260.

Qian, Z. and Blair, S. L. (1999). Racial/Ethnic Differences in Educational Aspirations of High School Seniors, in *Sociological Perspectives.* Vol. 42. No.4, 605-625.

Shapiro, T. M. (2005). *The Hidden Cost of Being African American.* Oxford: Oxford University Press.

Strauss, A. (1998). *Basics of Qualitative Research: Techniques and Procedures for Developing Grounded Theory.* New York: Sage.

Swail, W. S. (2002). Higher Education and the New Demographics. *Change.* (July/August) 15-23.

Terenzini, P. T., Springer, L., Yaeger, P. M., Pascarella, E. T., and Nora, A. (1996). First-generation college students: Characteristics, experiences, and cognitive development. *Research in Higher Education,* 37, 1-22.

Zhou, M. (1997). Growing Up American: The Challenge Confronting Immigrant Children and Children of Immigrants, in *Annual Review of Sociology.* Vol. 23, 63-95.

Chapter Seven
Examining Involvement as a Critical Factor: Perceptions from First-Generation and Non-First-Generation Students

Mona Davenport, Ph.D.,
Eastern Illinois University

Introduction

Research shows that even after controlling for pre-college characteristics and within-college experiences, differences remain in the persistence rates of certain student subgroups in higher education, with underrepresented students of color persisting to graduation at a lower rate than their White counterparts (Astin and Oseguera, 2005; Harvey, 2003). The research on first-generation students reveals that some of their academic and personal characteristics such as being less academically prepared for college, having lower rates of completion in higher-level mathematics courses in high school, and coming from families in lower socio-economic levels may affect their success in college (National Center for Educational Statistics, 2005).

Since student persistence has long been associated with parental educational levels, important differences between first-generation and non-first-generation students were not explained in the original conception of Astin's (1984) Student Involvement Theory (Braxton, 2002). Because parents transmit their values and attitudes to their children, the children from homes with more educated parents are more likely to value higher education (Pascarella and Terenzini, 1991, 1998, 2005; Pascarella, Pierson, Wolniak, and Terenzini, 2004). When examining student involvement on campus, some of the strongest predic-tors of college persistence usually include; effective academic advising, involvement with faculty, living environment, classroom experience, and extracurricular activities (Levin, 1998). Involvement for first-generation students has been found to be less frequent compared to traditional college students. First-generation students are less likely to have the time to participate in campus activities outside the classroom (McConnell, 2000). Considering barriers like background characteristics and family obligations, first-generation students find it hard to navigate and get involved in many "out-of-class" experiences. As we start to examine first-generation college students, it is clear that studies on specific sub-groups (ethnic minorities) of first-generation students are limited.

The purpose of this chapter is to provide findings from a research study that examined nine critical factors that affect persistence of ethnic minority first-generation and non first-generation undergraduates at Eastern Illinois University. It also sought to identify if there are differences between first-generation and non-first-generation college students' in each of the nine areas of involvement. Four research questions were addressed: 1) How do first-generation and non-first-generation students differ in terms of their experience across nine involvement components?; 2) Is there a difference between African American and Hispanic students and their involvement in the nine involvement components?; 3) Which areas of involvement are most predictive of students' perceived likelihood to be connected to the university?; 4) How are the students' perceptions of their overall involvement predictive of their perceived likelihood to graduate? Because the first-generation student is so unique with regard to involvement, this study also measured some of the important differences in social integration for these students. This chapter reviews an understanding of involvement and socio-cultural factors that influence first- generation and non first-generation minority students.

Research on First-Generation Students

In the late 1960s and early 1970s, access to higher education was again transformed when the report from the President's Commission of Higher Education established a more affordable education with the community college system (Humphrey, 2000). This was the beginning of equal educational opportunity for all students in the United States. In 1971, first-generation students represented 38.5 percent of all first-time college freshmen (Saenz, Hurtado, Barrera, Wolf, and Yeung, 2007). Research indicates that first-generation students differ from their peers in many ways prior to college enrollment, including their demographic characteristics, the importance they place on college, their aspirations, their perceived level of family support for attending college, their institutional choice and commitment, their pre-college knowledge and behaviors, and their entering academic skills and confidence levels (McConnell, 2000). Once first-generation college students enroll in college a lack of social and/or cultural capital—in the form of non-college educated parents—can serve to undermine the access to resources for first-generation college students (Saenz et al., 2007).

Challenges this group faces are sometimes overwhelming because they do not have parents who are familiar with higher education and they are not able to navigate as well as their non-first-generation counterparts. These first-generation students are also more likely to work more than thirty hours per week and be academically underprepared for college-level work (Thayer, 2000). Although the national average of first-generation students enrolled in college was 38.5 percent in

1971 among entering freshmen, the proportion was much higher for Latinos (69.6 percent), African Americans (62.9 percent), Native Americans (44.8 percent), and Asian/Asian Americans (42.5 percent) (Saenz et al., 2007).

Transition to college has also proven an obstacle for first-generation students. Because these students were breaking family tradition, college attendance often involved multiple transitions for their academic, social and cultural integration (Terenzini, Rendon, Upcraft, Millar, Allison, Gregg, and Jalomo, 1994). These transitions could include motivation, academic skills and cultural values. Attending and completing college carried the potential for radical changes in these students and the lives they led (Terenzini et al., 1994). One of the biggest challenges for first-generation students is deferring involvement in non-academic activities and life on campus until they felt they had their academic lives under control (Terenzini et al., 1994). This is in contrast with traditional non-first-generation students who typically were involved right away. In this study, the traditional students were worried about making new friends and getting socially connected even before mastering academic work. Because first-generation students do not have a familial experience providing support, what happens once they get to college (within and outside of the classroom) is a critical predictor for post-secondary outcomes (Hahs-Vaughn, 2004). Most of the studies that have been conducted on first-generation students examine the characteristics that make it difficult for them to persist in college. If a college student fails to receive support for college attendance from friends and family members, then early departure from college is likely (Elkins, Braxton, and James, 2000). Students who break their family traditions deal with issues such as: changing their identity, being perceived as different, leaving old friends behind, separating from their families, breaking family codes of unity and loyalty, and living between two worlds (Rendon, 1995). For minority students, leaving old friends and separation from family could be difficult. Nora, Cabrera, Hagedorn, and Pascarella (1996) found that the transition to college is smoother for minority students who have supportive family and friends from their past. Although some evidence indicates that emotional and financial support provided by families is key to the academic success of Latino students, other findings suggest that the struggle between familial obligations and requirements of school can contribute significantly to a difficult academic adjustment and to low retention rates in these students (Rodriquez, Mira, Myers, Morris, and Cardoza, 2003).

Hsiao (1992), in her review of research about first-generation students and minority students, concluded that having parents, siblings, and friends with no college experience resulted in the lack of an adequate support system for the student and possibly posed an obstruction to persistence in college. Billson and Terry (1982) took a different turn and examined how some of these barriers (opposed to characteristics) could prevent first-generation students from graduating. They wanted to study some of the barriers outside of academic areas such as: where students live and/or their lack of social integration (Billson and Terry, 1982). Billson and Terry (1982) also found that first-generation students were not as socially integrated as non-first-generation students because they were less likely to live on campus, be involved in campus organizations, establish their most important friendships on campus, or work on campus. Particularly as students began to take on the symbols of the college culture—be it style of dress, taste of music, or range of vocabulary—first-generation students often sense displeasure on the part of acquaintances, and feel an uncomfortable separation from the culture in which they grew up (Hsiao, 1992).

Minority Student Persistence

In 1954 the *Brown v. Board of Education* decision abolished segregation based on race in public schools. The *Brown* ruling is the most cited case in terms of desegregating elementary and secondary education which indirectly affected higher education attendance for African Americans (Allen, Jayakumar, Griffin, Korn, and Hurtado, 2005). Before *Brown*, Blacks were excluded from the American body public and defined as second-class citizens under the doctrine of "Separate but Equal," established in constitu-tional law by the 1896 case *Plessy vs. Ferguson* (163 U.S. 537 (1896)). It has been over fifty years since civil rights policies and federal legislation were established to promote equality in access to higher education for people of color, women and the economically disadvantaged. According to the 2006 American Council on Education (ACE) report, minority students made dramatic gains in college enrollment after the *Brown* decision, increasing by nearly 1.5 million students, or 50.7 percent. Although the number of minority students has increased over the last four decades, African American students show a declining proportion of first-generation representation, dropping by almost two-thirds from 1971 (62.9 percent) to 2005 (22.6 percent), (Saenz et al., 2007), a point illustrated in Table 7.1. The evidence that racial/ethnic groups and first-generation students may be less equipped for college is an important distinction that affirms the importance of increasing the attention paid to higher education institutions about this population (Zalaquett, 1999).

Black and Hispanic students are more likely to be first-generation college students and to come from low socioeconomic (SES) backgrounds. In addition to these family background characteristics that may put them at a disadvantage, students of color may be subject to adjustment difficulties rooted in the experience of being a minority student on a predominantly White campus (Fischer, 2007). As a category of students, "Black and Hispanics may not have had the advantages of being socialized and nurtured into having developed the competencies and framework for competitive learning in a middle-class place called college" (Betances, 2002; p. 47). Notable opportunities for these groups to participate and

Table 7.1. Racial/Ethnic Breakdown of First-Generation Students Over Time

U.S. Population (25 years or older) w/No College Education	1975	2005	% Change
African American People	84.50%	55.70%	-34.10%
Hispanic People	85.00%	69.10%	-18.70%
White People	72.80%	42.80%	-41.20%
Total/All People	73.70%	47.00%	-36.30%
First-Generation College Students			
African American People	51.50%	20.40%	-60.30%
Hispanic People	57.60%	35.80%	-37.80%
White People	28.90%	12.90%	-55.40%
Total/All People	31.20%	15.90%	-49.00%

From Cooperative Institutional Research Program, Higher Education Research Institute, 2007.

enroll in four-year institutions began with the start of education policies and financial aid initiatives which consist of programs like the State Student Incentive Grant programs during the mid and late sixties (Cross, 2001). Although the State Incentive Grant Programs were created to promote educational opportunities for the poor; the report of the federal Advisory Committee on Student Financial Assistance (2001), Access Denied, documented the gaps in college participation between the rich and the poor. Similar gaps in college participation exist between White youths, and African American, Native American and Latino students, driven at least in part by the strong correlation between race and income in this country (Heller, 2003). Between 1969 and 1979, minority students enrolled in predominantly White colleges in increasing numbers, due in part to the greater access afforded by affirmative action programs (Smedley, Myers and Harrell, 1993). Equal opportunity and affirmative action programs gave people of color, women, and others routinely pushed to society's fringes, the chance to prove their worth (Allen et al., 2005).

During this time, maintaining a culturally diverse student body, including adequate representation of minority students in the total student body was the educational goal for almost every university in this country. Gaining entry to college was a dramatic accomplishment for some but persisting to degree completion is what really mattered in the post-college world (Swail, Redd, and Perna, 2003). These affirmative action programs did not guarantee success; they merely provided the chance to compete and the opportunity to succeed (or fail). Some early findings by Tracey and Sedlacek (1985) found that the academic adjustment and achievement of African American and other minority students are influenced by different sociocultural and contextual factors (i.e., student satisfaction with college, peer group relations) than those that have an impact on White students. Culture is extremely important for students of color because, for them to be successful in college, these students need to affirm their own cultural identities in order to be successful (Tierney, 1999). He also pointed out that the more minority students affirm their own cultural identities, the more their chances for graduation increases.

Involvement Areas

To define theoretically how some of these factors contribute to first-generation and non-first-generation African American and Hispanic students' adjustment, nine areas were examined in this study. The areas that the researcher reviewed and identified as obstacles to the persistence of first-generation and non-first-generation African American and Hispanic students at Predominantly White Institutions (PWI) were interaction with intra-racial relations, interracial relations, interaction with faculty, campus involvement, academic and non-academic facilities, usage of the cultural center, athletic facilities, involvement in the Charleston community.

Intra-Racial and Inter-Racial Relations

It would seem that race and ethnicity have a fundamental impact on how college is experienced by minority students and therefore their adjustment process cannot be assumed to be the same as for White students (Smedley et al., 1993). Two of the most documented impacts on how minority students adjust on campus are the psychological and sociocultural stresses they face during their academic careers; for example, stresses that are experienced on campus or in the community (Smedley et al., 1993). These researchers explained that for some minority students, the source of college student stress may be compounded by actual or perceived weaknesses in academic preparation due to limited educational opportunities relative to their White peers' doubts about their abilities, or concerns that faculty and peers may question their legitimacy as college students. Smedley and his colleagues also mentioned that these factors (racism on campus and/or in the community, financial worries) threaten the effective adjustment for minority students, and they find it hard to concentrate on their studies and to trust faculty and administration.

Although stress has been studied for decades, more recent investigations have contributed to the understanding of the effects of race-related stress and forms of minority stressors to emotional, psychological, and physical outcomes among persons of color (Sanders-Thomas, 2002). Tierney (1992) suggested that academic and social integration for students of color might be different. The emerging research on the educational benefits of diversity is beginning to establish the theoretical and empirical links in determining the optimal conditions under which these benefits operate and how they may work differently for particular types of students (Hurtado, 2007). According to a study conducted by Chang, Astin, and Kim (2004), it has become increasingly evident that cross-racial interaction plays a key role in achieving the educational benefits associated with racial diversity. Their study examined both the effects of cross-racial interaction and the conditions that affect it (Chang, Astin and Kim, 2004). This longitudinal data was gathered at the initial entry to college and 4 years later, and the targeted population included all institutions of higher education listed in the 1994 Opening Fall Enrollment files of the U.S. Department of Education's Integrated Post-secondary Education Data System (IPEDS). The study revealed that regardless of the type of interaction or the level of diversity, students of color are uniformly more likely to engage in cross-racial interaction than White students. Their results indicated that the interaction between racial groups in the classroom had the most robust positive effect on all students, and it added to the value of undergraduate students' social skills, intellectual capacity, and level of civic interest (Chang et al., 2004).

It is important to also address the benefits that some students can accrue from "same-race" peers and environments, including social integration and comfort, in addition to learning and democratic skills (Hurtado, 2007). A related difference in the social adjustment of minority versus White students was that, unlike White students, minority students faced racial/ethnic accountability that undermined their sense of belonging (Morley, 2007). Racial/ethnic accountability refers to how students adhere to "preconceived notions" that minority students were either not as good as White students or did not belong to White social circles (Morley, 2007). To counterbalance these harsh realities at PWIs, some students of color have developed their own subcultures within the larger communities (Griffin, Nichols, Perez II, and Tuttle, 2008). For Latinos, finding a critical mass of students who are like them appears to be very important because they have a supportive community that may have some commonalities that they can relate to with each other (Hernandez and Lopez, 2007). In a study by Hernandez (2000), the results revealed that finding a Latino community on a predominantly White campus had a posi-tive impact on retention. This qualitative study revealed that meeting Latino students of similar backgrounds who were succeeding in college was an important motivating factor.

Interaction with Faculty

Student involvement in educationally related and distinctly academic interactions with professors appears to enhance student's academic performance (Anaya and Cole, 2001). Kuh and Hu (2001) conducted a study that examined the character and impact of student-faculty interaction on student learning and personal development in the 1990s. Using data from the College Student Experience Questionnaire (CSEQ) between 1990 and 1997, Kuh and Hu (2001) found that, compared with White students, Asian American students reported less frequent substantive inter-action with faculty, African American students had more interaction with faculty than any other group of minority students, and Latino students had more contact with a faculty member related to writing improvement. Anaya and Cole (2001) studied 836 Latino/a students using a national cross-sectional sample and found that student involvement in educationally related and distinctly academic interactions with professors appears to enhance student's academic performance. They even added that student achievement was enhanced when professors were perceived as accessible and supportive (Anaya and Cole, 2001).

When examining student-faculty interaction for minority students, concerns about the lack of same-race/ethnicity faculty sometimes hinder interaction (Lundberg and Schreiner, 2004). One of the most effective and most visible support systems for students is faculty with whom they can identify and receive strength (Owens, Reis, and Hall, 1994). Current research found that students were more comfortable with faculty members of their own race/ethnicity (Lundberg and Schreiner, 2004). Lundberg and Schreiner (2004) examined the difference in the frequency of interactions with faculty members and in satisfaction with faculty interaction based on ethnicity. The results revealed that such faculty interaction was a better predictor of learning for students of color than for White students.

Campus Involvement

Fleming (1984) conducted an extensive study and came to the conclusion that minority students perceive many traditional campus organizations as exclusive and insensitive to their social needs. DeSousa and King (1992) challenged the popular belief that Black students attending predominantly White institutions are alienated and maladjusted and, thus, they do not benefit from the college experience at levels comparable to White students. In this study, the researchers used the CSEQ to determine if African American students' level of involvement was consistent with past research. The results revealed that White students did not score higher on involvement than Black students and on all scales such as involvement with library experiences and clubs and organizations, Black and White students demonstrated comparable involvement levels. DeSousa and King (1992) did assert that Black students were more involved in organizations that were predominantly comprised of Black students compared to White students in organizations like student government, resident hall associations, etc. The researcher also noted that the students' involvement in predominantly Black organizations may provide a familiar cultural milieu for Black students and help them establish social networks and support systems not found in the classroom environment or residence halls (DeSousa and King, 1992).

Pascarella and Terenzini (2005) reviewed a large body of research that demonstrated that social interactions with peers may enhance the learning and performance of college students when these interactions are related to the achievement environment. Svanum and Bigatti (2006) conducted a study that examined social activities in terms of hours of time students devoted to student clubs, organizations and sororities and fraternities, and then assessed this in relation to other outside activities, course effort, and course grades. Their study is significant for institutions of higher education in assisting first-generation students, because the results revealed that outside activities did not directly influence course grades, but job activities negatively influenced course grades indirectly through reduced time to devote to course content. The students in the study felt their work and family demands lessened course effort which in turn lessened their GPA.

Academic and Non-Academic Facilities

Kuh and Gonyea (2003) examined data from more than 300,000 students who completed the CSEQ between 1984 and 2002 and concluded that libraries play an important role in helping the institution achieve its aca-demic mission. In their study, it was noted that students of color used the library as much or more than did other students (Kuh and Gonyea, 2003). Their findings noted that perhaps students of color find the academic library to be a safe haven, a place that supports and nurtures academic success in collabo-ration with peers of the same racial and ethnic background, much in the same way the campus union provides a venue for social gatherings (Kuh and Gonyea, 2003). For first-generation students, participating in an honors program, joining a fraternity or sorority, employment, and teachers' instructional skills have significantly more positive effects for academic success than those first-generation students that did not get involved (Pascarella and Terenzini, 2005). Not only first-generation but African American students at PWI's, regardless of institutional environment, spent more time than White students utilizing campus facilities and participating in clubs and organizations (Watson and Kuh, 1996).

Residence hall communities also play a major role in establishing an environment for students' involvement in campus-related and off-campus activities during their under-graduate years (Arboleda, Wang, Shelley, and Whalen, 2003). Arboleda et al. (2003) found that students who were more involved in their living community, both academically and socially, tended to be more satisfied with their living environment and found it easier to study and collaborate academically with others in their community.

Cultural Centers

Many PWIs and Black students attending these institutions perceived the creation of Black cultural centers as providing service and programs to help Black students "better" adjust to the college environment (Goggins, 2003). Black students of the 1960s and 1970s started the majority of these centers at several institutions in order to have a safe space in which to celebrate and recreate their culture (Williamson, 1999). Although the houses started off as safe havens for students of color, many centers now function with an underlining purpose to retain students of color by creating programming, academic, and cultural enrichment. A study by Patton (2006) revealed that centers make a powerful difference in student learning because they foster an environment that promotes leadership development, a sense of community, cultural identity, and a sense of mattering, all components for engagement in the learning process. Young (1991) stated that a properly functioning and effective ethnic minority cultural center can provide the dual service of advocating for minority students and of introducing cultural pluralism to majority students.

Athletic Facilities

The association between student participation in extracurricular activities and educational attainment has generally been found to be positive (Hanks and Eckland, 1976; Astin, 1984; Kuh and Umbach, 2004). According to Pascarella and Terenzini (2005), some evidence suggests that African American males participating in intercollegiate athletics may gain more in both academic and social self-concept than their White counterparts. They added that intercollegiate athletic participation has a positive impact on social involvement during college, satisfaction with college, interpersonal and leadership skills, and motivation to complete one's degree (Pascarella and Smart, 1991). Pascarella and Smart (1991) found that participation in intercollegiate sports can have a positive effect on degree attainment with some exceptions in Division I football and basketball.

For Division I intercollegiate athletes in the sports programs, the story can be somewhat different. Some of these student-athletes typically come from high schools with socioeconomic backgrounds different from those that of non-athletes (Pascarella and Smart, 1991; Hyatt, 2003 and Martin, 2009). Sports simply absorb so much physical and psychological energy that only a limited amount is left to make the kinds of intense investment necessary to one's academic experience (Pascarella, Truckenmiller, Nora, Terenzini, Edison, and Hagedorn, 1999). Different factors that may hinder successful social and academic integration in the student-athletes are often under enormous pressures to satisfy the goals set by the athletic departments at the institution (Hyatt, 2003) and limited time to integrate into the campus community. These problems, coupled with the students not being academically prepared, cause isolation and disassociation from campus resources and offices that could assist in balancing the dual roles (Martin, 2009).

Persistence Studies on African Americans

In *One Third of A Nation*, a report by the American Council on Education and the Education Commission of the States, predicted that by 2010 one-third of all school age children in America will represent members of ethnic minority groups (African American, American Indian, Asian American, and Hispanic), and this trend would also affect higher education institutions (Holmes, Ebbers, Robinson, and Mugenda, 2007). Several early scholars (Fleming, 1984; Sedlacek, 1987) have done extensive research on persistence of Blacks in higher education, and still today Blacks continue to lag significantly behind Whites in college enrollment, graduation, and advanced graduate study (Bowen and Bok, 1998). The reason this research will be valuable is because most of the theoretically based studies on student persistence in higher education have predominately focused on white, traditional-age college students. Some of the prominent studies on African American students were longitudinal and very informative with regard to attrition and retention in higher education. Pascarella (1985) investigated long-term persistence during a nine-year period among minority and non-minority students. He also reported that specific dimensions of social integration into the academic and social environments were more problematic for African Americans attending public and private four-year White institutions than for their counterparts attending historically Black colleges and universities. Freeman's (1999) study noted that personal commitments, such as bonding to the institution, were highly important for students attending Black institutions and lack of social and academic integration were strong "drop out" indicators in public and private PWI's but minimally so in historically Black institutions.

Historically Black Colleges and Universities (HBCUs) previously played a significant role in educating African American students. In the 1970s and 1980s they accounted for 26.4 percent (191,158) of the 723,326 total African American undergraduate students enrolled (Nettles, Wagener, Millett, and Killenbeck, 1999). The current research on African American students is extremely important because, according to figures from the Digest of Educational Statistics, only 15.9 percent of Black students in 2000 were enrolled in historically Black colleges and universities (NCES, 2002). In spite of the decrease of number of African Americans attending Black colleges, HBCUs still continue to produce an overwhelming percentage of African American leaders (Freeman, 1999).

One of the largest studies conducted on Black students on white campuses was a twenty-year study of African American students on predominantly White campuses. Sedlacek (1987) and other researchers felt that student affairs personnel throughout the United States should be aware of the growing concerns of Blacks entering in higher education. These researchers demonstrated the validity of the following variables: positive self-confidence, realistic self-appraisal, understands and deals with racism, demonstrated community service, prefers long-range goals, availability of strong support persons, successful leadership experience and non-traditional knowledge acquired which aids in the successful persistence of African American students.

The importance of student organizations, especially cultural student organizations, to minority student retention at PWIs has also been supported in the literature (DeSousa and Kuh, 1996; Sedlacek, 1987).

Persistence Studies on Hispanic Students

The Civil Rights movement of the 1960s and increased political participation by Hispanic Americans brought national focus to the educational disparities of this population (Olivas, 1997). According to analysis conducted by the Pew Hispanic Center (2004), many Latinos who do enroll for the first time at a baccalaureate institution do not graduate. They also state the following:

- The majority of Latinos in higher education are enrolled in two-year institutions, while the majority of White, Black and Asian/Pacific Islander students are enrolled in four-year institutions.
- Latino students are less likely to complete college through the traditional path (enroll within one year of high school graduation and attain the bachelor's degree within six years).

Like African American students, the retention of Hispanic students in higher education through graduation provides a great challenge for institutions that primarily serve this population (Salinas and Llanes, 2003). According to the research from the Pew report (2004), in attainment of bachelor's degrees, disparities are evident because White youth beginning at community colleges are nearly twice as likely as Hispanic youth beginning at community colleges to complete a bachelor's degree. Even when comparing the best prepared White and Latino college students at non-selective colleges and universities, 81 percent of whites complete a bachelor's degree compared to only 57 percent of Latinos (Salinas and Llanes, 2003).

Despite the surge in enrollment, Latinos remain notably underrepresented at all levels of higher education and have one of the lowest overall educational attainment rates of any ethnic or racial group (U.S. Census Bureau, 2004). While Hispanics are under-represented in four-year institutions, they are well represented in two-year institutions, where more than 55 percent of all Hispanic students enroll (Harvey and Anderson, 2005). Some states have engaged in programmatic efforts targeting community college students and among the most recognizable and a lauded effort is the Puente Project, a collaborative partnership between the California Community Colleges and the University of California system (Saenz, 2002). The Puente Project was established in 1981 and has improved the transfer rate of students from all ethnicities. This program's purpose is to increase the number of underrepresented students who enroll in four-year institutions and earn degrees with hopes that these students return to the community as mentors.

According to Hernandez and Lopez (2007), because of the heterogeneity and the diverse experiences and distinctive histories of each Latino group in the United States, there are no "cookie-cutter" approaches to increase access and retention rates of the Latino community (p. 116). They also state it is important to recognize that Latino college student retention begins well before students enter post-secondary education (Hernandez and Lopez, 2007). This research validated findings comparable to those of African American students: (a) the importance of connecting with faculty and staff, (b) beneficial campus involvement helped students succeed, and (c) finding a Latino community (Latino student organizations, programs,

Heritage month celebrations, etc.) to assist with coping with college assisted in students getting acclimated to the university and persisting.

Involvement and First-Generation Students/Minority Students

A small, but growing body of research has focused on first-generation students' experiences during college and the effect these experiences have on their learning and development (Filkins and Doyle, 2002). Terenzini, Springer, Yeager, Pascarella and Nora, 1995) conducted a longitudinal study of student learning which examined pre-college characteristics and college experiences of 825 first-generation college students and 1,860 traditional students at 23 diverse institutions nationwide. The results from this study noted significant differences between traditional and first-generation students. The results revealed: (1) The two groups had different curricular, instructional, and co-curricular experiences, as well as different perceptions of the environments of the institutions they were attending; (2) First-generation students (compared to their traditional peers) tended to take fewer courses in the "traditional fields" such as Business Administration, Computer Sciences, Education and instead took more technical and pre-professional courses; (3) First-generation students reported studying fewer hours because they spent more hours working; (4) First-generation students were less likely than traditional students to have positive experiences on campus. Because of their hours spent working, these students were less likely to perceive faculty members as concerned with their development and adjustment to college; (5) First-generation students were less likely to report that their institutions have an environment that encouraged being critical, evaluative, and analytical; and (6) First-generation students were more likely to report experiencing racial/ethnic or gender discrimination in the classroom (Terenzini et al., 1995).

Like first-generation students, minority students are less likely to get involved in some of the traditional organizations like student government (Sutton and Kimbrough, 2001). Sutton and Kimbrough also state that usually, when students of color get involved, they seem to want to be associated with multicultural organizations. Minority students perceive mem-bership within multicultural organizations will provide them greater opportunities to share their skills and talents with students from their same race (Sutton and Kimbrough, 2001). According to DeSousa and King (1992), an important next step in understanding the involvement of minority students at PWIs is to identify the specific factors that affect the quality as well as the frequency of student involvement in campus related activities.

Methodology

Eastern Illinois University is a comprehensive public university located in Charleston, Illinois, a city with a population of approximately 20,000. Ninety-eight percent of Eastern students come from Illinois, the largest percentage of them (41 percent) from Cook and adjacent counties in the Chicagoland area. In the fall semester 2009, Eastern Illinois University (EIU), minorities represent approximately 13.25 percent of the total student population: African American 992 (9.56 percent), Latino/a 324 (2.69 percent), Native American 44 (<1 percent), and Asian American 148 (1 percent). The graduation rate for each respective group varies from year-to-year with the African American and Latino/a students graduating at a lower rate than their White counterparts. In the 4 years prior to this research, the institution had increased the minority population from 10.52 percent (FY06) to 13.25 percent (FY09).

Study Design

The conceptual framework employed in this study is based on the theories of student persistence, which may, in turn, validate better retention of minority students at institutions of higher education. It is important to look at the college impact models that focus on the sources of change, such as different institutional characteristics, programs and services, student experiences, and interactions with students and faculty members (Pascarella and Terenzini, 2005) in order to increase the retention rate of minority students. The frameworks that were used in this study were Vincent Tinto's Theory of Student Departure (1987, 1993) and Alexander Astin's Theory on Student Involvement (1984, 1993). Both Tinto and Astin emphasize the importance of forging connections to individuals and groups on campus as key to student persistence. Tinto states that the greater the degree of integration into the institution's environment, the greater the student's commitment to educational goals and to his or her specific institution (Tinto, 1987, 1993, 2004). Tinto maintains that it is the interaction between institutional and educational commitments that will determine an individual's persistence behavior. Minority students may be an exception to the rule because, as these students interact throughout college, some pre-college friends perform a "bridge function" providing support and encouragement (Terenzini et al., 1995). Like Tinto, Alexander Astin also subscribes to the theory of academic and social integration. Astin's (1984, 1985, 1993) theory of student involvement occupies the middle ground between psychological and sociological explanations of student change (Pascarella and Terenzini, 2005). Astin developed one of the first college impact models. His Input-Environment-Outcome (I-E-O) model explained how college affects students related to incoming student characteristics, the campus environment and how the student leaves the campus.

Sample

Eastern Illinois University supplied a list of African American and Hispanic students who had been enrolled during FY08 and who met the criteria for this study. The criteria for selection were that the participants: had experienced at least one year of college and were currently enrolled at Eastern Illinois University during the 2008 Fall semester (FY09). The tenth day roster report from the Registrar's Office was compared with the FY08 list and the researcher discovered that of the 956-student total, 93 students had to be removed from the list because they were graduate students, provisional graduate students, or were not African American or Hispanic. This left a population of 863 students. The entire African American and Hispanic population who met the criteria were invited to complete the survey. The demographic profile of the students consisted of age, year in school, and race. Four-hundred four students completed the survey (46.8 percent response rate). Of those 404 students who participated in this research study, 71 percent (n= 288) were female and 29 percent (n= 116) were male. The race and ethnicity characteristics of the participant group were 82 percent (n=332) African American and 18 percent (n= 72) Latino/ Hispanic. The ethnicity demographics are fairly representative of the Eastern Illinois University minority population. According to the Planning and Institutional Research Office, approximately 71 percent of the minority population of the University is African American and approximately 19 percent is of Hispanic descent. Class standing of the participants reflected 13 percent (n=51) freshmen, 26 percent (n=105) sophomores, 25 percent (n=102) juniors, and 35 percent (n=140) seniors. Six (1 percent) of the students did not answer this question. The average age of the participants in the study was 20.56 years (SD=2.74). The demographic data for the generation profile showed that almost 68 percent of this group was non-first-generation and 32 percent were first-generation.

To determine if involvement is critical to first-generation minority students bonding to the university, a questionnaire was used to assess the students' involvement on campus. The instrument used in this study was a modification of the Participation in Campus and Community Activities (PCCA) designed by Dr. Marie Norby-Loud from the University of Northern Colorado. Additional questions were added to gather appropriate data specifically from students attending Eastern Illinois University. The PCCA contains eleven questions adapted from the College Student Experiences Questionnaire (CSEQ).

Data Analysis

For the purpose of this study, descriptive statistics were used for each group (first-generation, non-first-generation, African American and Hispanic) to measure percentages of responses, means, and standard deviations for each of the nine dependent variables in this study. Descriptive statistics were used to help the researcher summarize and describe the data (to give a full picture of the data). For each sample, means for the two groups (first-generation versus non-first-generation) were compared for each of the nine measures (use of nonacademic facilities, use of academic facilities, use of athletic facilities, experience with recognized student organizations, experience with faculty, relationships with students of the same race, relationships with students from other races, participation in university cultural centers and their participation in the community).

In addition to the descriptive statistics, the initial analysis utilized the Analysis of Variance (ANOVAS) to examine whether differences between first-generation and non-first-generation students are reliable and not due to random chance. This same process was used for ethnicity as well. To determine the combined effect on the experiences across the nine involvement variables, 2x2 factorial designs were used. To address research questions three and four, multiple regression equations and correlation of analyses were employed to determine how involvement in the nine areas might be predictive of how students connect to the institution and how their perceptions of their overall involvement were predictive of their likeliness to graduate. Specifically with question three, the researcher wanted to know if the different kinds of involvement were perceived predictors for connectedness to the university. Two regressions were tested to determine if there were differences between first-generation and non-first-generation students and African American and Hispanic students, simultaneously.

Quantitative Data Analysis

The data were examined in two sections: the frequency and nature of involvement on campus and the perceptions of connectedness to the institution. Two-by-two (ethnicity x generational status) factorial design was used to address research questions one and two simultaneously as well as to determine the possible combined effects of generational status and ethnicity on the experience across each of the nine involvement components. The third research question was to identify areas of involvement that were most predictive of students' perceived likelihood to be connected to the university, and the fourth research question was to determine whether students' perceptions of their overall involvement would be predictive of their perceived likelihood to graduate.

Research Question One

How do first-generation and non-first-generation participants differ in terms of their experience across the nine involvement components?

Table 7.2. Mean and Standard Errors of Involvement Measures by Generation

	First Generation M (SE)	Non-First Generation M (SE)	Mean Difference
Athletic Facilities Usage	10.94 (.556)	12.08 (.391)	1.14*
Intra-Racial Relations	17.56 (.621)	16.86 (.437)	0.7
Campus Involvement	15.04 (.675)	14.41 (.475)	0.63
Faculty Interaction	11.71 (.441)	11.13 (.311)	0.59
Academic Facilities	13.28 (.431)	12.75 (.304)	0.53
Inter-Racial Relations	15.62 (.560)	16.15 (.394)	0.53
Cultural Center Usage	6.63 (.353)	5.83 (.249)	0.47
Participating in Community	11.09 (.411)	10.90 (.289)	0.19
Non-academic Facilities	35.90 (1.75)	36.05 (.814)	0.15

*p<.05

In general, only involvement in the usage of athletic facilities was significantly different between first-generation and non-first-generation students, where non-first-generation students reported significantly higher usage. So across the nine involvement variables used in this study, there was no difference between first-generation and non-first-generation students overall with the exception of one variable which was slightly significant.

Research Question Two

Is there a difference between African American and Hispanic students with their involvement in the nine involvement components?

Table 7.3. Mean and Standard Errors of Involvement Measures by Race/Ethnicity

	African American (Black) M (SE)	Hispanic M (SE)	Mean Difference
Non-academic Facilities	40.40(.601)	31.55(1.28)	8.85*
Intra-Racial Relations	20.27(.323)	14.14(.687)	6.13*
Campus Involvement	16.34(.351)	13.10(.747)	3.24*
Faculty Interaction	12.35(.230)	10.50(.489)	1.85*
Academic Facilities	13.90(.224)	12.13(.478)	1.79*
Inter-Racial Relations	15.12(.291)	16.65(.620)	1.53*
Cultural Center Usage	6.67(.184)	5.79(.391)	.88*
Participating in Community	11.38(.214)	10.61(.455)	0.77
Athletic Facilities Usage	11.73(.289)	11.29(.615)	0.44

*p<.05

In general, the main effects of ethnicity indicated significant differences between African American and Hispanic students for several of the nine areas of involvement with the African American students reporting higher levels of involvement in six of those areas. The only area where Hispanic students reported higher levels of involvement were in interracial relations. So overall, there were differences between ethnicity in levels of involvement.

Combined Effects of Generation Status and Ethnicity

The results from the two-way factorial ANOVA revealed that none of the interactions between generation status and ethnicity were significant. That is, the differences between African American and Hispanic students were consistent for first-generation and non-first-generation students across all of the nine involvement measures.

Research Question Three

Which areas of involvement are most predictive of students' perceived likelihood to be connected to the University for first-generation and non-first-generation and for African American and Hispanic student groups?

To address the third question of this research, students responded to question 64 of the PCCA survey. The researcher performed a two-way univariate ANOVA to examine the effects of generational status and ethnicity on perceived connectedness. This statistical procedure was again selected because it allowed the analyses of ethnicity and generational status, as well as the combined effects of these two student variables, and perceived connectedness. That is, it simultaneously compares the levels of connected-ness between first-generation and non-first-generation students and African American versus Hispanic students; it also examines the difference between each generation across levels of ethnicity (i.e., African American and Hispanic students). The main effect of generation was not significant, $F(1, 400) = .0003, p=.99$; first-generation ($M = 4.88$, SE $=.182$) and non-first-generation ($M=5.02$, SE$=.128$) did not differ significantly in personal assessment of their connectedness to the institution. The main effect of ethnicity on connectedness to institution was significant, $F(1, 400) =4.92, p=.003$; African American students reported higher connectedness to institution ($M=5.16$, SE$=.094$) than Hispanic students ($M=4.74$, SE$=.201$). The interaction between ethnicity and generation standing was not significant, $F(1,400) =.288, p=.59$; the difference between African American and Hispanic students was consistent across the levels of generation status.

Overall, the main effect of generation (first-generation and non-first-generation) did not differ significantly in personal assessment of their connectedness to the institution and the main effect of ethnicity (African American and Hispanic) on connectedness to institution was significant. After simultaneously comparing the levels of connectedness between first-generation and non-first-generation students and African American and Hispanic students, the difference between African American and Hispanic students was consistent across the levels of generation status.

To address Research Question Three, multiple regression analysis was used to measure the predictive relationship between perceived connectedness to the institution and each of the nine independent variables (use of non-academic facilities, use of academic facilities, use of athletic facilities, experience with recognized student organizations, interaction with faculty, intra-racial relationships, interracial relationship, participation in the Cultural Center, and participation in the community) for each of the student groups (i.e., first-generation, non-first-generation, African American, Hispanic). These analyses were used to ascertain if the different categories of involvement were perceived predictors for connectedness to the university for each of the student groups.

First-Generation Students

Using the Enter method, a significant model emerged for first-generation students ($F_{9,121}$=9.205, $p<.001$), Adjusted R^2= .362. Regression analyses revealed a number of important findings. The Enter method allowed the researcher to enter all of the variables at the same time. Significant variables for connectedness were: Non-academic facilities (b = .523), Interracial Relationships (b = .192), and Academic Facility usage (b = –.216). These results show that first-generation students feel connected only through their involvement with of non-academic facilities.

Non-First-Generation Students

Using the Enter method, a significant model emerged for non-first-generation students ($F_{9,263}$= 16.483, $p<.001$), Adjusted R^2= .339. Regression analyses revealed a number of important findings. Significant variables for connectedness were: Campus Involvement (b = .224), Participation in Community (b = .161), and Non-Academic Facility usage (b = .217). The results from this regression analysis revealed that Non-first-generation students felt connected to campus through campus involvement.

African American Students

Using the Enter method, a significant model emerged for African American students ($F_{9,322}$= 20.324, $p<.001$), Adjusted R^2= .344. Regression analyses revealed a number of important findings. Significant variables for connectedness were: Non-Academic facility (b = .343), Campus Involvement (b = .194), Participation in Community (b = .114); and Inter-racial Relationships (b = .118). The results of this regression analyses revealed that African American students also felt connected primarily through being involved in non-academic facilities.

Hispanic Students

Using the Enter method, a significant model also emerged for Hispanic students ($F_{9, 62}$= 4.06, $p<.001$), Adjusted R^2= .280. Regression analyses revealed only one significant predictor. The significant variable for connectedness was: Usage of Athletic facilities (b = .281). The results in this regression analyses revealed that Hispanic students felt it was the usage of athletic facilities, which contributed most to their perceived connectedness.

Connectedness Summary

For the outcome of connectedness, multiple regression analysis explained 36 percent of the variance of first-generation students and 34 percent of the vari-ance in the non-first-generation students. For African American and Hispanic students, multiple regression analysis explained 34 percent and 28 percent of the variance, respectively. Additionally, the ANOVA model revealed no significant differences between first-generation and non-first-generation, but there were significant differences between African American and Hispanic students in their perception of connectedness to the institution. The regression models for each of these student groups were also different. Whereas African American students perceived greater connectedness to the university than Hispanic students, this difference between the African American and Hispanic students was not significantly different for first-generation and non-first-generation students. The inter-action was not significant.

Research Question Four

How are the students' perceptions of their overall involvement predictive of their perceived likelihood to graduate?

Correlation Analysis (Pearson r) was used to measure the relationship between overall involvement and the perceived likelihood to graduate for each of the student groups (i.e., first-generation, non-generation, African American, Hispanic) using question 70 on the PCCA survey. Overall involvement was calculated by summing involvement scores for the nine involvement areas (i.e., use of non-academic facilities, use of academic facilities, use of athletic facilities, experience with recognized student organizations, interaction with faculty, intra-racial relationships, interracial relationship, participation in the Cultural Center, and participation in the community) for each participant.

A Pearson product-moment correlation was used to determine if the overall involvement was related to the perceived likelihood to graduate for each group (first-generation; non-first-generation; African American and Hispanic students).

For first-generation and Latino students, the results revealed they did not perceive their overall involvement to assist with the likelihood to graduate. The relationship between perceived involvement and the likelihood to graduate was, at best, mild for non-first-generation and African American students in this study.

Summary of Findings

In general there were no statistically significant findings between first-generation and non-first-generation students with regard to their involvement in the nine areas. More directly, even students whose parents had a college degree did not differ from those students whose parents did not graduate from college. Although many of the findings were similar for first-generation and non-first-generation students, some findings in this study will be beneficial for Eastern Illinois University. For instance, only 36 percent of first-generation students lived on campus compared to over 55 percent non-first-generation students who resided in some type of on-campus facility, and over 80 percent of the students, both first-generation and non-first-generation, worked more than twenty hours per week.

In addition to the ANOVA findings, the multiple regressions were used to specifically answer the question on connectedness. This method did find some statistically significant results with the independent variables. The first-generation students felt connected though their involvement primarily using non-academic facilities, whereas non-first-generation students felt campus involvement made them feel connected. African American students also felt connected primarily through being involved in non-academic facilities, whereas Hispanic students felt the usage of athletic facilities contributed most to their perceived connectedness to the university. While there were no significant findings between first-generation and non-first-generation students in this study, there were a number of findings that will support new research on generation status versus ethnicity.

This quantitative study sought to examine the perception of involvement as a critical factor for first-generation and non-first-generation African American and Hispanic college students. The researcher also sought to determine if students' perceptions of their involvement contributed to their connectedness to the university as well as their perceived likelihood of graduating. The researcher examined this specific population because challenges that first-generation college students face, coupled with being a minority, have been noted throughout research to negatively contribute to students' educational aspirations, engagement, academic achievement, and academic integration (Giancola, Munz, and Trares, 2008; Lee, Sax, Kim, and Hagedom, 2004; Astin, 1997, 1993; Pascarella and Terenzini, 1991).

Discussion

In exploring the different types of involvement components, this study used two of the college impact models of student change as a means for understanding academic and social integration of first-generation and non-first-generation college students. These models were useful in understanding past research on the usage of some academic and non-academic facilities, participation in any type of clubs, organizations, and research with faculty, on-campus and off-campus employment, as well as interaction/involvement with first-generation/non-first-generation and ethnic minority students. Some of the findings from this study, coupled with current research, will help to clarify why some of the results were not statistically significant as well reveal the fact that some of the traditional theories of student retention and involvement may not be relevant for students of color regardless of their parents' educational background. As a consequence, the use of these models and theories created for majority students is well intentioned, yet it may not be appropriate when we add minority students to the group (Torres 2006).

The overall responses for the PCCA survey showed there were few differences in the involvement areas for first-generation and non-first-generation college students. Although there was a slight difference in the usage of athletic facilities with the non-first-generation using these facilities more, overall there was very little variance in means between both of these groups. Therefore, regardless of whether these students' parents had a college degree or not, there were no statistical significance in their involvement areas. Perhaps the reason why there were no differences in the involvement components with these two groups is because although there were differences with their generation status, their ethnicity rendered likeness on campus.

Another possible explanation for the results in the involvement of first-generation and non-first-generation not being different could be similarities in some of their demographic characteristics in this study. The demographic profile showed that some of the characteristics of the first-generation students, such as attending school part-time (Terenzini et al., 1995), from a lower family income level (Hernandez, 2000), and working while attending school (London, 1992), mirrored some of the characteristics of the non-first-generation students in this study. In this study, over 89 percent of both first-generation and non-first-generation students were enrolled as full-time students; and over 61 percent of both groups worked twenty hours or more during their undergraduate experience. Perhaps with these two groups having to work more hours and attending school full-time, both groups are similar in how they perceive their availability to get involved in the college experience.

Another factor that is important to note is both groups, regardless of generation, were ethnic minority students, either African American or Hispanic. For ethnic minorities attending a PWI, their adjustment may be different (i.e., educational attainment, and lower graduation rate) than for their White counterparts (Laird, Bridges, Holmes, Morelon, and Williams, 2004). So although they might not be the first in their families to attend college, their ability to get engaged and be involved on campus could be more similar to students who have parents with a higher education background because they are also students of color.

However, even though all the students were racial minorities, there were some differences between the African American and Hispanic groups in their involvement in the nine areas. In this study, African American students reported that they were involved in different areas (non-academic, intra-racial relations, campus involvement, faculty interaction and academic facilities) than the Hispanic students. Current research on Hispanic and African American students suggests that these two groups of students face serious challenges, but there are some differences in the challenges they face (Laird et al., 2004) like lack of engagement and culture backgrounds. The African American students were involved in more out-of-class experiences than the Hispanic students.

On the other hand, the Hispanic students in this study perceived more involvement in only one of the nine areas of involvement, which was their interracial interaction. This could have occurred because Hispanic students felt blending in with the majority population was more beneficial to them. According to stage one of Phinney's (1993) model of ethnic identity development, unexamined ethnic identity, individuals in this stage tend to accept the values and attitudes of the majority culture. This is consistent with current research on Hispanic students, because it is reported that some students feel it is important to become an integral part of the larger society (Torres, 2003). These students tended to associate with the majority culture, and they found diversity in the college environment as presenting conflicts (Torres, 2003). According to Phinney's (1993) model of ethnic identity development, the diversity could be presenting problems because, at phase two of this model, students are sometimes faced with a situation that forces them to "initiate an ethnic identity search" (Phinney, 1993, p. 69)

The main effect on generation with regard to students' perceived connectedness to campus showed that there was no significant difference between first-generation and non-first-generation students. Although there were no significant differences between the groups' perceived connectedness to the university, finding out if there were individual involvement variables that made them connect to the university was important. So a multiple regression model was then conducted to determine if these groups had differences in individual areas of involvement for connectedness. These areas were worth noting because they did show that there were slight differences in what these students were doing as a group to be connected to the campus in this study. For the first-generation students, they perceived the usage of non-academic facilities (i.e., attending events in the union, resident halls and hanging out in the union) as playing a role in connecting them to the university. Instead of using the non-academic facilities, non-first-generation students perceived campus involvement as an important variable for them. Perhaps again, the "campus community" is an important factor for this group because their parents may have been instrumental in helping them navigate and get acclimated. So overall, first-generation and non-first-generation students did not differ significantly in their perceived connectedness to the university, but when each group was examined individually, they both had different variables that connected them to the university. These findings are consistent with current literature that the campus environment plays a strong role in connecting students to the university (Pascarella and Terenzini, 1991).

On the other hand, there were differences between the African Americans and Hispanic students with their connectedness to the university. Although current research shows that both African American and Hispanic students have commonalities (i.e., low-income, first-generation, and family obligations) in their demographic profile, these two groups had different variables in how they interact and connect to the campus. The African American students reported more usage and/or involvement in six of the nine variables compared to the one involvement component indicated by the Hispanic students.

Perhaps the history of African American students on this particular campus plays a significant role in types of connections they have to the university. There is a stronger presence of student organizations with African American traditions on Eastern's campus for involvement (i.e., Miss Black EIU, Black Student Reunions). The African American students have multiple organizations (Black Student Union, NAACP, and National Association of Black Journalists) that have existed on the campus for more than thirty years. The Latin American Student Organization (LASO) is in its fourteenth year functioning on campus, and this currently is the only Latin American organization that exists. The Cultural Center is also used more frequently by African American students. This center could be used more by African American students because currently the center is named the Afro-American Cultural Center (the center is going through a name change that will take place after the next Board of Trustees meeting). According to Patton (2006), her research also validates that, in Black Cultural Centers, students learn about the importance of being involved on campus, about the skills for leadership, and helps develop a strong sense of identity. So perhaps, the history at this specific institution is making integration easier for African American students to engage more on the EIU campus than for the Hispanic students.

The final analysis in this study was to determine how students' perceptions of their overall involvement at the university were predictive of their likelihood to graduate. At Eastern Illinois University, the minority students' graduation rate is significantly lower than the majority students, 42 percent to 62 percent respectively. So this question was of significant interest in applying current research on involvement and understanding what this actually means for students of color and the graduation rate at Eastern Illinois University. A correlation analysis was used to determine the magnitude and direction of the association between the independent variables and the results. The results from the first-generation students emerged a non-significant model. This means that the first-generation student did not perceive their involvement in different areas on campus to be a predictor for graduation. There could possibly be two reasons for this result. First, first-generation students are unaware of the different involvement opportunities available on campus and therefore they feel involvement is not important for their progress toward graduation. Secondly, they might feel that academic involvement is strongly related to success in college so they do not perceive social involvement as important in assisting them in graduating.

On the other hand, the non-first-generation students in this study did feel that their involvement was perceived as a predictor for their likelihood to graduate. Again, when looking at non-first-generation students, we can assume that their parents have assisted them with knowledge of navigating through the college system so they are aware of the importance of involvement as a predictor for their persistence to graduation. Although the parents might know the importance of involvement, other results in this same study indicated non-first-generation students' level of involvement was no different than the first-generation students' involvement level. This again ties back to the research on students of color and some of the obstacles that might interfere with involvement, like alienation and the extent to which one is not comfortable and familiar with the norms and culture of the institution (Lundberg, Schreiner, Hovaguimian and Miller, 2007).

When the correlation analysis was conducted between the African American students and the involvement areas predictive of graduation, a significant result did emerge. Again, because African American students were involved in several out-of-class activities, they may perceive involvement to be helpful for graduation. African American students, regardless of the institutional type, seem to spend more time utilizing campus facilities and participating in clubs and organizations than White students (Sutton and Kimbrough, 2001; Watson and Kuh, 1996). This could be the reason these students feel participation will help with the persistence to graduation. On the other hand, with the Hispanic students, a significant result did not emerge connecting involvement to graduation. Because of the Hispanic students' lack on involvement on campus, this group perhaps did not relate involvement with graduation.

Although there were variables in this study that first-generation and non-first-generation students each found to be beneficial to their connectedness (usage of athletic facilities and campus involvement) to the university, the overall results revealed no statistical difference between the two student groups with connectedness. Students' whose parents had a college degree and were knowledgeable about how to navigate through higher education were no different in what they perceived to be connecting them to the university than students whose parents did not have a college degree.

While most of the findings in this study were not statistically significant, it is important not to overlook these results. The overall lack of differences in involvement and connectedness between the first-generation and non-first-generation may be due to the fact that these students' similarities as racial minorities on a predominantly White campus outweighed parental college background.

Implications for Practice

This study revealed no differences in the nine involvement levels between first-generation and non-first-generation students. However, it did identify some findings that similar four-year institutions and student affairs professionals will find relevant. For example, the number of hours these students report having to work may interfere with the time needed to engage in both on and off campus activities. Student affairs professionals could assist with finding financial resources and scholarships because working 15 hours or more is detrimental for the persistence of these students (Astin, 1984).

In this study, the results indicated that both first-generation students and ethnic minority students contribute uniquely to students' involvement patterns. Institutions cannot assume that addressing the needs of first-generation students will also address the needs of students of color (Lundberg et al., 2007). Institutions also need to be aware that even among students of color, it is not possible to create a "one size fits all" approach; each race/ethnic group appears to have its own unique needs (Jenkins and Walton, 2008). Student affairs professionals can work with services already existing on campus that target first-generation students only and offer these services for students of color, regard-less of parental education level. TRIO Programs have been extremely successful in graduating their students (Thomas, Farrow, and Martinez, 1998) and programs that offer tutoring, study skills workshops, and even cultural enrichment will help these students. Student affairs could provide an orientation that specifically educates the students on the importance of campus life, getting involved with student organizations and how partici-pating outside of the classroom can assist the student. Currently at Eastern Illinois University, the University Foundations course (freshmen seminar) is offered, and this course should be encouraged for first-generation and minority students. This 2-hour course offers topics on making connections, learning styles, mastering communication skills, building relationships, and campus activities.

Hispanic students reported higher levels of involvement in only one area in this study: interaction with students of a different race. Because their involvement was limited in this study, student affairs professionals need to encourage active participation in a full range of cocurricular activities. The current research notes that for Hispanic students, involvement in ethnic-based student organizations positively impacts retention (Hernandez and Lopez, 2007) because multicultural organizations serve as a major co-curricular experience for the majority of minority students at predominantly White campuses (Sutton and Kimbrough, 2001). Student affairs practitioners could disseminate information about the different multicultural organizations during student orientation and create more programming to include this population.

The most significant finding of this study was realizing that student affairs will need to examine what the institution is doing to assist students of color. If post-secondary institutions make a concerted and meaningful effort to affirm minority students' cultural identities, they stand to gain increased possibilities for ensuing the latter's success in college (Tierney, 1999). Cross-cultural researchers have suggested the need to compare people of color with one another rather than, or at least along with, Anglo American culture (Julian, McKenry, and McKelvey, 1994). The aforementioned findings can be useful to Eastern Illinois University as well as institutions that have similar demographics. Existing studies that have examined the role of race and first-generation status have put all non-White racial groups into one category, which overlooks distinctions among non-White racial and ethnic groups (Lundberg, Schreiner, Hovaguimian, and Miller, 2007). Most of the past literature groups underrepresented (first-generation, low-income, ethnic minority) students together. Perhaps we have been treating all groups as one and more research should focus on each individual group separately.

This study identified numerous challenges for first-generation and non-first-generation ethnic minority students that warrant examination. With threats of the elimination of grants and financial aid, more students in college are finding them-selves working full-time and attending college. The students in this study were those who persisted through their freshmen year of college, so looking at ways to engage second-year students and beyond would be beneficial. If these students are not getting engaged, the likelihood of graduation is slim.

Current research indicates that experiences of first-generation and ethnic minority student who attend Predominantly White Institutions (PWIs) complicate the college adjustment process and negatively affect student engagement, both inside and outside the classroom (Hawkins and Larabee, 2009). However, there is a lack of research that examines the differences or similarities comparing first-generation and non-first-generation students separately from ethnic minorities. This study showed that even when minority students had parents with an educational background, they were not at an advantage over first-generation students when navigating through higher education. Perhaps race and ethnicity outweighs generation on campus and more research is needed to re-examine these groups.

Pascarella and Terenzini (1991) contend that although structural and environmental characteristics of an institution shape students' social interaction and behavioral attitudes, it is the perceived environment that has the greatest influence on whether students of color have satisfying and rewarding social and academic experiences in college. It is up to institutions and student affairs divisions to address and transform the chilly and unwelcoming campus climates for students of color because environments can create climates that are debilitating to the success of these students (Steele, 2000). The time minority students spend developing a sense of community using of academic and non-academic facilities, the greater chance these students have to be engaged into the fabric of the institution. It is imperative that administrators' research minority student experiences on campus through data collection, which could provide information on possible cultural characteristic that affect educational outcomes for these specific ethnic groups.

Until persistence to graduation increases for first-generation and/or minority students, research on the retention of these students will continue to be a concern for higher education. Higher education institutions' "unwritten expectations" need to be a clear, explicit articulation for non-dominant groups unfamiliar with the academic culture at an institution (Schwartz, Donovan, and Guido-DiBrito, 2009). The need for additional research at multiple institutions will not only open the door for "new best practices" but new research will be able to create programming, support and initiatives to assist both first-generation and minority students. As we continue to provide greater insight into cross-cultural research-retention for racial/ethnic issues students, we will soon be able to shed some light on helping these populations obtain their baccalaureate degree!

References

Anaya, G., and Cole, D.G. (2001). Latina/o student achievement: Exploring the influence of student-faculty interactions on college grades. *Journal of College Student Development, 42*(1), 3-14.

Arboleda, A., Wang, Y., Shelley II, M. C., and Whalen, D. F. (2003). *Predictors of residence hall involvement,* 44(4), 517-531.

Astin, A. W. (1984). Student involvement: A developmental theory for higher education. *Journal of College Student Personnel, 25*(4), 297-308.

Astin, A.W. (1985). *Achieving educational excellence.* San Francisco: Jossey-Bass.

Astin, A. W. (1993). *What matters in college? Four critical years revisited.* San Francisco, CA: Jossey-Bass.

Astin, A. W. (1997). How 'good' is your institution's retention rate? *Research in Higher Education, 38*(6), 647-658.

Astin, A. W. and Oseguera, L. (2005). *Degree attainment rates at American colleges and universities* (Revised edition). Los Angeles, CA: Higher Education Research Institute, UCLA.

Betances, S. (2002). How to become an outstanding educator of Hispanic and African American first-generation college students. In F.W. Hale (Ed.), *What makes racial diversity work in higher education: Academic leaders present successful policies and strategies* (pp. 45-59). Sterling, VA: Stylus Publishing LLC.

Billson, J. M., and Terry, M. B. (1982). In search of the silken purse: Factors in attrition among first-generation students. *College and University*, 57-75.

Bowen, W. G., and Bok, D. (1998). *The shape of the river: Long-term consequences of considering race in college and university admissions.* Princeton, NJ: Princeton University Press.

Braxton, J. M. (2002). Conclusion: Reinvigorating theory and research on the departure puzzle. In J. M. Braxton (Ed.), *Reworking the student departure puzzle* (pp. 257-274). Nashville, TN: Vanderbilt University Press.

Chang, M. J., Astin, A. W., & Kim, D. (2004). Cross-racial interaction among undergraduates: Some consequences, causes, and patterns. *Research in Higher Education, 45*, 529-553.

Cross, T. (2001). Hopwood in doubt: The folly of setting a grand theory requiring race neutrality in all programs in higher education. *The Journal of Blacks in Higher Education. 29*, 60-84.

DeSousa, D. J., and King, P. M. (July 1992). Are white students really more involved in collegiate experiences than black students? *Journal of College Student Development, 33*, 363-369.

DeSousa, D. J., and Kuh, G. D. (1996). Does institutional racial composition make a difference in what Black students gain from college? *Journal of College Student Development, 37*, 257- 267.

Elkins, S. A., Braxton, J. M. and James, G. W. (2000). Tinto's separation stage and its influence on first-semester college student persistence. *Research in Higher Education, 41*(2), 251-268.

Filkins, J. W., and Doyle, S. K. (2002, June). *First-generation and low-income students: Using the NSSE data to study effective educational practices and students.* Paper presented at the annual forum for the Association for Institutional Research, Toronto, Canada.

Fischer, M. J. (2007). Settling into campus life: Differences by race/ethnicity in college involvement and outcomes. *The Journal of Higher Education, 78*(2), 126-161.

Fleming, J. (1984). *Blacks in college.* San Francisco: Jossey-Bass.

Freeman, K. (Fall 1999). HBC's or PWI's? African American high school students' consideration of higher education institution types. *The Review of Higher Education, 23*(1), 91-106.

Giancola, J. K., Munz, D. C. and Trares, S. (2008). First-verses continuing-generation adult students on college perceptions: Are differences actually because of demographic variance? *Adult Education Quarterly, 58*(3), 214-228.

Goggins, L. (2003). *The academic stars retention mode: An empirical investigation of its effectiveness.* Unpublished doctoral dissertation, University of Akron, Ohio.

Griffin, K. A., Nichols, A. H., Perez, D. H., and Tuttle, K. D. (2008). Making campus activities and student organizations inclusive for racial/ethnic minority students. In S. R. Harper (Ed.), *Creating inclusive college environments for cross-cultural learning and engagement* (pp. 121-138). Washington, DC: National Association.

Hahs-Vaughn, D. (2004). The impact of parents' education level on college students: An analysis using the beginning post-secondary students longitudinal study 1990-92/94. *Journal of College Student Development, 45*(5), 483-500.

Hanks, M. P., and Eckland, B. K. (1976). Athletics and social participation in the educational attainment process. *Sociology of Education, 49*, 271-294.

Harvey, W. B. (2003). *Minorities in Higher Education: 2000-2001.* The American Council on Education Eighteenth Annual Status Report.

Harvey, W. B., and Anderson, E. L. (2005). *Minorities in higher education: Twenty-first annual status report (2003-2004).* Washington, DC: American Council on Education.

Hawkins, V. M. and Larabee, H. J. (2009). Engaging racial/ethnic minority students in out-of-class activities on predominantly White campuses. In S. Harper and S. Quale (Eds.), *Student engagement in higher education: Theoretical perspectives and Practical approaches for diverse populations* (pp.179-188). New York and London: Routledge.

Heller, D. E. (2003). *State financial aid and college access* (Report No. HE035603). New York, NY: College Entrance Examination Board. (ERIC Document Reproductive Service No: ED472456).

Hernandez, J.C., and Lopez, M.A. (2007). The leaking pipeline: Issues impacting Latino/a college student retention. In A. Seidman (Ed.), *Minority student retention: The best of the journal of college student retention: Research, theory, and Practice* (pp. 7-28). Amityville, NY: Baywood Publishing Company, Inc.

Hernandez, J. C. (2000). Understanding the retention of Latino college students. *Journal of College Student Development, 41*, 575-588.

Holmes, S. L., Ebbers, L. H., Robinson, D. C., and Mugenda, A. G. (2007). Validating African American students at predominantly white institutions. In A. Seidman (Ed.), *Minority student retention: The best of the journal of college student retention: Research, theory, and practice* (pp. 79-98). Amityville, NY: Baywood Publishing Company, Inc.

Hsiao, K. P. (1992). *First-generation college students* (Report No. ED0-JC-004). Washington, DC: Office of Educational Research and Improvement. (ERIC Document Reproductive Service No: ED 351 079)

Humphrey, E. (April 2000). *An ex-post facto study of first-generation students.* Unpublished master's thesis, Virginia Polytechnic Institute and State University, Blacksburg, VA.

Hurtado, S. (Winter 2007) Linking diversity with the educational and civic missions of higher education. *The Review of Higher Education, 30*(2), 185-196.

Hyatt, R. (2003). Barriers to persistence among African American intercollegiate athletes: A literature review of non-cognitive variables. *Journal of College Student Development, 37*(2), 260-276.

Jenkins, T. S., and Walton, C. L. (2008). Student affairs and cultural practice: A framework for implementing culture outside the classroom. In S. R. Harper (Ed.), *Creating inclusive campus environments: For cross-cultural learning and student engagement* (pp. 87-103). United States: NASPA

Julian, R. W., McKenry, P. C., and McKelvey, M. V. (1994). Cultural variations in parenting: Perceptions of Caucasian, African-American Hispanic, and Asian-American parents. *Family Relations, 43*, 30-37.

Kuh, G. D., and Gonyea, R. M. (July 2003) The role of the academic library in promoting student engagement in learning. *College and Research Libraries, 64*(4), 256-282.

Kuh, G. D., and Hu, S. (2001). The effects of student-faculty interaction in the 1990's. *The Review of Higher Education, 24*(3), 309-332.

Kuh, G. D., and Umbach, P. D. (2004). College and character: Insights from the national survey of student engagement. *New Directions for Institutional Research, 122*, 37-54.

Laird, T. F. N., Bridges, B. K., Holmes, M. S., Morelon, C. L., and Williams, J. M. (2004, November). *African American and Hispanic Student Engagement at Minority Serving and Predominantly White Institutions.* Paper presented at the Annual Meeting of the Association for the Study of Higher Education, Kansas City, MO.

Lee, J.J., Sax. L.J., Kim, K. A., and Hagedom, L.S. (2004). Understand student's parental education beyond first-generation status. *Community College Review, 32*(1), 1-20.

Levin, J. S. (1998). Presidential influences, leadership succession, and multiple interpretations of organizational change. *The Review of Higher Education, 21*(4), 405-425.

London, H. B. (1992). Transformations: Cultural challenges faced by first-generation students. *New Directions for Community Colleges, 80*, 5-11.

Lundberg, C. A. and Schreiner, L. A. (2004). Quality and frequency of faculty-student Interaction as predictors of learning: An analysis by student race/ethnicity. *Journal of College Student Development, 45*(5), 549-565.

Lundberg, C.A., Schreiner, L. A., Hovaguimian, K. D., and Miller, S. S. (2007). First-generation status and student race/ethnicity as distinct predictors of student involvement and learning. *NASPA Journal, 44*(1), 57-83.

Martin, B. E. (2009). Redefining championship in college sports: Enhancing outcomes and increasing student-athlete engagement. In S. Harper and S. Quale (Eds.), *Student engagement in higher education: Theoretical perspectives and practical approaches for diverse students* (pp. 283-294) New York, NY: Routledge

McConnell, P. J. (2000). What community colleges should do to assist first-generation students. *Community College Review, 28*(3), 75-87.

Morley, K. M. (2007). Fitting in by race/ethnicity: The social and academic integration of diverse students in a predominately white university. In A. Seidman (Ed.), *Minority student retention: The best of the journal of college student retention: Research, theory, and practice* (pp. 243-270). Amityville, NY: Baywood Publishing Company, Inc.

National Center for Educational Statistics. (2002). *The condition of education 2002.* (NCES 2002-025). Washington, DC: U.S. Department of Education.

National Center for Educational Statistics. (2005). *The condition of education.* (NCES 2005- 094). Washington, DC: U.S. Department of Education.

Nettles, M. T., Wagener, U., Millett, C. M., and Killenbeck, A. M. (1999). Student retention and progression: A special challenge for private historically black colleges and universities. In G. H. Gaither (Ed.), *Promising practices in recruitment, remediation, and retention* (pp. 31-49). San Francisco, CA: Jossey-Bass.

Nora, A., Cabrera, A., Hagedorn, L. S., and Pascarella, E. (1996). Differential impacts of academic and social experiences on college-related behavioral outcomes acrossdifferent ethnic and gender groups at four-year institutions. *Research in Higher Education, 37*(4), 427-451.

Olivas, M. A. (1997). Indian, Chicago, and Puerto Rican colleges: Status and issues. In L. F. Goodchild and H. S. Wechsler (Eds.), *The history of higher education* (Second edition) (pp. 677-698). Needham Heights, MA: Simon and Schuster.

Owens, J. S., Reis, F. W., and Hall, K. M. (1994). Bridging the gap: Recruitment and retention of minority faculty members. *New Directions for Community Colleges, 22*(3), 57-64.

Pascarella, E.T. (1985). Students' affective development within the college environment. *The Journal of Higher Education, 56*(6), 640-663.

Pascarella, E. T., Pierson, C. T., Wolniak, G. C. and Terenzini, P. T. (2004). First-generation college students: Additional evidence on college experiences and outcomes. *The Journal of Higher Education, 75*(3), 249-284.

Pascarella, E. T., and Smart, J. (1991). Impact of intercollegiate athletic participation for African American and Caucasian men: Some further evidence. *Journal of College Student Development, 23*, 123-130.

Pascarella, E. T. and Terenzini, P. T. (1991). *How college affects students: Findings and insights from twenty years of research*. San Francisco: Jossey-Bass.

Pascarella, E. T., and Terenzini, P. T. (1998). Studying college students in the 21st century: Meeting new challenges. *The Review of Higher Education, 21*(2), 151-165.

Pascarella, E. T., and Terenzini, P. T. (2005). *How college affects students* (Second edition). San Francisco, CA: Jossey-Bass.

Pascarella, E. T., Truckenmiller, R., Nora, A., Terenzini, P. T., Edison, M., and Hagedorn, L. S. (1999). Cognitive impacts of intercollegiate athletic participation: Some further evidence. *The Journal of Higher Education, 70*(1), 1-26.

Patton, L. D. (May-June 2006). Black culture centers: Still central to student learning. *About Campus*, 2-8.

Pew Hispanic Center (2004). Changing channels and crisscrossing cultures: A survey of Latinos on the news media. Available from Pew Hispanic Center Web site: http://pewhispanic.org/datasets.

Phinney, J. S. (1993). A three-stage model of ethnic identity development in adolescence. In M. E. Bernal and G. P. Knight (Eds.), *Ethnic identity: Formation and transmission among Hispanics and other minorities* (pp. 61-79). Albany: SUNY Press.

Rendon, L. I. (1995, March). *Facilitating retention and transfer for first-generation students in community colleges*. Paper presented at the New Mexico Institute, Espanola, NM.

Rodriguez, N., Mira, C. B., Myers, H. F., Morris, J. K, and Cardoza, D. (2003). Family or friends: Who plays a greater supportive role for Latino college students? *Cultural Diversity and Ethnic Minority Psychology, 9*(3), 236-250.

Saenz, V.B. (2002). *Hispanic students and community colleges: A critical point for intervention.* (Report No. EDO-JC-02-08). Los Angeles, CA: ERIC Clearinghouse for Community Colleges. (ERIC Document Reproductive Services No: ED477908).

Saenz, V.B., Hurtado, S., Barrera, D., Wolf, D., and Young, F. (2007). *First in my family: A portrait of first-generation college students at four-year institutions since 1971.* Los Angeles: Higher Education Research Institute, UCLA.

Salinas, A., and Llanes, J. R. (2003). Student attrition, retention and persistence: The case of the University of Texas Pan American. *Journal of Hispanic Higher Education, 2*, 73-97.

Sanders-Thompson, V. L. (2002). Racism: Perceptions of distress among African Americans. *Community Mental health Journal, 38*(3), 111-118.

Schwartz, J. L. and Guido-DiBrito, F. (2009). Stories of social class: Self-identified Mexican male college students crack the silence. *Journal of College Student Development, 50*(1), 50-66.

Sedlacek, W. (1987). Black students on white campuses: 20 years of research. *Journal of College Student Personnel, 28*(6), 484-495.

Smedley, B. D., Myers, H. F., and Harrell, S. P. (1993). Minority-status stresses and the college adjustment of ethnic minority freshmen. *The Journal of Higher Education, 64*(4), 434-452.

Steele, C. M. (2000). "Stereotypes threat" and Black college students. *About Campus, 5*(2), 2-4.

Sutton, E. M. and Kimbrough, W. M. (2001). Trends in Black student involvement. *NASPA Journal, 39*(1), 30-40.

Svanum, S., and Bigatti, S.M. (2006). The influences of course effort and outside activities on grades in a college course. *Journal of College Student Development, 47*(5), 564-575.

Swail, W. S., Redd, K. E. and Perna, L. W. (2003). *Retaining minority students in higher education: A framework for success.* San Francisco, CA: Jossey-Bass.

Terenzini, P. T., Rendon, L. I., Upcraft, M. E., Millar, S. B., Allison, K. W., Gregg, P. L., and Jalomo, R. (1994). The transition to college: Diverse students, diverse stories. *Research in Higher Education, 35*(1), 57-73.

Terenzini, P. T., Springer, L., Yeager, P. M., Pascarella, E. T. and Nora, A. (1995, May). *First-generation college students: Characteristics, experiences, and cognitive development.* Paper presented at the annual meeting of the Association for Institutional Research, Boston, MA.

Thayer, P. B. (May 2000). Retraining first-generation and low income students. *Opportunity Outlook*, pp. 2-8.

Thomas, E. P., Farrow, E. V. and Martinez, J. (1998). A TRIO program's impact on participant graduation rates: The Rutgers university student support services program and its network of services. *The Journal of Negro Education, 67*(4), 389-403.

Tierney, W. G. (1992). An anthropological analysis of student participation in college. *The Journal of Higher Education, 63*(6), 603-618.

Tierney, W. G. (1999). Models of minority college-going and retention: Cultural integrity versus cultural suicide. *Journal of Negro Education, 68*(1), 80-91.

Tinto, V. (1987). *Leaving college: rethinking causes and cures of student attrition.* Chicago: University of Chicago Press.

Tinto, V. (1993). *Leaving college: rethinking causes and cures of student attrition* (Second edition). Chicago: University of Chicago Press.

Tinto, V. (2004). *Student retention and graduation: Facing the truth, living with the consequences.* Occasional Paper 1: The Pell Institute for the Study of Opportunity in Higher Education. Washington, DC: The Pell Institute.

Torres, V. (2003). Influences on ethnic identity development of Latino college students in the first two years of college. *Journal of College Student Development, 44,* 532-547.

Torres, V. (May/June 2006). A mixed method study testing data—Model fit of a retention model for Latino/a students at urban universities. *Journal of College Student Development, 47(3),* 299-318.

Tracy, T. J. and Sedlacek, W. E. (1985). The relationship of non-cognitive variables to academic success: A longitudinal comparison by race. *Journal of College Student Personnel, 26(5),* 405-410.

U.S. Census Bureau (2004). *Educational attainment in the United States: Table 1a percent. of high school and college graduates of the population 15 years and over, by age, sex, race and Hispanic origin: 2004.* Retrieved November 5, 2007, from http://www.cenus.gov/population/www/socdemo/education/cps 2004.html.

Watson, L. W. and Kuh, G. D. (1996). The influence of dominant race environments on student involvement, perceptions, and educational gains: A look at historical black and predominantly white liberal arts institutions. *Journal of College Student Development, 37*(4), 415-424.

Williamson, J. A. (1999). In defense of themselves: The Black student struggle for success and recognition at predominantly White colleges and universities. *The Journal of Negro Education, 68*(1), 92-105.

Young, L. (1991). The minority cultural center on a predominantly white campus. In H. E. Cheatham (Ed.), *Cultural pluralism on campus.* Lanham, MD: American College Personnel Association.

Zalaquett, C. P. (1999). Do students of non-college-educated parents achieve less academically than students of college-educated parents? *Psychological Reports, 85,* 417-421.

Quantitative Research Studies on Undecided and Non-Traditional College Students

Chapter Eight
Factors Impacting the Academic Achievement of Undecided College Students

Kimberly Brown, Ph.D.,
Virginia Tech University

Introduction

Higher education administrators have paid considerable attention to the retention and persistence of undergraduate students in hopes of reducing the percentage of students who leave college prematurely. Retention refers to an institution's ability to retain students from one year to another. Student persistence refers to students' conscious choice and ability to continue in their pursuit of their educational goals. Simply stated, persisters are students who enroll at an institution and continue their enrollment, though not necessarily in consecutive terms, until they have completed their degree requirements (Blecher, 2006). While the terms "retention" and "persistence" are often used interchangeably, it is important to note that retention is an institutional outcome and persistence is a student outcome (Hagedorn, 2003).

Retention and persistence are worthy of examination given that American colleges and universities consistently experience a first to second year persistence rate of only 75 percent. That is, one quarter of entering first year students do not persist to their second year of college (Braxton, 2000). It is important to understand why students are dropping out or have significant variability in enrollment patterns for institutions to respond to students' needs. The increased focus on student retention and persistence is warranted due to two important policy issues within higher education. First, student retention is a means of evaluating institutional performance (Green, 2002; Metz, 2004). Stakeholders today frequently request indicators of performance as a means of establishing institutional accountability and accountability is receiving a great deal of attention within the American higher education system. Retention rates are commonly used as a measure of student achievement and progress.

Second, retention also has significant financial implications that must be considered. When institutions are able to retain students from one year to another, they better position themselves to positively influence their revenue stream. This is particularly crucial given the increasing financial pressures placed on colleges and universities. An increased focus on improving retention rates, hence increasing revenues from tuition, is one strategy to address this issue. Another strategy includes improving student academic achievement. Academic achievement or a student's ability to meet or exceed the academic standards of a given institution, is important because it reflects a measure of students' acquisition of important skills and attributes considered necessary to demonstrate that student learning has occurred. Some benefits of student academic achievement represent public interests, such as increasing the United States' global competitiveness and increased civic engagement (Lopez-Claros, Porter, Schwab, and Sala-i-Martin, 2006; Jones, 1996). Other benefits of student achievement reflect private interests, including greater earning potential for individuals (College Board, 2006; Institute for Higher Education Policy, 1998, 2005).

Given the significant individual and societal benefits of academic achievement, it is important to consider the factors that influence academic achievement in higher education. Four factors have been identified in the literature as having an impact on academic achievement: student background characteristics, self-perception of abilities, degree aspirations, and choice of academic major. The specific set of background characteristics that students bring with them to college affects their academic performance (Astin, 1993b; Naretto, 1995). Background characteristics include age, gender, race, parental educational background, high school GPA, college admission test scores, and family income level, (Kahn and Nauta, 2001; Leppel, 1984; 2002; McGrath and Braunstein, 1997; Pascarella and Terenzini, 1991; Tinto, 1993). However, these characteristics do not account for all of the variation in academic performance. Another factor that contributes to student academic achievement is self-perception of abilities (Bryson, Smith, and Vineyard, 2002; Jackson, Smith, and Hill, 2003; Sedlacek, 2004). Specifically, students who report higher levels of self-confidence in their abilities tend to be academically successful. It is necessary for students to exhibit confidence in their abilities to achieve their academic goals (Sedlacek, 2004).

A third factor contributing to the academic achievement of students is their degree aspirations. Students reporting a desire to achieve educational goals beyond the bachelor's degree tend to achieve academically, persist, and graduate at greater rates than do students for whom a bachelor's degree is the ultimate educational goal (Walpole, 2007). While it may be beneficial for students to consider long-term goals such as the highest level of degree desired (e.g., earning a master's or doctorate degree), they must first complete a four-year degree and that process begins by selecting a major.

One particular group of students has been highlighted in the literature on academic achievement and academic major. Undecided students are those who are "unwilling, unable, or unready to make educational or vocational decisions" (Gordon, 1995, p. x). This population of students tends to produce lower scores than decided students in terms of high school grade point average, college grade point average, and American College Testing (ACT) Program composite scores

(Wood, 1990). Research also indicates that undecided students have lower academic performance and persistence rates (Leppel, 2001).

Despite a wealth of research on predicting the academic achievement of students, and programs and services designed to promote academic achievement among undecided students, no studies have focused exclusively on understanding the factors which impact the academic achievement of undecided students by examining their background characteristics, self-perception of abilities, and highest degree aspired to from a lens other than the deficiency perspective. In addition, existing literature on undecided students and academic achievement examine this population as a homogeneous group. The current study was designed to address these gaps in the literature.

Purpose Statement

The purpose of this study was to determine the differences between academic achievement and undecided student status. Specifically, this researcher determined how much of the variation in academic achievement could be explained by the pre-college characteristics for Specific Majors (SMs) and Non-Specific Majors (NSMs). These pre-college characteristics included background characteristics, self-perception of abilities, and degree aspirations. Academic achievement was defined as the cumulative GPA at the end of the second semester.

The factors which were examined to determine their impact on academic achievement of undecided students were variables measured by the 2005, 2006 and 2007 Cooperative Institutional Research Program's (CIRP) Annual Freshman Survey (AFS) (Higher Education Research Institute, 2007). The AFS variables used for this study were grouped into three categories: background characteristics, self-perception of abilities, and degree aspirations.

The sample was comprised of undecided, full-time students between the ages of eighteen and twenty at a single institution. The participants were first enrolled as students in the Fall semesters of 2005, 2006, or 2007, and completed the AFS during the summer prior to their matriculation.

Research Questions

The present study examined four research questions:
1. Are there statistically significant differences between Specific Majors (SMs) and Non-Specific Majors (NSMs) in terms of background characteristics?
2. Are there statistically significant differences between Specific Majors (SMs) and Non-Specific Majors (NSMs) in terms of self-perception of abilities?
3. Are there statistically significant differences between Specific Majors (SMs) and Non-Specific Majors (NSMs) in terms of degree aspirations?

4.   Are there statistically significant differences between Specific Majors (SMs) and Non-Specific Majors (NSMs) in terms of academic achievement (first year GPA)?

The study was significant for future practice, research, and policy within higher education. In regards to practice, this study provided results that may be of benefit to three constituencies. First, academic advisors were provided with information about the factors that predict academic achievement for undecided students. Advisors might use the findings to assess what services they deliver to undecided majors.

Second, the results of this study were significant for undecided students. This population of students might benefit from the results that highlight the background characteristics, self-perception of abilities, and degree aspirations that were most likely to predict academic achievement. Undecided students could use the findings to assess their own preparedness for academic achievement.

Third, admissions officers are charged with recruiting new classes of students to institutions each year with an expectation that the students will have the ability to succeed academically. This study provided admissions officers with information about the potential impact of background characteristics, self-perception of abilities, and degree aspirations on the academic achievement of undecided students. Admissions officers might use this information to refine their selection process or factors they consider in making their recommendation about which students should be offered admission, admitting students who better match the institution's strengths.

The study also served to promote future research. While end-of-year-one GPA was used as a measure of academic achievement, future investigations might examine academic achievement during the entire college career. Specifically, cumulative grade point average could be tracked at the end of each academic year for which undecided majors were enrolled. Such an approach would provide a broader time frame over which to measure academic achievement and might more accurately measure success for undecided students. This study defined achievement in college exclusively in terms of academic performance. Future studies might seek to broaden the definition of achievement to include both academic and non-academic indicators of achievement. Expanding the operational definition of achievement might provide the opportunity to highlight collegiate achievement in students not always evidenced by their grade point average.

Finally, future research might include an examination of students from other majors. While the current study focused on undecided students, this population constitutes only a fraction of the total enrollment of most higher education institutions. Such a future study might provide a greater awareness of the factors that impact academic achievement for students from various majors.

Policy implications were also evidenced in this study. Academic administrators charged with developing standards for internal transfer (i.e., changing majors within the same institution) could benefit from the results of the current study. The findings provided this group of policymakers with data regarding the factors that impact academic achievement among undecided students. They might use the results to evaluate the standards used to assess internal transfer applications.

Another way in which the results of the current study might influence policy is related to admission standards. Policymakers might use information about factors that impact achievement when determining admissions standards for undecided students.

Academic administrators concerned with retention of undecided majors might benefit from the results of this study as this population of students tends to have lower retention rates. The results provided insight into the effect of background characteristics, self-perception of abilities, and degree aspirations on the academic achievement of undecided students. The data might be used to develop policies geared towards the unique needs of this group of students.

Literature Review

This study was designed to address a gap in the literature regarding the academic achievement among undecided students during their first year of enrollment at a four-year public research institution. Specifically, differences in academic achievement between Specific Majors (SMs) and Non-Specific Majors (NSMs) in terms of pre-college characteristics were examined. In addition, the study examined whether the pre-college characteristics could be used to successfully predict the academic achievement of undecided students. The literature review is centered on these areas of study.

First, for purposes of this study, first-year college grade point average (GPA) was used as a measure of students' academic achievement. Therefore, GPA as a measure of academic achievement was reviewed. Next, it was necessary to examine the literature on pre-college characteristics that influence academic achievement.

Three groups of studies were reviewed. These included background characteristics, self-perception of abilities, and degree aspirations. Finally, since the study examined achievement among undecided students, research on that population of college students was explored.

GPA and Academic Achievement

In terms of academic achievement in college, grade point average (GPA) is commonly used as an indicator of student achievement. Specifically, first-year college GPA is a measure of the consistent academic achievement of a student across terms (Brashears and Baker, 2003). In addition, the value of using GPA as a measure of academic achievement has been highlighted as GPA has been found to be a significant predictor of persistence (Allen, 1999; Mitchel, Goldman, and Smith, 1999; Murtaugh, Burns, and Schuster, 1999) and serves as one indication of the degree to which students have responded to the institutional environment

(McGrath and Braunstein, 1997; Tinto, 1993; Tross, Harper, Osher, and Kneidinger, 2000).

Allen (1999) examined the existence of an empirical link between motivation and persistence. He concluded that regardless of students' racial/ethnic status (minority or nonminority), first-year college GPA exerts the largest influence on whether or not a student persists. In addition, the higher a student's GPA the greater the probability of retaining that student from the first to the second year of enrollment in college (Murtaugh, Burns, and Schuster, 1999).

Background Characteristics

Most studies suggest that background characteristics influence academic achievement only during the first year of enrollment. Six specific background characteristics have been identified: (a) high school achievement, (b) gender, (c) SAT scores, (d) ethnicity, (e) parental education, and (f) parental income (Terenzini, Theophilides, and Lorang, 1984).

Self-Perception of Abilities

Self-concept refers to an individual's image of him/herself. It is a multi-layered construct reflecting various dimensions of students' self-perceptions of their abilities and attitudes (Byrne, 1984; Hansford and Hattie, 1982). More specifically, Ethington (1990) has expanded the concept to include an academic component and has defined academic self-concept as a student's ability and intellectual self-confidence.

The vast majority of research in this area has focused on pre-school, elementary, and secondary school youth, with substantially less attention given to examining the self-perception of abilities of college students (Smart and Pascarella, 1986). A review of the current literature indicates the same trend to be true today. Minimal research exists regarding college students' self-perception of abilities compared to younger student populations. Despite the limited research on college students' self-perception of abilities, there is clear consensus among researchers on two related issues. First, academic achievement is positively influenced by self-perception of abilities (Bauer and Liang, 2003; Hamacheck, 1995; Hickman, Bartholomae, and McHenry, 2000;

Pritchard and Wilson, 2003; Zheng, et. al, 2002). Evidence supporting this conclusion includes Bauer and Liang's (2003) findings that students' personality type (encompassing self-perception of abilities) influences first-year GPA. Additionally, self-perception of abilities serves as a good predictor of future academic achievement (Pritchard and Wilson, 2003; Tross, Harper, Osher, and Kneidinger, 2000). The current study seeks to explain the variance in academic achievement for undecided students and because of its clearly established relationship with academic achievement, students' self-perception of abilities is included in the analysis.

Degree Aspirations

It is important to examine educational aspirations as they are a "fundamental part of the attainment process and yet are among the least understood concepts in higher education" (Carter, 2001, p. 6). Anecdotally, without aspirations college students' educational plans are not likely to come to fruition. However, research also confirms the relative strength of educational aspirations as a contributor to academic achievement. Pascarella (1984) investigates the influences of the college environment on students' educational aspirations and concludes "by far, the best predictor of educational aspirations at the end of the second year of college was the level of educational aspiration at entrance to college" (p. 767). In addition, others have reached similar conclusions noting that "the student's degree aspirations at the time of college entrance are the most potent predictors of enrollment in graduate and professional school" (Astin, 1977, p.112).

Defining aspiration can be difficult as it has been considered a concept that is synonymous with several other terms including expectation, educational plan, wish, dream, intention, and ambition (Carter, 2001). For the current study, aspirations are defined as the "goal that one intends or expects to attain" (Berman and Haug, 1975, p. 166). The goal under investigation in the current study includes the highest degree aspired to by first-year college students.

Aspirations have been studied since the late 1960s (Carter, 1999). However, when aspirations are investigated particular focus has been placed on research design and college students. Regarding design, researchers have studied aspirations as either an outcome or as a predictor of an outcome. For example, several scholars have concluded students' aspirations are directly affected by institutional characteristics and experiences (Carter, 2001; Hossler and Gallagher, 1987; Astin, 1993b; Smith, 1990). Fewer studies have used aspirations as anindicator of an outcome (Dey and Astin, 1993; Hull-Toye, 1995; Pascarella, Smart, and Stoecker, 1989).

The aspirations of college students are frequently examined in the literature. However, Carter (2001) notes more research related to aspirations for the high school-to-college population exists than research reporting on college students' plans to attend graduate school. The current study builds on this body of literature by examining the post-baccalaureate degree aspirations of college students as indicated prior to enrollment in their first term of college.

Undecided Students

One body of literature on undecided students recognizes the diversity of needs among this group of students by creating sub-types, or categories of undecided students. In one model, four general categories of undecided students were identified: tentatively undecided, developmentally undecided, seriously undecided, and chronically indecisive. Tentatively undecided students are characterized as happy and playful (Lucas and Epperson, 1988), are comfortable with themselves and have a relatively high vocational identity level. These undecided students are closer to making a decision than are the developmentally undecided students (Gordon, 1998).

Evidence exists to support the general perception within higher education for students who are undecided or have not declared a major are less likely to persist. In his study examining student attrition, Noel (1985) described uncertainty of major as a form of attrition and concluded "uncertainty about what to study is the most frequent reason talented students give for dropping out of college" (p. 12). This conclusion is also supported by Sprandel (1985) who argued undecided students experience less academic achievement because they do not have a purpose for attending school. Anderson (1985) believed undecided students ultimately fail to persist because they do not have a clear focus and they lack direction in terms of their educational and career goals. The general belief that undecided students are more attrition prone simply because they have not declared a major represents a more negative view of this student population.

A major shift in assumptions regarding undecided students and persistence occurred in the mid-1980s due to conclusions drawn from studies being conducted at the time. Notably, Lewallen (1992) disputes that undecided students are less likely to persist because the methodology of the majority of studies that draw such a conclusion is flawed. Although frequently cited on this topic, these findings "were not empirically derived from studying students, but were the result of respondent's opinions, perceptions, and judgments" (Lewallen, 1992, p. 29). Instead of drawing their conclusions from student data, the researchers surveyed administrators and staff.

Additional studies counter previous misconceptions that undecided students are more likely to drop out of college (Graunke et al., 2006; Lewallen, 1993). Graunke, et al. (2006) investigated the impact of institutional commitment, commitment to an educational goal, and commitment to an academic major on the probabilities of graduation for first-year students. Their results indicated commitment to an academic major, or decidedness, was negatively associated with probabilities of degree completion.

The current study seeks to expand existing literature on factors which impact academic achievement by investigating undecided students. Furthermore, it is important to note that not all undecided students have the same needs and concerns. Therefore, this study explores academic achievement by varying levels of undecidedness (Specific Majors and Non-Specific Majors). Using a multiple regression analysis, the background characteristics, self-perceptions of abilities, and degree aspirations of undecided students were examined in an effort to determine which factors have an impact on the academic achievement of this population.

Results of Study

The sample of undecided students is described by examining the differences between the NSMs and SMs in terms of their background characteristics, self-perception of abilities, degree aspirations, and academic achievement. These findings relate to the first four research questions. To address the final two research questions, the nature of the relationship between the two sub-groups of undecided students and their respective background characteristics, self-perception of abilities, and degree aspirations were examined to determine how much variance in academic achievement can be explained by these factors.

Comparing NSMs and SMs

The data set for this study provided the opportunity to investigate the similarities and differences between 852 undeclared students who were classified as either NSMs (n=538) or SMs (n=314). The literature describes academic achievement as an important measure of student persistence. In addition, a review of the literature notes a number of pre-college characteristics that influence academic achievement including background characteristics, self-perception of abilities, and degree aspirations.

Research Question One:
Background Characteristics

The first research question posed in the study focused on differences between SMs and NSMs by background characteristics. The background characteristics included sex, high school grade point average, parental income, race, parental education, and SAT score. Crosstab analysis was conducted on all background characteristics except SAT scores. Crosstabs are designed for discrete variables, usually those measured on nominal or ordinal scales. Because SAT scores are continuous variables that can assume many different values, crosstab analysis was not an appropriate form of analysis. Therefore, a t-test was used to examine differences in the two groups by SAT score.

The crosstabs analysis, as shown by the resulting chi squares, led to four significant differences between groups. First, a significant difference in terms of sex was revealed. Specifically, more NSMs were female (N=283) than male (N=255), while significantly more males (N=240) than females (N=74) were SMs. The differences by sex were significant at the level of p=.000 (see Table 8.1).

The findings also revealed significant differences between NSMs and SMs related to their high school grade point average. Table 8.1 reveals that NSMs tended to report higher grades earned during high school than SMs (p=.022). The three highest grade options students could report included: (a) A or A+, (b) A-, and (c) B+. The percentages of NSMs indicating these grade options were 21.19 percent, 33.09 percent, and 32.34 percent respectively for a total of over 86 percent. For the SM group the respective percentages were 16.56 percent, 25.80 percent, and 38.22 percent, or a total of only 80 percent.

The analysis also revealed that significantly more of the sample were students from the majority race category (White) in comparison to the non-majority race category (all other race categories) regardless of their major classification (NSM versus SM) (p=.007). Of the total sample, 685 students were of the majority and 167 were from the non-majority group. The original data included nine options for students to self-identify their race. However, the cell sizes for all groups other than Whites were too small to stand alone in the analysis. Therefore, it was necessary to create the majority and non-majority dichotomy for analysis purposes.

Parental education was grouped into three options: low, medium, and high. In each of these three groups, NSMs represented a larger percentage of the sample than SMs, with the exception that there were more SMs than NSMs at the low level. The difference between NSMs and SMs in respect to parental income was significant at the level of p=.022 (see Table 8.1).

There were no significant differences between the NSMs and SMs on the remaining two demographic characteristics. Specifically, Table 8.1 highlights the fact that regardless of whether students indicated their parents' income level as low, middle, or high no significant differences emerged between NSMs and SMs. In an effort to examine differences between the two groups in relation to their SAT scores, a t-test was conducted (see Table 8.2). Although the mean SAT score for the two groups varied (NSM mean=1194.89, sd=104.86; SM mean=1184.75, sd=102.35) the difference was not significant (p=.170).

Research Question Two: Self-Perception of Abilities

The second research question in the study examined differences between NSMs and SMs on self-perceptions of ability. Current literature indicates students' self-perception of abilities influences their projected academic achievement in college. This study examined self-perceptions of four abilities including analytic ability, artistic ability, leadership ability, and emotional health. Using crosstab analysis, findings suggested no significant differences between NSMs and SMs in terms of their analytic ability, leadership ability, and emotional health (see Table 8.3).

However, significantly more NSMs indicated higher self-ratings of their artistic ability (p=.019) than their SM counterparts.

Table 8.1. Results of Crosstabs Comparing NSMs (n=538) and SMs (n=314) on Background Characteristics Based on Chi Square Comparisons

Variables		NSM N	%	SM N	%	Total N	%	P-value
Sex	M	255	47.4	240	76.43	495	58.1	
	F	283	52.6	74	23.57	357	41.9	
	Tot	538	100	314	100	852	100	.000*
High School GPA	C+	1	0.19	0	0	1	0.12	
	B-	11	2.04	10	3.18	21	2.46	
	B	60	11.15	51	16.24	111	13.03	
	B+	174	32.34	120	38.22	294	34.51	
	A-	178	33.09	81	25.80	259	30.40	
	A/A+	114	21.19	52	16.56	166	19.48	
	Total	538	100	314	100	852	100	.022*
Parental Income	Low	44	8.18	32	10.19	76	8.92	
	Middle	110	20.45	74	23.57	184	21.6	
	High	384	71.38	208	66.24	592	69.48	
	Total	538	100	314	100	852	100	0.28
Race	Majority	448	83.27	237	75.48	685	80.4	
	Non-maj	90	16.73	77	24.52	167	19.6	
	Total	538	100	314	100	852	100	.007*
Parental Education	Low	101	18.77	84	26.75	185	21.71	
	Med	226	42.00	123	39.17	349	40.96	
	High	211	39.22	107	34.08	318	37.32	
	Total	538	100	314	100	852	100	.022*

Table 8.2. Results of T-test Comparing SAT Scores between NSMs (n=538) and SMs (n=314)

		N	Mean	SD	P-value
SAT Score	NSM	538	1194.89	104.86	.170
	SM	314	1184.75	102.35	
	Total	852			

Table 8.3. Results of Crosstabs Comparing NSMs (n=538) and SMs (n=314) on Self-perception of Abilities

Variables		NSM		SM		Total		
		N	%	N	%	N	%	P-value
Analytic Ability	Below avg	222	41.26	117	37.26	339	39.79	
	Average	190	35.32	115	36.62	305	35.8	
	Above avg	126	23.42	82	26.11	208	24.41	
	Total	538	100	314	100	852	100	0.476
Artistic Ability	Below avg	248	46.1	126	40.13	374	43.9	
	Average	141	26.21	72	22.93	213	25.0	
	Above avg	149	27.7	116	36.94	265	31.1	
	Total	538	100	314	100	852	100	.019*
Leadership Ability	Below avg	7	1.3	3	0.96	10	1.17	
	Average	390	72.5	242	77.07	632	74.18	
	Above avg	141	26.21	69	21.97	210	24.65	
	Total	538	100	314	100	852	100	0.332
Emotional Health	Below avg	217	40.33	126	40.13	343	40.26	
	Average	164	30.48	98	31.21	262	30.75	
	Above avg	157	29.18	90	28.66	247	28.99	
	Total	538	100	314	100	852	100	0.973

Research Question Three: Degree Aspirations

A final pre-college characteristic which has been found to have an impact on academic achievement is degree aspirations, the subject of the third research question posed in the study. While the literature on college students tends to examine degree aspirations as an outcome, the current study used it as a means to examine differences between NSMs and SMs and later its relative influence on academic achievement. For the current sample of 852 students, a p-value of .471 indicated no significant differences existed between the NSMs and SMs (see Table 8.4).

Table 8.4. Results of Crosstabs Comparing NSMs (n=538) and SMs (n=314) on Degree Aspirations

Variables		NSM		SM		Total		P-value
		N	%	N	%	N	%	
Degree Aspirations	Less than Bach deg	3	0.56	0	0	3	0.35	
	Bach deg	120	22.3	66	21.02	186	21.83	
	Post-Bach deg	409	76.02	246	78.34	655	76.88	
	Other	6	1.12	2	0.64	8	0.94	
	Total	538	100	314	100	852	100	0.471

Research Question Four: Academic Achievement

As noted in previously, first-year grade point average is frequently used as a measure of student achievement and has been found to have a significant impact on persistence in the literature. Therefore, in the current study, the first-year GPAs of 852 undecided students were analyzed using an independent sample t-test to determine if significant differences in first-year GPA existed for NSMs and SMs. The findings revealed there is a statistically significant difference between the two groups in terms of their academic achievement as measured by their cumulative, first-year GPA ($t=6.431$, $p=.000$). The mean first-year GPA for NSMs (3.02) was significantly higher than that for SMs (2.73) (see Table 8.5).

Table 8.5. Results of T-test Comparing First-Year GPA between NSMs (n=538) and SMs (n=314)

		N	Mean	SD	P-value
Academic Achievement	NSM	538	3.02	0.6	.000*
	SM	314	2.73	0.68	
	Total	852			

*$p<.05$

Discussion

Results of this study are discussed in relation to the four research questions posed in the study. The first four research questions examined whether differences existed between NSMs and SMs in terms of their background characteristics, self-perceptions of abilities, degree aspirations, and academic achievement.

Background Characteristics

The first research question presented in this study examined whether significant differences in background characteristics existed for NSMs and SMs. To explore this question a crosstab was used based on the belief that background characteristics might be causally influencing students' undecided status. Findings revealed significant differences with respect to four background characteristics: (a) sex, (b) high school GPA, (c) race, and (d) parental education.

Gender

First, in terms of sex, the SM group included more males (76.43 percent) than females (23.57 percent). This finding was not completely surprising as the gender distribution of the study's total sample was comprised of 58.10 percent males and 41.90 percent females and institutional data indicate the gender distribution of first-year undecided students for 2005-2007 consisted of 59.57 percent males and 40.43 percent females. Nevertheless, males represented a significantly larger portion of the SM group. One plausible explanation for this difference relates to the nature of the SM population. At the institution at which this study was conducted, the majority of students in the SM group were denied admission into a single degree option, general engineering, which tends to have a first-year student gender distri-bution includes more males than females. Specifically, the gender distribution for the first-year students in engineering during 2005-2007 for males and females was 84.25 percent and 15.75 percent, respectively. Therefore, the gender demographics of the SM group more closely matched those of their most frequently cited choice of major.

A noteworthy finding, however, is revealed regarding sex and the NSM group which was composed of significantly more females (52.60 percent) than males (47.40 percent). This finding deviates from both the sample population as well as the first-year, undecided student population during 2005-2007, so the reasons that females make up a greater portion of the NSM group cannot be easily explained. It is possible students' reasons for choosing a major can provide some context to interpreting this finding. Malgwi, Howe, and Burnaby (2005) found that females' aptitude in a particular subject was a significant influence on their choice of major. In light of their finding, females at the university from which the current sample was derived may not initially had confidence in their aptitude in the majors for which the institution has its greatest reputation: Engineering and Architecture. If their confidence was lower in these areas, perhaps they felt the need to explore more options before committing to major. On the other hand, males to choose their major based on perceived potential for career advancement and higher salary expectations (Malgwi, Howe, and Burnaby, 2005). Therefore, they would have selected a major during the admission process regardless of their aptitude and preparedness to begin the major. These influences on students' choice of major may explain why the NSM group has significantly more females than males.

High School GPA

The institution at which this study was conducted is considered selective in terms of their admission standards. Specific evidence of this includes the fact that in 2007 the average high school GPA of students who were offered admission to the institution was a 3.85. In light of these high academic credentials of potential first-year students, it is startling to note the significant difference in high school grades between the NSM and SM groups. Specifically, a greater percentage NSMs (54.28 percent) indicated an average high school grade of an A than SMs (42.36 percent). In addition, a smaller percentage of NSMs (45.72 percent) reported their average high school grade as a B or less than the NSM group (57.64 percent). Both findings support the idea that NSMs had higher levels of academic performance in high school than the SMs.

This finding is counterintuitive given the assumption that students who are committed to a particular major or degree program experience greater levels of academic achievement as a result of their goal commitment and focus. That is, the SMs were undecided only because they were not accepted into their first choice major, hence could be considered committed to an academic program. However, the lower levels of average high school grades for the SM group might be explained by the fact that many of these students were denied entry into their first choice of major because their high school credentials, including grades, were not as competitive as those who were offered admission. If the SM group had average high school grades which mirrored the overall average GPA for students admitted to the university, more SMs would have been directly admitted into their first choice of major instead of enrolling in the undecided option.

Race

A third significant difference in background characteristics between NSMs and SMs was found in relation to race. Due to the small number of students representing racial backgrounds other than Caucasian, the analysis of differences by race were based on a comparison of majority and non-majority students. Findings revealed the overall sample's racial distribution between majority and non-majority students to be 80.40 percent and 19.60 percent, respectively. However, closer examination reveals differences between the undecided student statuses. The racial distribution among the NSM group was very similar to the sample distribution: majority (83.27 percent) and non-majority (16.73 percent) students. For the SM group, though, there is a greater deviation from the sample population with 75.48 percent majority and 24.52 percent non-majority students. Clearly, the SMs have a greater representation of non-majority students than the NSM group. Societal forces again may partially explain the impact of race on undecided major status. The non-majority SM group members may have experienced more pressure from parents and their communities to begin their college enrollment focused on a particular major. This would decrease or better manage the time required to complete their degree. While the intent of these expectations may have been to encourage and provide focus for non-majority students, these students may have ultimately chosen to apply for admission to a major for which they were not prepared to succeed.

Parental Education

The final background characteristic for which significant differences between NSMs and SMs were revealed is parental education, with significantly more SMs (26.75 percent) having parents with lower levels of education than NSMs (18.77 percent). This finding is interesting in light of the fact that only 21.71 percent of the sample population indicated low parental educational levels. One possible explanation could be related to the difference found in race. Since a significant portion of the SM group was comprised of non-majority students, it would follow that their parents were also considered non-majority. As non-majority parents they may have less education than the majority parents. Other feasible explanations for this finding are not available but the current finding warrants future investigation.

Self-Perception of Abilities

The second research question posed in this study examined whether significant differences in self-perceptions of abilities could be identified for NSMs and SMs. Respondents' self-perceptions of abilities were represented by one item on the AFS that included 21 sub-items. These 21 sub items were collapsed into four groups based on previous research in which factor analysis was conducted on the 21 sub-items in order to cluster related items. The factor analysis yielded the following clusters and their corresponding labels: (a) analytical ability (academic and mathematical ability), (b) artistic ability (artistic ability and creativity), (c) leadership ability (leadership and public speaking ability, and intellectual and social self-confidence), and (d) emotional health (drive to achieve, emotional health, and initiative) (Zheng, et. al, 2002). These four factors were included in a crosstab analysis to explore potential differences between the two groups.

Of the four self-perceptions of abilities examined, the only significant difference between NSMs and SMs was in the ratings of their artistic abilities. Specifically, a greater percentage of SMs (36.94 percent) rated their artistic ability as above average than NSMs (27.70 percent). Given that artistic ability is a measure students' artistic and creativity, this finding does not come as a surprise because of the nature of the institution at which the study was conducted. This university has top-ranked engineering and architecture programs. These programs tend to attract students with interests in design and creativity. Recall that the SM group included students who were denied admission to their first choice major. The overwhelming majority of students in the SM group were denied admission into Engineering and Architecture. Specifically, 478 first-year students were denied admission to majors within the architecture college and 833 within general engineering from 2005 to 2007 out of a total undecided population of 3990 students. Both of these academic majors place a major emphasis on creativity and design which might explain the higher self-ratings of self-perception of artistic abilities by SMs. Both engineering and architecture and design students have to demonstrate a skill set based on artistry and creativity.

Degree Aspirations

Examining whether significant differences in degree aspirations could be identified for NSMs and SMs was the purpose of the third research question. The analysis employed to address this question was a crosstab. The 10 response options related degree aspirations from the Annual Freshman Survey were collapsed into four groups: (a) less than a Bachelor's degree, Bachelor's degree, post-Bachelor's degree, and other. The greatest percentage of responses indicated students aspired to a Bachelor's degree (21.83 percent) or post-Bachelor's degree (76.88 percent) regardless of students' affiliation with either the NSM or SM group. No significant difference was found between NSMs and SMs in terms of their degree aspirations (p=.471).

There are a couple potential explanations for this finding. First, the institution from which the sample was drawn is a major research university with highly competitive admission standards. The average SAT score for entering classes in the three years in which the sample matriculated was 1203. Also, faculty members were awarded $5,888,585,133 in research grants during those years and there is a growing emphasis on engaging undergraduates in research activities. Finally, the students in the sample completed the AFS prior to enrolling at the institution. It is possible that they had high aspirations prior to selecting a university to attend and that their selection of this particular university was, in part, due to their assumption that a degree from the school would facilitate their post-baccalaureate degree plans, regardless of their undecided status (NSM or SM).

Alternatively, the finding might be explained by the types of academic programs offered at the institution where the study took place. As noted previously, the university is host to top-rated programs in architecture and engineering. There are also major programs in sciences, business, natural resources, and agriculture. Many of these are fields in which advanced degrees are the norm for career success.

This might explain why both groups in the study (NSMs and SMs) reported high degree aspirations.

Academic Achievement

Perhaps the most interesting finding of this study came from the finding related to the fourth research question: Are there significant differences between NMSs and SMs in terms of their academic achievement, as measured by their first-year cumulative college GPA? The mean first-year GPAs for NSMs and SMs were 3.02 and 2.73, respectively. Though both mean GPAs are commendable and would indicate academic success at most institutions of higher learning, the results reveal the difference is highly significant at the level of $p=.000$. Most surprising is the fact that NSMs generally earned higher GPAs than SMs. This finding is counterintuitive in that there is a generally held belief that the more certain a student is about his/her major choice the more likely that student is to be academically successful (Anderson, 1985; Leppel, 2001, Sprandel, 1985). In the case of the current study, SMs are students who originally applied for admission into a specific major but were not accepted because of additional entrance requirements beyond those of the institution. SM status would indicate students have a more focused and deliberate plan to declare their intended major as quickly as possible in comparison to NSMs. They have usually researched what it will take to transfer and are able to clearly articulate the requirements and procedures that must be completed prior to initiating the transfer process. On the other hand, NSMs are characterized as truly undecided students who want to spend some time exploring all of the various degree programs and options available at the institution.

Interpreting this finding is challenging. Perhaps the flexibility of course scheduling for NSMs facilitates greater levels of academic achievement. In particular, as truly undecided students, NSMs have more opportunities during their first year of enrollment to select a variety of courses that satisfy both degree requirements and personal interests, while also providing students the chance to explore various academic fields and disciplines. Students who are more interested in their coursework may experience higher levels of academic achievement. The same options are not available to SMs. Because these students have a specified academic plan in place and often have to complete prerequisite courses before they can even be considered for admission into their intended major, their course scheduling options are more rigid. SMs are often also under time constraints and need to complete these required courses within a predetermined time frame in order to be considered competitive applicants for internal transfer. This situation can jeopardize the success of SMs who may not have selected the most appropriate major and are attempting to complete course work for which they are not as prepared.

However, it is important to note that this finding should have been predictable to some degree because of the finding related to high school grades. Recall that there was a significant difference between NSMs and SMs in terms of high school grades. Prior research has shown that a consistent predictor of first year college GPA is high school GPA (Daugherty and Lane, 1999; DeBerard, Spielmans, and Julka, 2004; Noble and Sawyer, 2002). The results of the current study indicate high school GPA is a factor in which a significant difference exists between NSMs and SMs. Logic would suggest that higher academic achievement in high school would produce high academic achievement in college.

Limitations of the Study

Limitations have been revealed throughout the course of conducting and analyzing the data set. Specifically, three limitations emerged involving the generalizability of the results, the narrow definition of achievement, and the classification of undecided students.

One limitation of the current study centers on its generalizability, or the ability to use the findings to draw general conclusions about other groups of undecided students. The sample included students from only one institution and it is not clear whether their academic success (GPA) is related to the selectivity of the institution. The results should be generalized with caution to undecided students at institutions other than selective research universities.

A second limitation involves the definition of achievement. For purposes of this study, achievement was measured as a function of academic success; first-year GPA. Although previous literature affirms that GPA is a consistent measure of academic achievement, there are alternative measures of achievement. For example, for undecided students, achievement could be measured by students' ability to make a decision about and transition into a major that is congruent with their skills, interests, and abilities. In addition, achievement could be measured by assessing the number of times students change their major after exiting an undecided program. More major changes would be a good indication that a student continues to face difficulty in deciding on an appropriate field of study. Other measures of academic achievement might have led to different results.

A final limitation relates to the classification of undecided students into two sub-categories: NSM and SM. While background characteristics, self-perceptions of abilities, and degree aspirations explained a larger amount of variance for students in the NSM group than the SM group, it is clear that much is still unknown about the factors that impact the academic achievement for both groups. More variation may exist within the population of undecided students than can be adequately assessed using simply two groups to differentiate its members.

Despite these limitations, significant information has been provided by the results of the current study in terms of the differences between NSMs and SMs. In addition, the amount of variance in academic achievement explained by these variables for both groups was highlighted. Previous literature has investigated the factors that impact academic achievement in many student populations but those studies have excluded undecided students. In addition, when research was conducted on undecided students in prior studies it frequently involved a comparison between undecided students and students from degree-granting majors. My results provide a unique perspective by which to evaluate undecided students.

In conclusion, the significant findings in the current study were not surprising, as each of the factors revealed in my study had been previously reported in the literature as having an impact on academic achievement for other populations of students. For both groups, the models presented explained a statistically significant portion or variance. However, for practical purposes the percentage of variance explained was relatively low (NSM=16.6 percent and SM= 6.8 percent). More research regarding the factors that influence the academic success of this population is warranted. With increased academic achievement, it is expected that this population will also increase in retention rates. Improved retention rates are a means of assessing institutional accountability (Green, 2002; Metz, 2004; Trow, 1996) and increasing institutional revenues (Jones, 1996). Since undecided students comprise a growing percentage of matriculating college students, improving their academic achievement, hence their retention rates, has important implications for colleges and universities.

References

Allen, D. (1999). Desire to finish college: An empirical link between motivation and persistence. *Research in Higher Education, 40*(4), 461-485.

Anderson, E. (1985). Forces influencing student persistence and achievement. In Noel, L., Levitz, R., Saluri, D. and Associates. *Increasing student retention: Effective programs and practices for reducing the dropout rate.* San Francisco, CA: Jossey-Bass.

Astin, A. W. (1977). *Four critical years: Effects of college on beliefs, attitudes, and knowledge.* San Francisco, CA: Jossey-Bass.

Astin, A. W. (1993b). *What matters in college: Four critical years revisited.* San Francisco: Jossey-Bass.

Bauer, K. W. and Liang, Q. (2003). The effect of personality and precollege characteristics on first-year activities and academic performance. *Journal of College Student Development, 44*(3), 277-290.

Berman, G. S. and Haug, M. R. (1975). Occupational and educational goals and expectations: The effects of race and sex. *Social Problems, 23*, 166-181.

Blecher, L. (2006). Persistence toward bachelor degree completion of students in family and consumer sciences. *College Student Journal, 40*(3), 469-484.

Brashears, M. T., and Baker, M. (2003). *A comparison of the influence of traditional predictors and individual student talents upon collegiate success: A longitudinal study.* Paper presented at the Southern Agricultural Education Research Conference, February 1-3, Mobile, AL.

Braxton, J. M. (2000). *Reworking the departure puzzle.* Nashville: Vanderbilt University Press.

Bryson, S., Smith, R., and Vineyard, G. (2002). Relationship of race, academic and nonacademic information in predicting first-year success of selected admissions first-year students. *Journal of the First Year Experience and Students in Transition, 14*(1), 65-80.

Byrne, B. M. (1984). The general/academic self-concept nomological network: A review of construct validation research. *Review of Educational Research, 54*, 427-456.

Carter, D. F. (1999). The impact of institutional choice and environments on African-American and white students' degree expectations. *Research in Higher Education, 40*(1), 17-41.

Carter, D. F. (2001). A *dream deferred? Examining the degree aspirations of African American and White college students*. New York: Routlegdge Falmer.

College Board. (2006). *Education pays: Second update*. Retrieved October 10, 2007, from http://www.collegeboard.com/prod_downloads/press/cost06/edu cation_pays_06.pdf

Daugherty, T. K., and Lane, E. J. (1999). A longitudinal study of academic and social predictors of college attrition. *Social Behavior and Personality, 27*(4), 355-362.

DeBerard, M. S., Speilman, G. I., and Julka, D. L. (2004). Predictors of academic achievement and retention among college freshmen: A longitudinal study. *College Student Journal, 38*(1), 66-80.

Dey, E. L., and Astin, A. W. (1993). Statistical alternatives for studying college student retention: A comparative analysis of logit, probit, and linear regression. *Research in Higher Education, 34*(4), 569-581.

Ethington, C. A. (1990). A psychological model of student persistence. *Research in Higher Education, 31*(3), 279-293.

Gordon, V. N. (1995). *The undecided college student: an academic and career advising challenge*. Springfield, Ill.: Thomas Publishing.

Gordon, V. N. (1998). Career decidedness types: A literature review. *Career Development Quarterly, 46*, 386-403.

Graunke, S. S., Woosley, S. A., and Helms, L. L. (2006). How do their initial goals impact students' chances to graduate? An exploration of three types of commitment. *NACADA Journal, 26*(1), 13-18.

Green, K. C. (2002). In search of academic accountability. *Converge, 5*(1), 44-46.

Hagedorn, L. S. (2003). *How to define retention: A new look at an old problem*. Unpublished reports from TRUCCS to the Los Angeles Community College District. Los Angeles.

Hamacheck, D. (1995). Self-concept and school achievement: Interaction dynamics and a tool for assessing the self-concept component. *Journal of Counseling and Development, 73*, 419-425.

Hansford, B. C., and Hattie, J. A. (1982). The relationship between self and achievement/performance measures. *Review of Educational Research, 52*, 123-142.

Hickman, G. P., Bartholomae, S., and McHenry, P. C. (2000). Influence of parenting styles on the adjustment and academic achievement of traditional college freshmen. *Journal of College Student Development, 41*(1), 41-54.

Higher Education Research Institute. (2007). CIRP freshman survey. Available from the Higher Education Research Institute web site, http://www.gseis.ucla.edu/heri/researchers/instruments/CIRP/2007SIF.PDF.

Hossler, D., and Gallagher, K. S. (1987). Studying student college choice: A three-phase model and the implications for policymakers. *College and University, 62*(3), 207-221.

Hull-Toye, C. S. (1995). *Persistence based upon degree aspiration.* Paper presented at the Annual Meeting of the Association for the Study of Higher Education, Orlando, FL. (ERIC Document Reproduction Service No. ED 391-414).

Institute for Higher Education Policy. (1998). *Reaping the benefits: Defining the public and private value of going to college.* Washington, D.C.: Institute for Higher Education Policy.

Institute for Higher Education Policy. (2005). *The investment payoff: A 50-state analysis of the public and private benefits of higher education.* Washington, D.C.: Institute for Higher Education Policy.

Jackson, A. P., Smith, S. A., and Hill, C. L. (2003). Academic persistence among Native American college students. *Journal of College Student Development, 44*(4), 548-565.

Jones, E. A. (1996). National and state policies affecting learning expectations. *New Directions for Higher Education, 96,* 7-18.

Kahn, J. H., and Nauta, M. M. (2001). Social-cognitive predictors of first-year college persistence: The importance of proximal assessment. *Research in Higher Education, 42*(6), 633-652.

Leppel, K. (1984). The academic performance of returning and continuing college students: An economic analysis. *Journal of Economic Education, 15*(1), 46–54.

Leppel, K. (2001). The impact of major on college persistence among freshmen. *Higher Education, 41*(3), 327-342.

Leppel, K. (2002). Similarities and differences in the college persistence of men and women. *The Review of Higher Education,* 25(4), 433-450.

Lewallen, W. C. (1992). Persistence of the undecided: The characteristics and college persistence of student's undecided about academic major or career choice. *Dissertation Abstracts International, 53,* 12A, 4226.

Lewallen, W. C. (1993). The impact of being "undecided" on college student persistence. *Journal of College Student Development, 34,* 103-112.

Lopez-Claros, A., Porter, M. E., Schwab, K, and Sala-i-Martin, X. (2006). *The Global Competitiveness Report 2006-2007.* England: Macmillan Publishers Limited.

Lucas, M. S. and Epperson, D. L. (1988). Personality types in vocationally undecided students. *Journal of College Student Development, 29*(5), 460-466.

Malgwi, C. A., Howe, M.A., and Burnaby, P.A. (2005). Influences on students' choice of college major. *Journal of Education for Business, 80*(5). 275-282.

McGrath, M. and Braunstein, A. (1997). The prediction of freshmen attrition: An examination of the importance of certain demographic, academic, financial, and social factors. *College Student Journal, 31*(3), 396-408.

Metz, G. W. (2004). Challenge and changes to Tinto's persistence theory: A historical review. *Journal of College Student Retention, 6*(2), 191-207.

Mitchel, D. F., Goldman, B. A., and Smith, M. (1999). Change factors affecting college matriculation: A re-analysis. *Journal of the First-Year Experience and Students in Transition, 11,* 75–92.

Murtaugh, P.A. Burns, L. D., and Schuster, J. (1999). Predicting retention of university students. *Research in Higher Education, 40*(3), 355-371.

Naretto, J. A. (1995). Adult student retention: The influence of internal and external communities. *NASPA Journal, 32,* 90-97.

Noble, J. P. and Sawyer, R. L. (2002). Predicting different levels of academic success in college using high school GPA and ACT composite score. *ACT Research Report Series,* 1-22.

Noel, L. (1985). Increasing student retention: New challenges and potential. In L. Noel, R. Levitz, and D. Saluri (Eds.), *Increasing student retention* (pp. 1-27). San Francisco: Jossey-Bass.

Pascarella, E. T. (1984). College environmental influences on students' educational aspirations. *Journal of Higher Education, 55,* 751-771.

Pascarella, E. T. Smart, J. C., and Stoecker, J. (1989). College race and the early status attainment of black students. *Journal of Higher Education, 60(1),* 82-107.

Pascarella, E. T., and Terenzeni, P. T. (1991). *How college affects Students: Findings and insights from twenty years of research.* San Francisco: Jossey-Bass.

Pritchard, M. E. and Wilson, G. S. (2003). Using emotional and social factors to predict student success. *Journal of College Student Development, 44*(1), 18-28.

Sedlacek, W. E. (2004). *Beyond the big test: Non-cognitive assessment in higher education.* San Francisco: Jossey-Bass.

Smart, J. C. and Pascarella, E. T. (1986). Socioeconomic achievements of former college students. *Journal of Higher Education, 57*(5), 529-549.

Smith, D. G. (1990). Women's colleges and coed colleges: Is there a difference for women? *Journal of Higher Education, 61*(2), 181-195.

Sprandel, H. Z. (1985). Career planning and counseling. In Noel, L., Levitz, R., Saluri, D. and Associates. *Increasing student retention: Effective programs and practices for reducing the dropout rate.* San Francisco, CA: Jossey-Bass.

Terenzini, P. T., Theophilides, C., and Lorang, W. (1984). Influences on students' perception of their personal development during the first three years of college. *Researching Higher Education 21,* 178–194.

Tinto, V. (1993). *Leaving college: Rethinking the causes and cures of student attrition* (2nod edition). Chicago, IL: University of Chicago Press.

Tross, S. A., Harper, J. P., Osher, L. W., and Kneidinger, L. M. (2000). Not just the usual cast of characteristics: Using personality to predict college performance and retention. Journal *of College Student Development, 41*, 323-334.

Trow, M. (1996). Trust, markets and accountability in higher education: A comparative perspective. Center for Studies in Higher Education Research and Occasional Paper Series CSHE.1.96. Retrieved at http://cshe.berkeley.du/publications/docs/ROP.Trow.Trust.1.96.pdf.

Walpole, M. (2007). *Economically and educationally challenged students in higher education:Access to outcomes.* Series: ASHE Higher Education Report, v. 33, no. 3.

Wood, P. H. (1990). *The comparative academic abilities of students in education and other areas of a multi-focus university* (Report No. SP032663). Bowling Green State University. (ERIC Document Reproduction Service No. ED327480).

Zheng, J. L., Saunders, K. P., Shelley, M. C., and Whalen, D. F. (2002). Predictors of academic success for freshmen residence hall students. *Journal of College Student Development, 43*(2), 267-283.

Chapter Nine
An Analysis on Retention Among Traditional and Non-Traditional Students in Select North Carolina Community Colleges

J. Michael Harpe, Ed.D.,
Mount Saint Mary's University
Theodore Kaniuka, Ed.D.,
Fayetteville State University

Introduction

While there is growing literature on the topic of retention for baccalaureate institutions, few researchers have attempted to address the issue for community colleges. Since this line of research is relatively new, a comprehensive and shared understanding of the role of the community college and the degree to which it successfully meets the needs of its students and its communities has been ambiguous because of limited applicable research. This identity crisis has existed since the inception of the community colleges and it has been exacerbated through the years as enrollment levels increased at the same time as community colleges attempted to become increasingly responsive to community and even national needs.

The purpose of this study was to analyze retention and persistence rates among traditional and non-traditional students categorized by demographic and academic performance factors. This study was conducted using a cohort of degree-seeking traditional and non-traditional students enrolled in North Carolina Community Colleges from the fall 2006 to the spring 2008 semesters. The factors that were selected were based on previous findings of traditional and non-traditional students.

Review of Literature

Nearly half of all undergraduates in this country and more than half of all new college entrants begin their post-secondary education at the community college. The importance of community college retention becomes greater as more students choose these institutions as their pathway into higher education. Many higher education institutions report record enrollments as nearly 75 percent of high school graduates receive post-secondary education within two years of receiving their diplomas (Ramaley, et al., 2002). Over the past thirty years, community college credit enrollment has more than doubled and continues to expand at a rapid pace. For example, according to the Planning, Accountability, Research, and Evaluation section in the NCCCS (2006), a study was conducted to ascertain the number of students enrolled in curriculum or occupational extension courses in North Carolina community colleges. The results of the data indicated that the enrollment of 2005-2006 high school graduates in community colleges in the academic year of 2006-2007 was 25,804, representing a 7.3 percent increase from the previous years of enrollment.

While these institutions have experienced phenomenal growth, especially over the last forty years, they have also been plagued with questions about effectiveness, quality and purpose. According to McCabe (2000) study, community colleges serve every type of student from the well prepared high school graduate to the under-prepared high school graduate, from the academically gifted to the academically at-risk, from the high school student taking a few courses, to the senior citizen interested in personal enrichment. This makes the student body at any given community college remarkably complex.

Neutzling's (2003) research revealed that many students plan to take a small number of courses and then transfer to a four-year school. Other students may intend to graduate but either transfer out or, for a variety of reasons, fail to complete a program of study. Neutzling observed that these circumstances increase time to degree completion and potentially increase dropout rates. This is reinforced by Smith (2002) who notes that community college students are often adults who are employed on a part- or full-time basis and who are reentering or nontraditional students. In fact, according to research by Smith just 17 percent of today's college students are considered "traditional." For example, students who begin with a full-time load, the community college three-year retention to graduation rate stands at 28.9 percent (ACT, 2006). This rate has dropped 3.5 percentage points since 2000, when the rate was 32.4 percent (ACT, 2000). The first to second year retention rate of students at two-year public institutions was 52.5 percent in 2006 (ACT, 2006). These low rates of retention and graduation attainment have fostered a dubious image of the community college. Thus, the "open door admissions" policy that allows all students the opportunity to participate in higher education now is questioned as to where that open door leads.

There is a comparative paucity of research pertaining to community colleges despite the large numbers of students who attend. In the 1997 article, *It's Time We*

Started Paying Attention to Community College Students, prominent researcher Ernest Pascarella chides himself for his lack of attention to the community college student. Speaking about his initial research on the topic, *How College Affects Students*, which synthesized the results of over 2,600 research project participants, Pascarella noted that it would be a liberal estimate to say that even 5 percent of the studies reviewed focused on community college students (1997, p.15). In a second edition of the same title, the authors put considerably more focus on the community college, with highlights that illustrate attainment and persistence levels as they compare to four-year schools, as well as transfer success of community college attendees. Pascarella determined that as a result of limited research, a comprehensive and shared understanding of the role or identity of community colleges and the degree to which it successfully meets the needs of its students and its communities, has been elusive.

Exactly why community college retention rates are low is constantly debated in the academic community. Due to the nature of their student populations, most two-year colleges have higher rates of student withdrawal than four-year institutions. According to Schmid and Abell, (2003) it is not unexpected that these institutions enroll a greater number of students who are: academically underprepared, ethnic minorities, financially independent, low socioeconomic status, and/or single parents of low socioeconomic status. Many studies tend to simply describe the differences between those students who leave and those who stay, while the best studies predict future behavior by explaining how these differences arise within the context of a specific institution.

Retention research has grown increasingly complex as the student population at these institutions has continued to diversify. Much of the research that led to previous models of student retention was built upon the characteristics of traditional college students and not germane to students at community colleges. Few of the students in community colleges match those characteristics. According to Choy (2001) while previous research is helpful for understanding retention in general, it does not necessarily benefit individual institutions trying to improve the retention efforts with their own students. Students' campus experiences are unique, and so are their reasons for leaving. An example would be the previous research of Bean and Metzner (1985) that found that the most important (retention) variables were likely to differ for subgroups such as older students, part-time students, ethnic minorities, women, or academically underprepared students at different types of institutions. In fact, Pascarella's and Terenzini's (2005) research correlated with Bean and Metzner's prior research suggesting that the academic and social correlates of attrition may be different for different kinds of students. Accordingly, Tinto (2004) indicated concerns about the applicability of his model to non-traditional students and institutions. Tinto's assertion was that "it [the model] fails to highlight the important differences in education careers that mark the experiences of students of different gender, race, and social status backgrounds" (p. 689).

Non-Traditional Students

While retention issues associated with a changing student population are relevant to most colleges and universities, they are of particular concern to institutions that have high percentages of non-traditional students. The term "non-traditional" is used to cover a wide range of individual student characteristics, including age, ethnicity, residence, disability, status, and gender. The NCCCS categorizes these students as the *adult population* and assesses the percentage of this adult population in each college's service area enrolled in either curriculum or continuing education classes (NCCCS, 2006).

The Bean and Metzner (1985) model of non-traditional student attrition proposed four sets of variables affecting dropout: academic performance, intent, defining variables (e.g., age, ethnicity, gender), and environmental variables not controlled by the institution (e.g., finances, outside encouragement). They found non-traditional student attrition was affected more by the environment than social interaction variables which tended to influence traditional student attrition. Later research by Bean and Metzner found that grade point average and institutional commitment directly affected dropout through the perceived usefulness of higher education in gaining employment, satisfaction and transfer opportunities.

Even though Tinto's model has provided a basis for much of the research on student retention and attrition, there are some that think that this type of model has the propensity to produce ambiguous results. According to Byun (2000) Tinto's model has become the most widely recognized theory of student retention; yet its applicability to nontraditional student populations has not been validated. The research of Nitzke and Wacker (2001) address this concern in that the research used to develop the model was conducted on traditional student populations attending four-year, residential institutions. Fewer students can now be classified as traditional. Yet, some research has confirmed Tinto's argument that institutional fit is a good predictor of persistence or dropout (Nora and Rendon, 1990; Pascarella and Terenzini, 1980). In other studies, social integration has been found to be negatively associated with persistence. Bean's (1985) research found that student's peers are more important agents of socialization than the informal faculty contacts presented by Pascarella and Terenzini (1980). Bean argues that students play a more active role in their socialization then once thought, and college grades are more a product of selection than socialization.

Conflicting findings exist among many of these studies as to whether gender, student goals, the need for remedial education, student grade point averages, contact with faculty, or hours studied can be related to student retention. Pascarella and Terenzini (2005) found that academic integration, measured by grade point average, intellectual development and faculty interaction, is the most influential for retention of non-traditional students. Unlike traditional students, adult learners usually do not live on campus, many are married with children, and most work full time. Most adult learners have very little social interaction at college; instead, they have social links to organizations outside of the college community.

Degree completion is the goal for some but not all adult students. Students are generally more concerned with the "hands-on" applicability of a degree, have a greater sense of responsibility than younger students, and have more varied experiences to draw upon. According to research by Kerka (2003), the idea of having a career culture at college may be a key factor in retaining adult students. Usually, career advancement is a more motivating factor for adult students than the need for growth or self-development. According to Kerka (2003), there are three important strategies for retaining adult students. First, it should be recognized that diverse groups of students are retained by different methods. Second, either before or after enrollment, adult students should be encouraged to clarify career and academic goals. Third, institutions should recognize that not all students' objectives include obtaining a degree and that measuring retention success should take that into account.

Students often juggle many roles in addition to being a student, such as employee, spouse, and parent. Work and family responsibilities, commuting distance to campus, and finances may all have an impact on students' persistence. Seidman (2005a) contends that often students may be forced to leave school for reasons out of their control and beyond the control of the institution. Because commuting and non-traditional students are more likely to balance multiple roles and responsibilities, the environment external to the institution plays a significant role in their persistence (Seidman, 2005a). Furthermore, students with multiple roles off-campus are at an increased risk for attrition. Studies have found that family obligations have been among the top reasons for student departure at commuter institutions like most community colleges (Bean and Metzner, 1985). These additional responsibilities compete with the academic and social realms of the college, thereby lessening a students' integration, which has the result of decreased persistence (Seidman, 2005a). Having a spouse and children to support increases the need to complete college and obtain a higher paying job, but attempting to support that family while in school leaves less time for studying (Leppel, 2002). Specifically, women have been shown to be more sensitive to these responsibilities and have higher rates of withdrawal due to family issues (Tinto, 1993).

Bradburn (2002) examined the characteristics associated with departure at two- and four-year colleges. The results showed that 62 percent of the married students withdrew within three years, compared with 15 percent of the students who had never been married. Other studies have reported a negative correlation between marriage and persistence for women, but found a positive correlation for men (Johnson, 1996). Women may be more likely to leave school because a spouse relocates or due to lack of spousal support. Jacobs and King (2002) studied the relationship between marital status and time to graduation. Single students with no children graduated at a higher rate than married students. Divorce has also been found to decrease an individual's chances for persistence; however, this may be because it forces the student to attend part-time while they pursue full-time employment (Jacobs and King, 2002).

Community colleges face even more difficult challenges as they serve as the gateway to higher education for traditional students without the academic background to enter most four-year colleges and universities. A collaborative study was conducted by Brown, Brown and Yang (2008) from the University of North Carolina General Administration and the North Carolina Community College System Office (2006). These researchers' analyzed the enrollment patterns of students from the UNC colleges and universities and the N.C. community colleges that encompassed ten years of cohort data from 1997-1998 to 2006-2007. The researchers concluded that the traditional first-time freshmen enrollment in N.C. community colleges increased 81.2 percent from 12,891 in 1997-98 to 23,364 in 2006-07. For the past ten years, the proportion of females enrolled in NCCCS has been steady at 54 percent, with male enrollment at about 46 percent. American Indian enrollment, between 1 and 1.5 percent, was slightly higher than that in UNC system. Asian students increased about 2.5 percent from 1.6 percent in 1997-98 to 4.1 percent in 2006-07. Blacks gained about 1 percent increase over the ten years. Hispanic enrollment kept about the same, 2 percent, over the years. The "other" category increased about 3 percent. Similarly, white students' enrollment decreased 7 percent from 75 percent to 68 percent in the past ten years.

Institutions have been grappling with how to enhance student achievement, satisfaction, and graduation rates for decades. Yet, according to Brahm (2006) despite programs and services designed to help first-year students make the transition to college, graduation and retention rates have not measurably improved for many institutions. All community colleges face the difficult challenge of finding solutions to attract, retain and graduate students and the problems associated with attrition. Every year, a substantial number of college students join the growing ranks of students who fail to complete their college education. According to St. John (2000), attrition is believed to be caused by an extremely complex interaction of a multitude of variables, not just academics. Yet Jones (2002) findings affirm that students at community colleges are four times more likely to leave school due to non-academic reasons than for academic reasons.

Ethnicity

Of the 557,000 degrees conferred at two-year colleges in the United States in 2006, the vast majority were awarded to Caucasian students. Only 11 percent were awarded to African American students, 10 percent to Hispanic students, 5 percent to Asian students, and a mere 1 percent to Native American/Alaska Native students (National Center for Education Statistics, 2005). Community colleges currently enroll the highest proportion of minority students, yet their graduation rates are not proportional to rates of enrollment (Bailey, Jenkins, and Leinbach, 2005).

There are several reasons for this disparity. Tinto (2006) indicated that commonly identified retention variables had different effects on minority students than on white students. Nettles, Thoeny, and Gosman's (1986) previous research noted that black students typically have "significantly lower levels of pre-college preparation than white students, are less academically integrated, have less satisfaction with their universities, experience more interfering problems, and have less well-developed study habits" than their white peers (p. 309).

Levin and Levin (1991) reported that (a) academic preparedness, high school grade point average and class rank, (b) enrollment in college preparatory courses, (c) adaptability, and (d) commitment to educational goals are student characteristics that have the largest impact on at-risk minority student persistence. Nettles, Thoeny, and Gosman (1986) noted that SAT scores, student satisfaction, peer relationships, and other intrusive problems had different predictive validity for the retention status of black and white students. SAT scores, in particular, were not as strong predictors for black students. However, Eimers and Pike (1997) reported the academic performance of minority students did not help predict intentions to stay at the institution. More recent research by Opp (2002) insisted that many minority students experience a variety of personal, environmental, and institutional barriers in college. The research by Opp found that students of color also may find it more difficult to transition into the college setting. Factors such as cultural values and upbringing define the way in which students experience college (Szelenyi, 2001). They enter college with different value and belief systems, which may result in feelings of alienation and social isolation (Larimore and McClellan, 2005;Shield, 2005). Additionally, without a strong peer group or mentoring relationship, students of color may struggle with the pressures to assimilate, experience racism and harassment, and the incongruence between the campus culture and their own (Opp, 2002).

There are studies that have found that many ethnic groups have a much higher dropout rate than average (Bailey, Jenkins, and Leinbach, 2005; Clark, 2004; Cofer and Somers, 2000; Hawley and Harris, 2005; Scoggin, 2005; Zhai and Monzon, 2004). The research of Zhai and Monzon (2004) studied the community college student retention and discovered that students of African American or Hispanic decent had a much lower persistence rate than the general student population.

Scoggin (2005) did another study investigating the factors related to withdrawal from community colleges, and observed that African American students had the highest rates of attrition among any group. The study by Clark (2004) of within-year retention at a community college also revealed lower persistence rates among minority students. Bailey, Jenkins, and Leinbach (2005) reported similar results. In their research on minority community college students in the United States, these researchers found that African American students had the lowest completion rates at 37 percent, followed by Hispanic students, who graduated at a rate of 42 percent. In comparison, over half of all white students persist until degree completion at these institutions.

Gender

Researchers have explored the role of gender in retention and persistence. Colleges throughout the United States have experienced an increase in female enrollment.

Concerned that women have been historically marginalized within the academy, researcher Hayes (2000) examined how the educational environment and, in particular, faculty interactions, institutional culture, and the curriculum can affect the manner in which women learn. Hayes noted that the use of certain textbooks and teaching styles reinforce gender stereotypes and ultimately affect the success of female students. Due to rising costs, more women have chosen to return to work to contribute to their family income. A rise in divorce rates has also forced women into the world of work. Due to the increasing need for higher level of skills necessary for the workforce, many of these women are attending postsecondary education.

Results of studies conducted on the gender differences in persistence have been mixed. Hagedorn (2005) analyzed the withdrawal patterns of 2,906 students at a large research university. The results of the study found that graduation rates for female students were 20 percent higher than that of male students. Nippert's (2001) study of community college students also found gender to be significant, with females persisting at higher rates. Chen and Thomas (2001) looked specifically at the gender differences in persistence for vocational and technical school students. Again, females were found to persist at higher rates. Thus, higher persistence rates in women can be attributed to the finding that they interact more with peers while on campus, which increases their level of social integration.

However, there is also sufficient evidence to propose that men persist at higher rates. Bradburn (2002) conducted a study that examined the student background characteristics associated with departure at two- and four-year colleges and found that women were more likely than men to leave their institutions. Zhai and Monzon (2004) conducted a study in which over half of all female students withdrew during their first semester of college, a much higher rate than for males. Yet, there are other studies that have examined the impact that gender has on attrition and have discovered no significant difference between the retention rates of males and females (Cambiano, Denny, and Devore, 2000; Leppel, 2002; McGrath and Braunstein, 1997). According the National Center for Education Statistics, males and females were equally likely to have attained a college degree (National Center for Education Statistics, 2005). Bailey, Jenkins, and Leinbach (2005) researched data from postsecondary institutions in the United States and also found no difference in the completion rates of males and females.

Program of Study

A limited amount of research has been conducted on the influence of the student's chosen academic major on persistence. In several studies, a student's college major has been shown to impact student retention (Astin and Oseguera, 2005), but the evidence has not yielded consistent patterns. Majors that are more in demand by the labor market and programs leading to careers with higher occupational status and greater economic potential have also been shown to promote persistence (St. John, Hu, Simmons, Carter, and Weber, 2004).

Students who choose programs of study that are underrepresented for their gender may also have lower persistence rates due to social forces such as stereotyping and lack of emotional support from friends and family members. Leppel (2002) found this to be true in her research on the relationship between program of study and persistence. The results of the study confirmed that students in non-traditional fields of study for their gender had lower persistence rates. Females in education and health related programs had higher persistence rates than females enrolled in business programs. For men, the opposite was true. Male business majors had one of the highest overall persistence rates, while male education majors had the lowest. In Leppel's research, retention rates were found to vary by major, even when other factors were held constant.

St. John et al. (2004) discovered a relationship between the economic potential of the major and retention. For programs that yield lower-paying careers, students are more likely to see less benefit in completing college. These students may be less committed to their education, and therefore more prone to withdrawal (Leppel, 2002). St. John et al. (2004) found that students enrolled in majors associated with high-demand, better paying careers, such as business, healthcare, engineering, and computer science, exhibited the highest rates of retention.

St. John, Carter, Chun, and Musoba (2006) found that minority students persisted less in health, business, education, and computer science majors, while the study by Johnson (1999) established that females had lower persistence rates in art, education, or science programs, and males were more likely to withdraw from science and engineering programs of study. Program of study also has been shown to be a significant predictor of persistence (Bailey, Jenkins, and Leinbach, 2005; Chen and Thomas, 2001). Bailey, Jenkins, and Leinbach (2005) found that nationwide, students enrolled in certificate or diploma programs had persistence rates of 41 percent, compared to a 51 percent completion rate among students in associate degree programs.

Many of those enrolling on these campuses did not plan to attend college but requirements of today's workforce changed those plans. The American Association of College and Universities reports that 53 percent of students entering these colleges and universities are academically underprepared, *i.e.,* lacking basic skills in at least one of the three basic areas of reading, writing or mathematics" (Tritelli, 2003). This is a 33 percent increase in the number of academically prepared students since 2001 (National Center for Educational Statistics, 2005).

Even so, McCabe (2000) found that "each year more than half a million (academically underprepared) college students successfully complete remediation" and go on to "do as well in standard college courses as those students who begin fully prepared." Boylan (2001) maintains that this success can be attributed to the use of a developmental approach when working with underprepared students. Boylan further supports King's (2004) assumptions when he says that students fail to do well in college for a variety of reasons and only one of them is lack of academic preparedness. Factors such as personal autonomy, self-confidence, ability to cope with racism, study behaviors, or social competence have as much or more to do with grades than how well a student writes or how competent a student is in mathematics.

Based upon the work of Tinto (2004) and Boylan (2001), those academicians who sought to improve success rates for academically underprepared students lobby for a developmental education program that encompassed a three pronged approach that laid the groundwork for success with effective academic advising; provided content and structure (e.g., pre-college basic skills courses, tutoring, and topical workshops); and developed resilient students who, despite sometimes improbable circumstances, can succeed. Tinto (2004) maintained that campuses support the development of underprepared students and enhance retention and graduation when they provide effective academic advisement.

First-Semester Grade Point Average

Research from various studies has found that college grade point averages to be the single most important predictor in student persistence. Specifically, first-term grade point average has been found to be positively associated with persistence. First-semester grade point average can serve as an early gauge of college success, and is also indicative of academic intent (Hyers and Zimmerman, 2002). Grades can be likened to a reward system for students. The more rewarding their academic accomplishments are, the more likely the student is to persist. In earlier research, Bean and Metzner (1985) tested their own model concerning this factor and found grade point average to be the strongest predictor of dropout. Chen and Thomas (2001) looked at vocational and technical college student persistence and found that first-semester grade point averages were also significant for this population. Research examining the persistence of commuter students found the same results (Tharp, 1998; Weissberg, Owen, Jenkins, and Harburg, 2003).

Bradburn (2002) examined the student background characteristics associated with departure at two- and four-year colleges. She found that first-year grade point average was a significant predictor of retention at all of the institutions in the study. Byun (2000) found that grade point average had a large impact on the semester-to-semester persistence of associate degree students. Zhai and Monzon (2004) also revealed that community college students who withdrew from college had lower grade point averages than persisters. Similar results were discovered by Somers (1995) who found that for each one-point increase in grade point average, the odds of persisting increased by 45.9 percent.

A study by Murtaugh, Burns, and Schuster (1999) on first- to second-year persistence rates also revealed that students with higher first-term grade point averages experienced increased odds of persisting. Ninety-one percent of the students achieving grade point averages ranging from 3.3 to 4.0 persisted compared to only 57 percent of the students with grade point averages below 2.0. These results corroborated with Cofer and Somers' (2000) study pertaining to the within-year persistence of two-year college students. They found that students with lower grade point averages were almost ten percent less likely to persist than students with a grade point average of at least 2.5. Hyers and Zimmerman (2002) also found that graduation rates for students with first-semester grade point averages of 3.0 and higher were 5.6 times more likely to graduate than students with less than 3.0 averages.

Research Questions

Quantitative methodology was used to analyze data on the random sample of community college students from the fall of 2006 to the spring 2008 semesters to examine the association between identified first-time full-time traditional and non-traditional student's attributes with their fall-to-fall retention rates. To achieve this the following research questions were used:

1. What is the association between the retention rates of traditional and non-traditional community college students as related to selected demographic characteristics?
2. What is the association between the retention rates and the academic performance of traditional and non-traditional community college students?
3. What factors are related to the semester-to-semester and overall persistence of traditional and non-traditional community college students?

Sample Population

The sample population was 1,000 first-year, degree-seeking (traditional and non-traditional) students who were admitted in the fall 2006 cohort in North Carolina community colleges. This study analyzed the nature of the relationship pertaining to retention patterns over a two-year period of first-semester students enrolled in associate, certificate and diploma programs starting in the fall 2006 semester and tracked to the spring 2008 semester. By analyzing two years, the study was able to capture degree completion data for the cohort if applicable. Only degree-seeking students were used in this study, as students without long-term educational goals are not comparable to those students who discontinue their progress towards a specific degree (NCCCS, 2006). The population set was classified into two categories: persisters and non-persisters. Individuals were classified as persisters if they re-enrolled at the institution the subsequent fall semester. Conversely, individuals were classified as non-persisters if they did not re-enroll at the institution the subsequent fall semester.

Descriptive Data on the Sample

The sample cohort consisted of 533 (57 percent) traditional students and 467 (43 percent) nontraditional students. In addition, there were 644 (60.3 percent) students enrolled in an academic program of study, 114 (16.5 percent) students enrolled in a technical program, and 160 (23.2 percent) students enrolled in a vocational program. Based on the available data for the degree-seeking students that entered in the fall semester of 2006, the majority of the population was female (51.1 percent) and white (70.4 percent). The data also revealed that 647 (79.3 percent) students were the recipients of some form of student financial aid and 143 (20.7 percent) students were no recipients. The mean age of the traditional students was 22.687 years of age and the mean age of the non-traditional students was 34.882 years. The mean age for the entire sample was 29.655 years.

Of the 1,000 subjects, 558 or 62.1 percent of the traditional students listed their race as White, while 70 or 21.4 percent listed their race as Black; 55 or 6.7 percent listed their race as Hispanic/Latino, whereas 51 or 1.1 percent American Indian was the selected race; 14 or 1.8 percent listed their race as Asian/Pacific Islander, while 8 or .02 percent listed themselves as Other. In contrast, of the non-traditional students 505 or 69.4 percent listed their race as White, 105 or 25.4 percent listed Black as their race, 27 or 3.1 percent listed Hispanic/Latino as their race, while Asian, and Other showed 21 students or 1.0 percent.

Data Analysis

All data was analyzed using techniques of stepwise logistical regression, utilizing a .05 level for statistical significance. Logistical regression was considered to be the most effective method for this study given the possible outcomes for these questions to be dichotomous. The dependent variable of this study was student retention which was premised upon the student's graduation rates. The predictive factors used in the model are shown in Table 9.1.

Findings

This study sought to determine the extent to which certain student demographic and academic factors could be used to enhance the understanding of how they are related to persistence. This study was also designed to begin to fill the void on scholarly research on the dynamics of student persistence and retention in the community college environment.

Demographic Factors and Retention

The first question addressed in this study was whether or not certain student demographic characteristics- age, gender, and race were related to retention for traditional and non-traditional students. The cohort's ages were calculated as of the first day of class for their initial semester enrolled. The mean age of the traditional students was 22.687 years and the mean age of the non-traditional students was 34.882 years. Clearly non-traditional students who are older imply that these students have a significantly different set of prior experiences and potentially possess different career paths compared to younger students. The mean age of persisters was 20.21 years, while the mean age for non-persisters was 20.38. While this difference was small; it indicated that persistence was not influenced by the age of the student and other factors that were related to whether a student remained in college or left.

Table 9.1. Logistical Regression Variable Values

Variable Name	Description of Variable
Age	0 = > 25 or younger; 1 = < 25 or older
Gender	1 = Female; 0 = Male
Ethnicity	1 = White; 2 = Black; 3 = Hispanic/Latino; 4= Asian/Pacific Islander; 5 = American Indian; 6 = Other
Application Date	1 = Submitted application 61 days or more prior to start of fall semester; 0 = 60 days or less
AAS Major	1 = AAS major; 0 = Otherwise
Certificate	1 = Certificate; 0 = Otherwise
Diploma	3 = Diploma; 0 = Otherwise
No Financial Aid	1 = Did not receive financial aid; 0 = Otherwise
Pell Grant Recipient	2 = Received Pell Grant as the only form of financial aid; 0 = Otherwise
Lottery Grant Recipient	3 = Received the Lottery Grant as the only form of financial aid; 0 = Otherwise
Other Single Forms of Financial Aid	4 = Received other single form of financial aid; 0 = 0 = Otherwise
Multiple Forms	5 = Received multiple forms of financial aid; 0 = Otherwise
First Semester GPA	1 = 4.0 – 3.0; 0 = Otherwise
	2 = 3.0 – 2.0; 0 = Otherwise
	3 = 2.0 – 1.0; 0 = Otherwise
	4 = 1.0 – 0.0; 0 = Otherwise
Persisters/Non-Persisters	1 = Persist to Spring 2008; 0 = Did not persist

An interesting find was that the gender of the student was significantly related to retention such that male students were 1.9 times more likely to persist as compared to females. Combining this with the small age difference for persisters and non-persisters may imply that females, while focused on the importance of education, face other life related demands which could cause them to leave. The analysis of the cohort data pertaining to race indicates that black students are less likely to enroll in associate degree programs and/or persist than the white students. However, the additional categories of *other* race positively correlated to program of study which means that these students were inclined to enroll in associate degree programs at almost twice the rate of white students in the cohort. These findings are aligned with previous research regarding an association between race and persistence.

While seemingly contradictory, this implies that certain ethnic categories included in this study were less likely to persist than other students. It appears that this contention depends upon the type of institution of higher education the student attends. For example, Black students who began at public four-year colleges or universities were more likely than their Hispanic peers to leave within three years (21.4 percent versus 13.4 percent). This may imply that black students emphasized the short-term goal of quick entry into the job market more than their white and other counterparts and, therefore, enrollment in the community college was the portal to facilitate this initiative.

Academic Factors and Retention

The second question addressed in this study was whether or not academic enrollment behaviors (i.e., first-semester grade point average, financial aid status, application submission date and program of study) were factors related to retention. Descriptive statistics indicated the mean grade point average for persisters in this study was 2.39, while the mean grade point average for non persisters was 1.45. It was interesting to note the effect of grade point average (GPA) on attrition in this study. The research findings consistently indicated that the first-semester cumulative grade point average was a reliable predictor of retention. Students with a lower cumulative GPA were less likely to be retained than were students with higher GPA's. Students with GPAs under 2.50 in their first year were more likely to leave than students with GPAs of 2.50 or higher (25.8 percent versus 11.3 percent at four-year institutions and 47.9 percent versus 37.8 percent at two-year colleges).

The correlation between grades and retention was supported by earlier research by Murtaugh, Burns, and Schuster, (1999) and from recent research from Reason (2003) that found that grade point averages achieved during the first semester of college, had a stronger association with retention and persistence-to-graduation than many other variables researched. Moreover, this research indicated that the combined effects of an individual's gender, ethnicity, and socio-economic status are less a predictor of persistence than the individual's first-semester grade point average. This research may imply that students falter in college due to the gap between their high school experience and college expectations. Many students may find that their college courses are fundamentally different than their high school courses. Thus, a consistent yet troubling situation is made prevalent when making the transition to college for some of these students.

The findings in this study related to the significance of obtaining financial aid as a predictor of retention appear to be in accord with most research. The results of this study revealed that students who received financial aid were almost 2.5 times more likely to be retained than students who did not receive financial aid. Earlier research from Tinto (1987) found that students with a financial aid need tended to be unfamiliar with the financial aid process, tended to have other financial obligations, and often juggled school, work and family. Consequently, the student often became overwhelmed and withdrew.

However, when comparing individuals who received financial aid in any amount with those individuals who did not receive aid, Bradburn (2002) did not find any significant differences in retention. He did note that community college students who left the institution were more likely to indicate the need to work as the reason for withdrawing than were dropouts attending four-year colleges and universities. Therefore, it was interesting to note the inference concerning financial aid and persistence in this study. College students who have less financial worries are more likely to return the following semester than those students who receive little or no financial aid. These overall results suggest that attending to students' financial concerns is pivotal to enable students to be retained and persist to graduation at these institutions.

The data pertaining to the relationship regarding the persistence rate at community colleges to the cohort's major program of study is inconclusive due to the lack of definitive research that relates this factor to retention. A review of literature revealed that students with higher career or degree aspirations were more likely to persist than those with lower degree aspirations (Feldman, 1993; Horn and Nevill, 2006). This contention is aligned with Tinto (2006) who claimed that the higher the educational goal, the more likely the student will be retained which challenges the findings of this study. It was interesting to note that the researcher found that nearly one-third (31.7 percent) of 2006-07 cohort beginning post-secondary students left without a degree or credential and did not return by spring 2008. According to the American Association of Community Colleges (2006) these students in the two-year institutions were much more likely than those in the public four-year colleges or universities to leave without completing a degree or credential (43.6 percent versus 18.8 percent).

This study revealed that a significant number of students enroll in community colleges for personal enrichment and to upgrade job skills training which embodies the purpose of these institutions. It was interesting to note that students who considered themselves to be primarily employment- related students were more likely to leave without a credential than those who described themselves as primarily or exclusively students (25.6 percent versus 18.3 percent). For some of these individuals attending a community college, degree completion of any type was never a goal. This poses as an imminent problem for community college faculty and staff as they are indoctrinated to encourage degree or certificate completion as compared to their peers at four-year institutions. This is due to the nature of these institutions enrolling students who are considered a demographic risk factor and are not prepared for the rigor of college-level work. Because of the limited research, however, additional research is recommended.

In Research Question 3, significant association between the student's date of application relative to his or her first semester of college and fall-to-fall persistence was interesting to note. The study indicated that students who submitted their applications for admission 121 days or more before the start of the fall semester were likely to persist more so than students who submitted their admission application 60 days or fewer before the start of the fall semester.

In contrast to this study, research conducted by Goodman (2000) at Walters State Community College found that students who applied to the institution more than two months prior to the first day of classes were more likely to persist. The population in Goodman's study, however, only included all students who attended WSCC from fall 1992 through fall 1997, with the exception of those students who were listed as *special*. No other studies regarding the association of the student's application date and persistence were located. The results of this study could imply that these students are more likely than those who attend four-year colleges and universities to delay submission of an application to enter college due to reservations associated with the lack of college preparatory skills to meet the academic requirements of the institution. Another reason could be due to full-time working and other peripheral commitments that would prohibit full-time enrollment, thus making part-time enrollment the only option. Therefore, additional research is warranted.

Conclusion

Special retention initiatives should be directed toward first-year students, as the majority of these students depart during their first two semesters at the institutions. Demographic factors were found to have a significant impact on student persistence, indicating that institutions can use this background information to predict which students are most at-risk for attrition before the students even begin classes.

The majority of the most significant predictors of persistence were among the academic factors, indicating that students' level of academic success and integration is a major determinant in whether a student persists or leaves the institution. The best predictors of student persistence were first-semester grade point average, application submission dates, enrollment status, and ethnicity.

Recommendations for Practice

It is clear from this research that the relationship between select student academic and demographic factors and persistence and retention is inconsistent and multifaceted. This presents difficulty for educators who are charged with improving the educational outcomes of students by simply examining student characteristic prior to enrollment. It is clearer for students who have a history at the college; however this may be too late for interventions for some students. Therefore, given the complexity associated with student retention and persistence the following recommendations are cautiously provided.

1. Because first-semester grade point average has such a strong impact on student persistence, the academic support systems within the institution should be improved to assist students in earning higher grade point averages. The use of a well-advertised tutoring program, arranged early in the semester, and supplemental instruction for difficult classes, can aid in retention.
2. Retention data should be generated at the academic unit level as well as the institutional level. This will create a system of accountability and force programs with low retention to create plans and activities designed to reduce student attrition.
3. A thorough exit interview process should be implemented and utilized for leavers, to shed light on students' reasons for departure, in an effort to develop strategies to increase student persistence. Re-entry programs should be conducted, involving communication with the student after they have withdrawn, these programs are designed to encourage leavers to return to the institution the next semester.
4. Because student's goals and objectives for attending community colleges are very diverse, these reasons should be taken into consideration when assessing student retention. Non-persistence to graduation may not always be a negative; therefore, persistence rates must not be looked at in a vacuum. Information on student goal attainment may provide additional useful information to the institution. More specific research should attempt to link goal attainment to specific outcomes experienced by the student.

Recommendations for Further Study

Based upon the findings of this study, the researcher recommends the following initiatives for further research:
1. More research is necessary to determine which retention program initiatives are most successful with two-year community colleges. Research should be conducted on students who participate in intervention services, to assess the effectiveness of such programs.
2. A qualitative study should be conducted on subgroups of students attending two-year institutions such as younger students, students of ethnic minority, students with disabilities, and lower-achieving students, to increase the understanding of why these various subgroups of students choose to persist or leave.
3. More research is necessary to investigate additional factors influencing student retention, including social factors that may have an indirect effect on persistence). It is critical that institutions conduct research on these factors, and additional ones, in an effort to predict the likelihood that the student will persist or leave. For at-risk students, early, intensive, and continuous interventions should be employed to assist the student in persisting to graduation.

References

American Association of Community Colleges (AACC). (2006). *2006 American Association of Community Colleges (AACC) facts.* ERIC Document Reproduction Service No. ED 94816)

American College Testing (ACT), Inc. (2006). *National collegiate retention and persistence to degree rates.* Retrieved September 18, 2008, from https://www.noellevitz.com/.

Astin, A.W., and Oseguera, L. (2005). Pre-college and institutional influences on degree attainment. In A. Seidman (Ed.), *College student retention: Formula for student success* (pp. 245-276). Westport, CT: American Council on Education and Praeger Publishers.

Bailey, T., Jenkins, D., and Leinbach, T. (2005). *What we know about community college low-income and minority student outcomes: Descriptive statistics from national surveys.* New York: Columbia University Teachers College, Community College Research Center. (ERIC Document Reproduction Service No. ED484354).

Bean, J.P. and Metzner, B.S. (1985). A conceptual model of nontraditional undergraduate student attrition. *Review of Educational Research, 55* (4), 485 -540.

Boylan, H. R. (2001). *Making the case for developmental education.* Research in Developmental Education, 12 (2), 1-4. Retrieved 1/31/05 from http://www.nade.net/documents/Articles/MakingtheCase.pdf.

Bradburn, E.M. (2002). Short-term enrollment in post-secondary education: Student background and institutional differences in reasons for early departure. *Education Statistics Quarterly, 4*(4). Retrieved September 11, 2008, from http://www. nces.ed.gov/.

Brahm, G. (2006). Personal coaches can boost each student's academic experience-and your retention rate. *Business Officer NACUBO* (39)12, 17-20.

Brown, J.K., Brown, K. J., and Yang, X. (2008). *Enrollment patterns and completion status: Students in North Carolina Public Post-secondary Institution.* Paper published for 2008 NCAIR and SCAIR Joint Conference. April, 2008.

Byun, K. (2000). A study on the applicability of Bean and Metzner's nontraditional student attrition model for older students using four different measures of persistence. *Dissertation Abstracts International, 61*(07), 2615. (UMI No. 9978249).

Cambiano, R.L., Denny, G.S., and DeVore, J. B. (2000). College student retention at a midwestern university: A six-year study. *Journal of College Admission, 166,* 22-29.

Chen, S., and Thomas, H. (2001). Constructing vocational and technical college student persistence models. *Journal of Vocational Education Research, 26*(1), 26-55.

Choy, S. (2001). *Students whose parents did not go to college: Post-secondary access, persistence, and attainment* (NCES 2001-126). Washington, DC: U.S. Department of Education, National Center for Education Statistics.

Clark, C.R. (2004). The influence of student background, college experience, and financial aid on community college within-year retention. *Dissertation AbstractsInternational, 64*(07), 2400. (UMI No. 3099265).

Cofer, J., and Somers, P. (2000). Within-year persistence of students at two-year colleges. *Community College Journal of Research and Practice, 24*(10), 785-807.

Eimers, M. T. and Pike, G. R. (1997). *Minority and nonminority adjustment to college.* Englewood Cliffs, NJ: Prentice-Hall.

Feldman, M. J. (1993). *Factors associated with one-year retention in a community college.* San Francisco: Jossey Bass.

Goodman, P. (2000). Pre- and post matriculation correlates of student retention within a community college setting (Doctoral dissertation, East Tennessee State University, 2000). *Dissertation Abstracts.*

Hagedorn, L.S. (2005). Square pegs: adult students and their "fit" in post-secondary institutions. *Change, 37.* 22-29.

Hawley, T. H., and Harris, T.A. (2005/2006). Student characteristics related to persistence for first-year community college students. *Journal of College Student Retention, 7*(½), 117-142.

Hayes, E. (2000) Social Contexts. In E. Hayes and D.D. Flannery (Eds.). *Women as Learners: The Significance of Gender in Adult Learning.* San Francisco: Jossey-Bass.

Horn, L., and Nevill, S. (2006). *Profile of undergraduates in U.S. post-secondary education institutions: 2003-04: With a special analysis of community college students (NCES 2006-184).* Washington, DC: National Center for Education Statistics.

Hyers, A. D., and Zimmerman, A. (2002). Using segmentation modeling to predict graduation at a two-year technical college. *Community College Review* 30: 1-26.

Jacobs, J.A., and King, R.B. (2002). Age and college completion: A life-history analysis of women aged 15-44. *Sociology of Education, 75*(3), 211-230.

Johnson, G. M. (1996). Gender differences in university attrition. *Education and Society, 14*(1), 33-47.

Jones, Steven (2002). No magic required: Reducing freshman attrition at the community. *Journal of College Student Retention*, Vol. 1, No. 3, pp. 239-253.

Kerka, S. (2003). *Career Development of Diverse Populations.* (ERIC Document Reproduction Service No. ED484354).

King, N. (2004). *Advising Underprepared Students.* Presentation: NACADA Summer Institute on Advising.

Larimore, J.A., and McClellan, G.S.(2005). Native American student retention in U.S. postsecondary education. *New Directions for Student Services, 109,* 17-32.

Leppel, K (2002). Similarities and differences in the college persistence of men and women. *Review of Higher Education: Journal of the Association for the Study of Higher Education, 25*(4), 433-450.

Levin, J. R., and Levin, M. E. (1991). A critical examination of academic retention programs for at-risk minority college students. *Journal of College Student Development, 32*, 323-334.

McCabe, R. (2000). *Underprepared Students. Measuring Up 2000: The State by State Report Card for Higher Education.* Retrieved July 8, 2008 from http://www.measuringup.highereducation.org.

McGrath, M.M., and Braunstein, A. (1997). The prediction of freshmen attrition: An examination of the importance of certain demographic, academic, financial, and social factors. *College Student Journal, 31*(3), 396-408.

Murtaugh, P.A., Burns, L.D., and Schuster, J. (1999). Predicting the retention of university students. *Research in Higher Education, 40*, 355-371.

National Center for Education Statistics. (2005). *Digest of Education Statistics.*

Nettles, M. T., Thoeny, A. R., and Gosman, E. J. (1986). Comparative and predictive analyses of black and white students' college achievement and experiences. *Journal of Higher Education, 57*, 289-318.

Neutzling, E. (2003). Crossing the finish line: A strategic approach designed to help Nontraditional Students?" Adult Education Quarterly (43)2, 90-100.

Nippert, K. (2000/2001). Influences on the educational degree attainment of two-year college students, *Journal of College Student Retention, 2*(1), 29-40.

Nitzke, J., and Wacker, M.E. (2001). *Dropping out at Western Iowa Tech Community College: A report summarizing focus group interviews.* Sioux City, IA: Office of Institutional Effectiveness. (ERIC Document Reproduction Service No. ED473193).

Nora, A. and Rendon, L.I. (1990). Determinants of predisposition to transfer among community college students: A structural model. *Research in Higher Education*, 31 (3), 235-257.

North Carolina Community College System. History of the NCCCS.

North Carolina Community College System. Office of Institutional Effectiveness.

Opp, R. D. (2002). Enhancing program completion rates among two-year college students of color. *Community College Journal of Research and Practice, 26*(2), 147-163.

Pascarella, E.T. (1997). Its time we started paying attention to community college students. *About Campus,* 14-17 January/February.

Pascarella, E.T. and Terenzini, P.T. (1980). Predicting freshman persistence and voluntary dropout decisions from a theoretical model. *Journal of Higher Education, 51* (1), 61-75.

Pascarella, E.T. and Terenzini, P.T. (1991). How college affects students: Findings and insights from twenty years of research, Jossey-Bass Publishers, San Francisco, CA.

Pascarella, E. T., & Terenzini, P. T. (2005). *How college affects students: A third decade of research* (First edition). San Francisco, CA: Jossey-Bass.

Ramaley, Judith, Leskes, Andrea, and Associates. (2002). Greater expectations: A new vision for learning as a nation goes to college. Association of American Colleges and Universities.

Reason, R. D. (2003). Student variables that predict retention: Recent research and new developments. NASPA Journal, 40, 172-191.

Schmid, C. and Abell, P. (2003). Demographic risk factors, study patterns end campus involvement as related to student success among Guilford Technical Community College students. *Community College Review*, Vol. 31, 2003.

Scoggin, D. (2005) Factors associated with student withdrawal from community college.*Community College Enterprise*.

Seidman, A. (2005a). *College student retention: Formula for student success.* Westport, CT: American Council on Education/Praeger Series on Higher Education.

Smith, A.B., Street, M.A., and Olivarez, A. (2002). Early, regular, and late registration and community college student success: A case study. *Community College Journal of Research and Practice, 26*(3), 261-273.

Smith, L. (2002). Understanding our students. *NASPA Net Results,* 1-2.

Somers, P. (1995). First-to-second semester persistence: a case study. *Journal of the Freshman Year Experience,* 7(2), 43-62.

St. John, E.P. (2000). The impact of student aid on recruitment and retention: What the research indicates. *New Directions for Student Services, 89*(61-75).

St. John, E.P., Hu, S., Simmons, A., Carter, D.F., and Weber, J. (2004). What difference does a major make? The influence of college major field on persistence by African American and White Students. *Research in Higher Education, 45*(3), 209-232.

St. John, E.P., Carter, D.F., Chun, C.G., and Musoba, G.D. (2006). *Diversity and student aid.* In E. P. St. John (Ed.), *Readings on Equal Education Vol. 22: Public Policy and Education and Education Opportunity: School Reforms, Post-secondary Encouragement, and State Policies on Higher Education* New York: AMS Press.

Szeleny, K., (2001). Minority retention and academic achievement. *ERIC Digest,* No. ED 451859.

Tharp, J. (1998). Predicting persistence of urban commuter campus students utilizing student background characteristics from enrollment data. *Community College Journal of Research and Practice*, 22(3), 279-294.

Tinto, V. (1987). *Leaving college: Rethinking the causes and cures of student attrition.* Chicago: University of Chicago Press.

Tinto, V. (1993). *Leaving college: Rethinking the causes and cures of student attrition.* Chicago; London : University of Chicago Press.

Tinto, V. (July 2004). *Student retention and graduation: Facing the truth, living with the consequences.* The Pell Institute http://www.pellinstitute.org.

Tinto, V. (2006). Research and practice of student retention: What next? *College Student*, 8(1), 1-19.

Tritelli, D. (Winter 2003). Association of American Colleges and Universities. Retrieved September 16, 2008 from http://findarticles.com.

Weissberg, N.C., Owen, D.R., Jenkins, A.H., and Harburg, E. (2003). The incremental variance problem: Enhancing the predictability of academic success in an urban, commuter institution. *Genetic, Social, and General Psychology Monographs, 129* (2), 153-180.

White-Shield, R. (2004/2005). The retention of indigenous students in higher education: Historical issues, federal policy, and indengous resilience. *Journal of College Student Retention*, 6 (1), 111-127.

Zhai, L., and Monzon, R.I. (2004). Studying community college student retention: Student retention: Student characteristics and reasons for withdrawal. *Insight into Student Services Journal*, 7.

Index

271

Editors

Terence Hicks is a research professor and former Department Chair of the Department of Educational Leadership at Fayetteville State University. Dr. Hicks is a noteworthy scholar who has conducted important research analysis on the adjustment and psychological well-being of college students. His work has been cited in the USA Today, the Research Alert Yearbook, Detroit News and the Fayetteville Observer. He has published and disseminated research findings on college students at the local, regional and national levels. To date, he has over 60 combined publications and presentations and has been cited by over 65 combined nationally/ internationally researchers. He also serves as an advisory editor for the *Negro Educational Review* journal and the *American Journal of Health Behavior.* Dr. Hicks has provided valuable research findings and evaluation data on college students for the following federal and state funded grants: US DHHS National Institutes of Health, National Center of Minority Health and Health Disparities and the Maryland Higher Education Commission for the College Preparation Intervention Program (CPIP) in support of Gaining Early Awareness and Readiness for Undergraduate Programs. Most recently, he co-edited a book entitled, *"The Educational Lockout of African Americans in Prince Edward County, Virginia (1959-1964): Personal Accounts and Reflections,"* University Press of America. In addition, a companion guide has been developed to accompany the educational lockout book. This guide is entitled, *"An Instructional Companion Guide for the 21ˢᵗ Century Educational Leader in the Classroom and Beyond,* the companion guide is authored by Terence Hicks, Abul Pitre and Kelly Jackson Charles. Dr. Hicks earned his bachelor and master degrees from Virginia State University and a doctorate degree in Educational Leadership from Wilmington University, Delaware. Currently, he is completing a second doctorate degree, a Ph.D. in Counseling Education from North Carolina State University.

Abul Pitre is the former Carter G. Woodson Professor of Education at Edinboro University of Pennsylvania. Currently, he is the Department Chairperson for the Leadership Studies Program at North Carolina A&T State University, N.C. Dr. Pitre is the author of several articles and books. Most notable is his work on the educational philosophy of Elijah Muhammad and Malcolm X.

279

Book Contributors

Bryan Andriano is the Director for Graduate International Education and Programs at The George Washington University.

Kimberly Brown is the Director of Academic Advising at Virginia Tech. In 2010, she served as the university's interim associate vice provost for academic support services where she provided university leadership for institutional support programs and services for students. Dr. Brown has presented at the local, state, and national level at various professional conferences on topics related to assessment of advising, advising undecided students, utilization of technology in advising, and developing an effective advising program for orientation. She's the co-author of a chapter entitled "Applying Quality Educational Principles to Academic Advising." She earned her B.A. degree (1993) in Psychology from the University of Richmond, M.A. degree (1996) in Counselor Education from Radford University, and Ph.D. degree (2009) from Virginia Polytechnic Institute and State University.

Ron Brown is the Associate Vice Chancellor, Lone Star College System, Division of Educational Partnerships & P16 Initiatives for the Lone Star College System, Texas. He has extensive knowledge in the areas of Higher education and K-12, and is currently responsible for the development and implementation of long-term outreach and initiatives designed to influence and raise the awareness of P-16 students. He holds a M.Ed. from Prairie View A&M University and a Ph.D. in Education Administration and Human Resource Development from Texas A&M University. His articles and reviews have appeared in the National Forum of Multicultural Issues and the National Forum of Applied Educational Research Journal.

Mona Y. Davenport is the Director of Minority Affairs and the African American Cultural Center at Eastern Illinois University. She earned her B.A. and B.S. in Sociology and African American Studies; Master's degree in Educational Psychology from Eastern Illinois University and a Ph.D. in Higher Education Administration from Illinois State University. She has taught courses in Cross-Cultural Counseling and Multicultural Competence in Higher Education. Davenport's research interests are student involvement and purposeful engagement of underrepresented students. She has prior professional experience in the areas of residence life, student activities and TRIO programs at Illinois State University and Governors State University.

J. Michael Harpe is faculty member in the School of Education and Human Services for Mount Saint Mary's University, Maryland.

Adriel A. Hilton serves as the executive assistant to the President and assistant secretary of the Board of Trustees at Upper Iowa University in Fayette, Iowa. A graduate of the Higher Education (Ph.D.) program at Morgan State University in Baltimore, Maryland, Dr. Hilton has been a Frederick Douglass Scholar at Clarion University of Pennsylvania, in the College of Education and the Office of the Provost and Vice President for Academic Affairs. He earned his master's degree in Applied Social Science with a concentration in public administration from Florida Agricultural and Mechanical University and completed his undergraduate degree as a cum laude graduate in Business Administration with a concentration in finance from Morehouse College.

Theodore Kaniuka is an Assistant Professor in the Department of Educational Leadership at Fayetteville State University. He has worked as a district super-intendent, associate and assistant superintendents, principal and classroom teacher. His research interests are high school reform, instructional decision-making and social justice.

Pamela A. Larde is an Assistant Professor of Research and Education in the Tift College of Education at Mercer University in Atlanta, Georgia. She received her Ph.D. in Leadership for the Advancement of Learning and Service from Cardinal Stritch University in 2009, completing her dissertation on Factors that Predispose African American and Mexican American First-Generation Students to Pursue Higher Education. She has presented at national conferences including the National Conference on Race and Ethnicity, the American College Personnel Association, and the National Association for Student Personnel Administrators.

James L. Moore III is a professor in Counselor Education in the College of Education and Human Ecology and coordinator of the School Counseling Program. Dr. Moore is also the inaugural director of the Todd Anthony Bell National Resource Center on the African American Male and has faculty affiliations with the Ohio Collaborative, John Glenn Institute, and Criminal Justice Research Center at The Ohio State University. Dr. Moore has a national- and international-recognized research agenda that focuses on (a) how educational professionals, such as school counselors, influence the educational/career aspirations and school experiences of students of color (particularly African American males); (b) socio-cultural, familial, school, and community factors that support, enhance, and impede academic outcomes for preK-20 African American students (e.g., elementary, secondary, and post-secondary); (c) recruitment and retention issues of students of color, particularly African Americans, in K-12 gifted education and those high-potential college students in science, technology, engineering, and mathematics (STEM) majors; and (d) social, emotional, and psychological consequences of racial oppression for African American males and other people of color in various domains in society (e.g., education, counseling, workplace, athletics, etc.). In ten years of professorship, he has made significant contributions in *school counseling, gifted education, urban education, higher education, multicultural education/ counseling, and STEM education*. To this end, Dr. Moore has published over 75 publications. He has also given over 150 different scholarly presentations throughout the world (e.g., United States, Canada, China, England, France, India, and Spain) and has obtained over $4.5 million in extramural funding.

Ashley Rondini is currently an Assistant Professor of Sociology at Transylvania University in Lexington, Kentucky. She was awarded the 2010-2011 American Sociological Association Sydney S. Spivack Applied Social Research and Social Policy Congressional Fellowship, through which she served as a Post-Doctoral Research Fellow with the United States House of Representatives Committee on Education and Labor, as well as a Policy Analyst in Higher Education with the Domestic Social Policy Division of the United States Congressional Research Service. She received a joint Ph.D. in Sociology and Social Policy from the Graduate School of Arts and Sciences and the Heller School of Social Policy and Management at Brandeis University (2010), with concentrations in Qualitative Research Methods, Sociology of Race, Sociology of Gender, and Policies and Programs related to Assets and Inequalities. She also holds an M.A. in Social Policy from the Heller School of Social Policy and Management at Brandeis University (2006), and an M.A. in Women's Studies from the University of Sussex in Brighton, England (1999). She has worked as a mentor to students with the Posse Foundation, and as an instructor with Brandeis University's Transitional Year Program. Her dissertation was based on an interdisciplinary,qualitative study of how low-income, first-generation college students and their parents understood and experienced intergenerational educational mobility.

Desireé Vega is currently a School Psychologist with the Omaha Public Schools District in Omaha, Nebraska. She earned her B.A. in Psychology at Binghamton University, and her M.A. and Ph.D. in School Psychology at The Ohio State University. Her research interests focus on the following: (a) the relationship between psychological, social, and school factors and academic outcomes among African American and Latina/o youth, (b) African American and Latina/o parental involvement in urban public schools, (c) access to higher education among first-generation urban and undocumented Latina/o youth, and (d) access to gifted and college preparatory curricula for African American and Latina/o youth. Both while pursuing her undergraduate and graduate education, she has received numerous honors and recognitions. More recently, she was selected as a Bell Doctoral Fellow, for scholastic achievements and strong interests in becoming a college professor.

Gregory J. Vincent was named Vice President for Diversity and Community Engagement in 2006, when President William Powers Jr. created a new division as one of his four strategic initiatives for The University of Texas at Austin. Since that time, the Division of Diversity and Community Engagement has become one of the most comprehensive divisions of its kind in the nation. It has grown to encompass more than fifty units and projects, including the exemplary rated UT Elementary School, the university's Office of Institutional Equity, a new Community Engagement Center, the University Interscholastic League, the Hogg Foundation for Mental Health, and a number of initiatives that work to increase the number of first-generation college students and students from under-represented populations in the higher education pipeline.

A native of New York City, Dr. Vincent came to The University of Texas in 2005 as Vice Provost for Inclusion and Cross Cultural Effectiveness. He is currently a professor in the School of Law and a professor in the Department of Higher Education and holds the W. K. Kellogg Professorship in Community College Leadership.

J. Luke Wood is an Assistant Professor in the Department of Administration, Rehabilitation and Postsecondary Education (ARPE) at San Diego State University. Dr. Wood is Co-Editor of the Journal of African American Males in Education (JAAME) and Chair of the Multicultural & Multiethnic Education (MME) special interest group of the American Educational Research Association (AERA). Luke received his Ph.D. in Educational Leadership and Policy Studies with a concentration in Higher Education from Arizona State University.

CPSIA information can be obtained at www.ICGtesting.com
Printed in the USA
BVOW040400300412

288958BV00002B/2/P